The
Sporting Terrier

BY THE SAME AUTHOR

NON FICTION

Modern Ferreting
Tales of a Rat-Hunting Man
Adventures of an Artisan Hunter
Rogues and Running Dogs
The Complete Lurcher: A Manual
The Complete Jack Russell Terrier
The Fell Terrier
Merle: The Start of a Dynasty
Omega
Off the Beaten Track
North and North Again
The Cottage at the Edge of the World
In Pursuit of Coney
The Working Terrier
Diary of a Hunter
Practical Lurcher Breeding
Sighthounds

FICTION

Nathan
Lepus: The Story of a Hare
Trog: A Novel

The
Sporting Terrier

D. BRIAN PLUMMER

THE BOYDELL PRESS

First published 1992 by The Boydell Press, Woodbridge

The Boydell Press is an imprint of Boydell & Brewer Ltd
PO Box 9, Woodbridge, Suffolk IP12 3DF, UK

ISBN 0 85115 314 3

British Library Cataloguing-in-Publication Data
Plummer, David Brian
Sporting Terrier
I. Title
636.7
ISBN 0–85115–314–3

This publication is printed on acid-free paper

Printed in Great Britain by
St Edmundsbury Press Ltd, Bury St Edmunds, Suffolk

Contents

THE TERRIERS OF SCOTLAND

TERRIERS AND THEIR QUARRY

Acknowledgement is made
to Wendy Bent
for her contribution of breed photographs

I dedicate this book to Paul and Sheila Jackson who, in true Biblical fashion, fed me when I was hungry, gave me shelter when I had none and cared for me when no one else seemed to care. This dedication is such a paltry repayment for the friendship you have given me over the years!

Introduction

Terriers, together with the English bulldog perhaps, can be considered as the most typically British breed of dog. No other country seems to have produced types of dogs which were specifically tailored to go to ground and join battle with foxes, badgers or otters. True, the German dachshund, a hound bred on terrier lines would seem to best describe the dog, was used to seek out foxes, badgers etc., but the dachshund was first and foremost always a hound; as at home hunting above ground as below, although, as the name implies, it was often used as a badger-digging dog. It was suggested by Turbeville in 1575 that a type of terrier-cum-hound or hound-cum-terrier, existed in the Low Countries, a crooked-legged smooth-coated beast, that hunted above ground, but would also follow quarry into its lairs. Turbeville had probably seen a primitive basset and while it is true that most breeds of hounds will enter the lairs of foxes and badgers – Lake District beagles were notorious for running to ground, and several fox hounds have been lost when they went to ground and dug on to find their foxes – it would be ludicrous to classify such dogs as terriers.

True, since the turn of the twentieth century breeds of terrier have begun to appear in other parts of the world but these terriers are the result of hybridising various British breeds of terrier rather than the refinement of certain native breeds of dogs that showed a tendency to go to ground in a manner befitting a terrier. The Jadghund is clearly a Germanic edition of the Old English rough-coated black-and-tan terrier. The Japanese terrier is simply a rather leggy Jack Russell-type terrier said to be a hybrid between the Manchester terrier and the miniature bull terrier. Likewise the Cesky terrier, the creation of Czechoslovakian Frantisek Horak, is the result of mating a Scottish or Aberdeen terrier (Scottish Rose) to a Sealyham terrier (Buganier Urquelle) though Horner suggests that Dandie Dinmont terrier blood was also used to refine the type. The American toy fox terrier, a breed that never really became popular in Britain or America, is simply a small Jack Russell-type terrier of the sort commonly seen at working terrier shows during the early 1960s.

Why Britain should be the only country in the world to produce dogs that were specifically tailored to go to ground, seek out and sometimes destroy vermin, is the subject of some speculation. Britain certainly does not have a monopoly on earth- or set-dwelling vermin, and stoats, weasels, rats, rabbits, foxes, badgers and otters are as common in the rest of Europe as they are in Britain. It is, however, likely that the British have a racial tendency to breed dogs for specific purposes and to produce animals that excel in a single activity. British setters and pointers are specifically tailored to seek out and point game after which the retrieving of the game brought down by gunmen is the domain of other types of dogs – retrievers and sometimes spaniels. Continental breeds of gun dog are invariably dual purpose animals (H. P. R. – hunt, point and retrieve-type breeds) which epitomise versatility rather than specialisation.

It is possible that small dogs throughout Europe were sometimes used to help dig out vermin as well as perform other functions, and that the British passion for specialisation (and, it should be added, the British penchant for developing and perfecting certain special qualitities in their livestock) brought about the evolution of that most typically British type of dog – the terrier.

The History and Development of Terrier Types

Various theories are put forward to explain the origin of the British terriers: one of the most logical of which is that offered by A. and R. Fiennes in their *Natural History of the Dog* (1968). The Fiennes believe that the hounds described by Oppian, a third century Greek historian with a very tenuous knowledge of Britain, may well have been the ancestors of certain types of terriers. Oppian describes small hounds which were used to hunt vermin and it is possible that Oppian did in fact refer to a type of beagle or basset rather than a terrier.

The Roman bronze statuette excavated at Covertina's Wells at Carrawburgh is invariably credited with being a model of a terrier – the statuette does resemble an early Aberdeen terrier – but there is little to substantiate the claim that the statuette represented an earth dog. The figure may well be that of a hunting dog, a guard dog or simply a household pet for its resemblance to present-day terriers is superficial to say the least and it could be stated that the statuette closely resembles the pariah dogs described by Zeuner in his book *The History of Domestication*.

However the vocation of terriers was known by the Abbess Juliana Berner who in her curious book *The Boke of St Albans* makes mention of 'terrours' or 'earth dogges' but does little to describe the type and makes only scant reference to the use of these dogs.

Modern cynologists tend to place far too much store on the researches of John Caius, author of *De Canibus Brittanicus* (British Dogs) (1570), who makes reference to that most uniquely British of dogs, the terrier. Caius did in fact have little interest in dogs, let alone in terriers, and his book was in fact simply a translation of letters he sent to the Swiss naturalist Conrad Gesner. Gesner had contacted 'Caius' (who had deliberately Latinised his name, John Keyes) in order to obtain information on British dogs, particularly mastiffs in which Gesner had a great interest. Keyes, or Caius, was a physician and scholar, but knew little of British dogs. The pair conducted their correspondence in Latin, as Caius knew no German and Gesner had no knowledge of English, and the epistles were later to be translated somewhat inaccurately and misleadingly by Abraham Fleming in 1576.

Caius refers to a small mastiff – he calls it a 'degenerate' – which in all probability was a bulldog, for the term bulldog was not used before 1632, or a type more akin to the bull terrier than the modern bulldog, and he also makes mention of terriers which were used to pursue foxes and badgers underground and bring them to the surface, but he neither describes these terriers nor elaborates on their use. Caius' letter was in fact simply an effort to please his friend or colleague, though it is likely Caius would have been the very last person to credit himself with any knowledge of cynology and it is fortunate that Caius did not choose to elaborate on the British terrier or its use. The Victorian cynologist George R. Jesse, in his book *Researches into the History of the British Dog* (1866), states 'it is plain from these and other remarks of Caius that he knew little of dogs or the chase.'

George Turbeville, *The Noble Art of Venerie and Hunting* (1575), is equally ill at ease when describing terriers and refers to two types of terrier(?): a short-legged breed found in the Low Countries or Flanders and a shaggy straight-legged breed that would hunt above and below ground. It is also worth noting that Jacques du Fouilloux, in his book *Venerie* (The Art of Hunting) (1561), makes elaborate references to badger and fox hunting and refers to the dogs used to seek out such quarry as 'bassets'. It is fairly obvious that Turbeville, writing some fourteen years later, borrows heavily from du Fouilloux's text, but fortunately omits mentioning that du Fouilloux states that one way of entering a basset to badger or to fox was to 'take some old foxes or badgers and cut off the entire jaw where the big teeth are, so that the beast can show the utmost fury without being able to do any harm'.

Nicholas Cox, *The Gentleman's Recreation* (1674), knew much about hounds perhaps, but borrows from Turbeville regarding the ways of terriers and foxes and adds 'Now to say the truth, there is not much pastime or pleasure in hunting a fox underground; for as soon as that subtle creature perceiveth the terriers, if they bay hard and lie near to them, they will bolt out immediately unless it be when the bitch (vixen) hath young cubs then they will sooner die than stir'. Cox also adds that terriers were sometimes treated with brimstone and oil of cade before being put to ground and this concoction so stank out the earth that no fox or badger would inhabit the lair for a month or so.

Tom Horner, *Terriers of the World*, states that Richard Blome author, or perhaps editor, of yet another *Gentleman's Recreation* (1686) was held in little esteem by his contemporaries, yet Blome was the first English writer to suggest how terriers could be bred. Blome suggests that a suitable terrier could be bred by mating a mongrel mastiff (the degenerate mastiff of *De Canibus Britannicus* perhaps) to a beagle.

> the above mentioned cross usually proves good, the result thereof hath courage and a thick skin as participating of the cur and is mouthed like a beagle.

While Blome's theory is always questioned by cynologists and ridiculed by others, his notions are certainly logical and many breeds of terrier certainly owe much of their ancestry to the influence of both hound and bull terrier crosses and Oliver Goldsmith in his book *Animated Nature* (1774) is wont to refer to a terrier as 'a type of small hound' that was used to bay at quarry lodged below ground and drive it to the surface.

However, by 1760 terriers were considered important enough not merely to mention in print but also to describe. William Daniel, *Field Sports*, is reputed to have kept a large kennel of terriers which he describes thus

> There are two sorts of terrier, the one rough short-legged and long-backed, very strong and most commonly of a black or yellowish colour mixed with white; the other is smooth-haired and beautifully formed having a shorter body and a more sprightly appearance, generally of a reddish-brown colour or black with tanned legs. Both these sorts are the determined foe of all vermin kind and in their encounters with the badger very frequently meet with severe treatment which they sustain with great courage and a thoroughbred well-trained terrier often proves more than a match for his opponent.

If Daniel is correct – and he is reputed to have kept many terriers – then in all probability terriers similar in shape and type to dachshunds may well have been bred in Britain during the fifteenth century and the description of the first type of terrier depicts a dog not dissimilar to a Dandie Dinmont terrier or a wire haired dachshund. Certainly houndy terriers still abounded and Buffon, *Natural History*, who attempts some form of scientific classification of species of animal, also divides terriers into two similar types but still refers to them as 'hounds'.

Later Sydenham Edwards in his *Cynographica Britannica* (1800) also mentions that two distinct types of terrier were worked in Britain one short and crooked-legged the other longer-legged – black, tan-legged terriers were common and white terriers greatly prized by the huntsmen of the era. Sydenham Edwards also adds that rough-coated terriers were generally considered to be the harder biters – though this was not always so.

It is possible that the short bent-legged type of terrier was confined to the north of Britain and gave rise to the low slung Scottish types of terrier and also the common stock that spawned the Dandie Dinmont and the Bedlington terrier, but many paintings of the terriers of the time depict both tan and black-and-tan terriers as well as terriers with top-knots and hirsute flowing coats. It seems possible that both types were found throughout the length and breadth of Britain and that the low-slung hirsute kind fell out of popularity in the south of Britain but continued to be bred in the north of England and Scotland. It is also

Early eighteenth century punt showing three distinct types of terrier

possible that the Scottish types of terrier the Cairn, the West Highland white, the Skye and the Scottish or Aberdeen terrier are descended from or closely related to the short-legged terriers described by Sydenham Edwards and Daniel.

However Cuvier in 1862, in his book *Animal Kingdom*, seems to indicate that a distinct type of terrier had begun to emerge – the rough coated black-and-tan terrier a long straight-legged animal which despite its title was black, tan, black-and-tan, blue-and-tan, grizzle, brindle and sometimes smooth-coated as well as more copiously jacketted. This type of terrier referred to as the Old Adam of terriers by Horner in his book *Terriers of the World* seldom exceeded fifteen inches at the shoulder, was kept to bolt foxes, to assist in the digging of badgers and to flush otters from their holts as well as to kill rats, stoats, weasels, polecats and other vermin.

A. Compton in his book *The Twentieth Century Dog* (1904) has this to say of the type.

> The terrier of the old days was nearly always a black-and-tan or dark-coloured dog. During the seventeenth century such terriers were kept chiefly by grooms, stablemen, huntsmen etc. to assist in their work and at that period were commonly used in the hunting field.

Various strains of black-and-tan rough-coated terrier were kept by many hunt servants and a particularly fine type of terrier was kept by the Duke of Beaufort though many of these terriers were blue-and-tan and seldom exceeded twelve pounds in weight. Word of mouth stories of the prowess of the Beaufort hunt terriers are legion, but while certain fox-hound kennels continued to inbreed these strains of terrier, white-bodied working terriers, both fox terrier and heterogenous Jack Russell type terriers were soon to usurp the rough-coated black-and-tan terriers long before the start of the twentieth century.

However there is evidence to suggest that long after the rough-coated black- and-tan terrier had fallen into disfavour at the majority of fox hunt kennels the type was still to be found in certain kennels in Wales and the Lake District and was to emerge as the Welsh and later still as the Lakeland terrier. There is some, albeit scant, evidence to suggest that a very pure form of the type was still bred at the Ynysfor Otter-hound Kennels in North Wales until the late 1950s. Earlier in that decade Major Roche M.O.H. had sent a terrier to Harry Smith the huntsman for the Kendal and District Otter Hounds and the terrier later entered into the lines of fell terrier bred by Keith Clement of Kendal. Local legend however states that Major Roche's terrier was not of the Ynysfor strain but was sired by a Coniston-bred fell terrier, but this tale confirms rather than repudiates that the Ynysfor terriers and the fell strains bred around Kendal were similar in type, attitude and working qualities and that both fell and native unregistered Welsh terriers are fairly pure forms of the Old English rough-coated black-and-tan terrier.

What caused the appearance of white-bodied working terriers – both the fox terrier-types and the shorter-legged types which shelter under the umbrella of the title Jack Russell terriers – is the subject of much debate and speculation. Three theories as to the origin of the white-bodied types have been put forward.

a. The type is the result of breeding from white-bodied 'sports' appearing in litters of black-and-tan terriers.
b. That the type was a result of crossing native terriers with bulldogs to increase the valour of the strain of terrier.
c. Further additions of beagle blood could have produced a new type of terrier.

The theory that the type appeared as white-bodied sports in black-and-tan litters has much to commend it. Sydney Castle in his *A Monograph of the Fox Terrier* states that he is unhappy about the theory that further additions of either hound or bulldog blood produced white-bodied fox terriers and states that he is confident that 'though possibly these strains of terriers may have been the victims of occasional mis-alliances with something the equivalent to a beagle or bull terrier cross, yet for practical purposes the breed has been of the terrier order for centuries'.

Certainly it is not uncommon for certain strains of fell terrier to throw an occasional white-bodied puppy in their litters and the appearance of white-bodied Lakelands has done much to strengthen and improve the strains of modern Parson Jack Russell terriers. It is also possible that if Blome was correct and terriers were created by mating beagles to degenerate mastiff types many strains of rough-coated black-and-tan terrier would have carried 'white-bodied genes' and once white-bodied terriers had appeared as sports in litters of black-and-tan terriers these sports would breed true to type. It is said that John Russell mated his first white-bodied terrier bitch Trump to his father's black-and-tan terrier dog and began his strain from the progeny – though there is little to authenticate this theory – though there is some evidence to suggest that dogs bred or kept by the Reverend John Russell eventually became some of the foundation stock for the modern wire-haired fox terrier.

Certainly Castle's theory is given some credence by records appertaining to the eighteenth century spendthrift Colonel Thornton who in addition to being an afficianado of coursing greyhounds (he bought up Lord Orford's famous greyhound kennels when Orford died) also kept a terrier called Pitch 'from whom are descended most of the white terriers in this Kingdom'. Castle also offers as proof of his theory that in 1795 'a picture was painted of Viper – a fox terrier short in head but otherwise very similar to terriers we have seen'. However Viper was a heavily marked dog – almost hound-marked one should add and had the heavy jaws one associates with dogs bred from bull terrier crosses!

There is, however, considerable evidence to suggest that crosses with bulldog or bull terrier blood may well have produced the white-bodied terrier. John Russell at least, according to Davies one of Russells biographers, is said to have avoided using smooth-coated fox terrier blood to create his strain because he believed that this smooth coat was an

Black and tan and early Jack Russell/fox terrier type terriers

indication of the presence of bull terrier blood in the breed. Certainly the painting of Viper the smooth fox terrier mentioned by Castle shows a dog with a strong heavy short muzzle of the type often bred from bull terrier cross-breds.

Edward Ash, *Dogs*, quotes Taplin (1803) (scarcely an accurate source of information, one should add) that there was an absolute mania for crossing all breeds of terrier with bulldogs to breed more valourous animals and Stonehenge (A. H. Walsh) mentions that the now extinct Old English white terrier was known to be a crass coward unless crossed with bulldogs. Yet Stonehenge was against crossing terriers with bulldogs as 'the bull cross makes a dog lie too close to his game . . . often absolutely preventing his bolting by hanging on to him'.

Yet there is much to substantiate Ash's statement that there was an absolute mania for crossing all breeds of terrier with bulldogs (bull terriers) for few breeds of English or Welsh terrier are not descended from stock that owes at least some of its origin to the bull terrier cross. Airedales were said to be the result of mating bull terriers to otter hounds to produce a large ratting terrier capable of working the banks of the river Aire. Lucas, *Hunt and Working Terriers* (1931), is bold enough to actually name the first hound to serve the bull terrier! Early Airedale breeders often fought these terriers against other dogs and this fact is often offered as proof of the bull terrier origins of the Airedale. This is clearly ridiculous for terriers of all breeds (bull blooded or not) have been pitted against other dogs since time immemorial. Such is the nature of terrier owners one supposes! It is also said that John Tucker Edwardes used small Cheshire terriers – catch-weight bull terriers of between twelve and twenty pounds in weight – to give strength of jaw and courage to the Sealyham terriers he was endeavouring to create. Likewise it is said that small bull terriers were used in the creation of Norfolk and Norwich terriers. Furthermore Geoffrey Sparrow *A Terrier's Vocation* suggests that every ten generations or so a strain of working terrier needs a dash of bull terrier blood to maintain courage and head size.

Many of the best strains of bulldog were either pied or totally white – the famous Paddington white bull terrier/bulldog strain was almost invincible in the pits – and hence it is likely that white-bodied terriers began to appear in litters of rough-coated black-and-tan terriers that carried bull terrier genes.

In passing it is worth mentioning why terrier breeders sought to add the blood of fighting dogs to an already fiery breed: the Old English rough-coated black-and-tan terrier, and it should be mentioned that fell terriers – the most pure form of the Old English rough-coated black-and-tan terrier – are regarded as some of the hardest and toughest terriers in the world. Thus the uninitiated must certainly wonder why breeders would seek to produce even harder terriers by mating indigenous terriers to bulldogs.

Three factors certainly encouraged terrier breeders to produce even tougher harder-biting terriers.

a. The brown rat became a common sporting quarry.
b. Badger baiting increased in popularity.
c. Badger digging clubs were set up and the sport became more popular than hitherto.

At the start of the eighteenth century the black rat was a threatened, if not an endangered, species in Britain. Improved sanitation had made life harsh for this rodent and its numbers had declined accordingly. Into the void created by the decline of the black rat (*Rattus rattus*) crept the brown or Hanoverian rat (*Rattus norvegicus*) a more vigorous, tougher and larger species that not only thrived in the temperate climate Britain afforded it and became a pest but provided the British sporting public with a hard biting ubiquitous and unpopular sporting quarry. Not only did the brown rat provide a fascinating quarry to hunt however, but it also became an unwilling or reluctant participant in that most bizarre of sporting spectacles, the rat pits.

Mayhew, *London Labour, London Poor,* gives a vivid account of this macabre spectacle. Rat pits were commonly constructed at the rear of public houses and landlords would provide a hundred, or on the odd occasion as many as a thousand, rats for a terrier to kill in a set period of time. Some dogs became amazingly adept at the technique of killing rats neatly, quickly and efficiently without scattering the rodents to the four corners of the pit. Huge mounds of rodents frequently over-faced terriers which were unwilling to attack members of a huge pile of terrified rodents (it is not merely by chance that Mayhew mentions a black-and-tan terrier that did not have the courage to perform against such a group of rats). Other dogs set to work systematically, killing the outlying rats quickly and deftly with the minimum of disturbance so as not to disturb the terrifed occupants of the mound that huddled against the edge of the rat pit. Billy, a famous rat-killing terrier, once slew a hundred rats in five minutes in 1823 while the pugilist Jem Shaw's Jacko saw off a thousand of these rodents in an hour and forty minutes.

Few terriers emerged from such pits unscathed. Rats bite hard and many dogs are loathe to pursue the killing of rats once they are badly bitten. As time goes on – and it took the fabulous Jacko over an hour and a half to slay one thousand terrified rats – lips, muzzles, noses and ears smart and sting. In fact it takes a very special sort of dog to despatch a huge quantity of rats. Such a dog must be determined, quick to kill his rats, phlegmatic of disposition (for an excitable dog would scatter the pile of rats making the process of killing them an extremely lengthy one) and almost immune to the pain many rats would inflict on him. It is unlikely that the Old English rough-coated black-and-tan was tough

Brown rats: a hard biting quarry

enough to cope with the killing of rats in number, so bulldog blood was introduced into the type of terrier required to perform in the rat pits.

It is hard, if not impossible, for modern man reared as he is on an antiseptic diet of nicer-than-nice pleasantries to imagine just how popular the rat pits were. The film *The Great Train Robbery* (1978), featuring Sean Connery, shows an enormous and varied crowd descending on an inn to watch a terrier kill a dozen or so rats. It was not uncommon to see several hundred people watching this disgusting and barbaric spectacle as photographs of the last days of the Leicester Rat Pit in 1911 attest, and the popularity of these pits caused a metamorphosis in the strains of working terrier.

The cessation of bull baiting in 1835 produced a void that the British sporting public were wont to fill. It is likely that had not Pease pushed through an Act of Parliament to bring about the abolition of the spectacle, bull baiting may well have died a natural death. However, once the activity was made illegal there was a revival of interest in dog fighting and the curious spectacle of badger drawing. A badger was placed in a

Matching small terriers against large rats was a passion in Victorian England.

barrel or tunnel and a dog encouraged to rush into the darkness, seize the badger and draw it from its sanctuary. Once clear of the barrel an official promptly bit the tail of the dog thereby causing him to release its hold on the badger which shot back into the, albeit temporary, sanctuary of the tunnel, whereupon the whole rather pointless spectacle began yet again until the dog, wounded and bruised beyond belief, refused to enter the darkness to face the badger. It is unlikely that the Old English black-and-tan rough-coated terrier was tough enough, strong enough or impervious to pain enough to participate in such an activity so bulldog blood was once again introduced into the gene pool of the working strains of terrier to produce an animal suitable for such activities.

Yet another factor that influenced the metamorphosis and possibly hastened the decline in popularity of the Old English rough-coated black-and-tan terrier was the formation of badger digging clubs during the late nineteenth and early twentieth centuries. Such clubs were formed ostensibly to further the working qualities of terriers. Badgers dug by such clubs were usually released unharmed rather than killed and dug yet again a week or so later. Arthur Heinemann founded such a club as did Larcombe and the Ilfracombe Badger Digging Club was famous throughout Britain. Badgers subjected to such treatment adopt an entirely different attitude to dogs sent to harrass them. When a badger is first dug a yapping darting terrier will usually bring him to bay and keep him pinned in a chamber of the set. However a badger subjected to such torment week after week becomes a furious adversary and rushes his foe inflicting terrible damage on the terrier that is harrassing him. After a while such a badger will over-match all but the most determined terrier that is sent to face him and to produce such badger digging dogs bulldogs were crossed with working terriers.

It must be even more baffling for the reader to understand why beagle blood was now added to this very potent mix to ameliorate the fiery disposition of these bulldog blooded working terriers. Conventional fox hunting, riding to fast hounds, was unknown before the mid 1600s but in 1660 the Old Charlton Hunt met at a hunting box of the Earl of Arundel in Midhurst, Sussex and the popularity of the sport caused monumental changes in stock breeding throughout Britain. At first strong but slow horses followed equally slow but 'musical' hounds kept for their deep baying 'music' rather than their efficiency in the field. Within a century however faster Arab blooded horses followed fleet, fast moving hounds less musical perhaps than their ancestors, but swifter and more efficient at the task of hunting foxes. Fox hunting became an efficient pageant as much as a sporting event and hence hunt terriers were required to bolt a fox rather than go to ground and destroy the creature. In 1710 *Memoirs of The Old Charlton Hunt* suggests that should a terrier be too hard to bolt a fox 'a fighting biting cur' it should be mated to a nymph or small pocket beagle of the type used to run 'stinked out rabbits' rather than hares for this cross gave voice and sense to the resulting hybrid. Lucas *Hunt and Working Terriers* suggests that the cross was made simply 'to get a terrier that would run with hounds' but it is likely the beagle cross was made to produce a terrier that bolted rather than slew its fox.

In point of fact hound blood has frequently been used to produce new or improved breeds of terrier. Airedales were supposedly bred by crossing bull terriers with otter hounds to produce dogs which took to water more readily and had better noses. It is often stated that otter hound blood was used to create the Dandie Dinmont, the Bedlington terrier and possibly the Border terrier and John Gordon in his book *The Dandie Dinmont Terrier* goes to some pains to show how early Dandie Dinmont terriers resembled certain strains of otter hound. Certain schools of thought also believe that the Sealyham terrier was not a creation of John Tucker Edwardes but simply a descendant of the rough-coated hounds of the Lowlands that were 'wont to go to ground'. This however is a very tenuous notion based on the fact that Pembrokeshire – 'a little England beyond Wales' – was settled by Flemish Huguenots and that these Huguenots brought these Lowland hounds with them. However hound-marked white-bodied terriers, both fox terriers and Jack Russell terrier-types are both spectacular and commonly seen.

Thus it came to pass that by the advent of the mid-1800s three distinct true breeding types of terrier had begun to appear in Britain.

1. The English and Welsh terrier group.
2. The Scottish terrier group.
3. The Irish terrier group.

ENGLISH AND WELSH TERRIER TYPES

Lakeland and Fell Terrier Types

It has been said that the Lakeland and fell terrier types are perhaps some of the purest forms of the Old English rough-coated black-and-tan terrier, for whereas the hunt kennels in the rest of England began to breed the fashionable and attractive white-bodied fox terriers, the Lake District continued to produce hard-bitten fell terriers that had changed but little over the century or so since they had first appeared in Britain.

It has been argued that the reason for the fact that the Lake District clung to its tradition of breeding an old type of terrier whereas the rest of England embraced the newly created white-bodied fox terrier, was simply due to the way that the inhabitants of the Lake District regarded the fox. The advent of conventional fox hunting, riding to hounds, the production of fast elegant Arab-blooded horses and faster more elegant greyhound-blooded fox hounds had allowed the Shire-dwelling sportsman to regard the fox as a sporting quarry rather than vermin and terriers with what John Russell referred to as 'gentlemanly qualities' became desirable; terriers which would go to ground and bolt rather than kill a fox, thereby affording the hounds stationed near the earth a lengthy and spectacular chase.

Pageant played no less a part in fell hunting and indeed much of the native Lake District poetry is concerned with the chase, the valour of the terriers, the tenacity and determination of the huntsmen and the abilities of famous hounds. Nevertheless the fox was regarded as vermin, a destroyer of lambs and poultry rather than simply a sporting adversary. Terriers were required to go to ground and bolt (or if the quarry would not bolt, kill) the fox and while is was obviously more spectacular to see a fox overtaken and slain by pursuing hounds if the destruction of a fox was deemed necessary – and it invariably was, these terriers were put to ground to kill a fox that had 'run in'. The more 'gentlemanly' characteristics (a curious expression) of the southern terriers was not considered desirable and terriers capable of killing foxes swiftly and efficiently greatly prized by Lake District terrier men. Thus a very hard biting extremely game type of Old English rough-coated black-and-tan terrier had evolved in the fells and it must be added that these terriers were seldom as large and powerful as folk legend would have us believe. True fell-type terriers were required to follow the hounds but mounted packs required a more leggy terrier to keep pace with hounds (allowing a

Lakeland terrier

terrier to run with hounds is a questionable practice by any standards one should add) whereas fell terriers accompanied foot followers and hence proceeded at a more leisurely pace (these terriers were frequently further encumbered by running terriers in linked couples). It is therefore worth noting that while a fox terrier of fifteen and a half inches at the shoulder is not undesirable: a Lakeland terrier of more than fourteen and a half inches at the shoulder would be considered untypical.

Archie Kirk *The Lakeland Terrier* (1964) states that he believes that the modern Lakeland terrier is a composite of the Old English rough-coated black-and-tan terrier, the Bedlington terrier and Irish terrier and while it might be argued that the original fell-bred strains were relatively pure forms of the Old English terrier there is some evidence to suggests that long before the fell strain had standardised enough to be considered Lakeland terriers, foreign blood had been added in prodigious quantities.

There was according to Ash, *Practical Dog Book* (1930), a mania for crossing southern types of terrier with bulldogs to give the terriers bred from such unions greater courage and perhaps stamina to endure lengthy battles below ground. Likewise when fell strains were considered to be becoming below par it was practice to mate certain bitches to Bedlington terrier dogs to give the progeny greater courage and tenacity. There is every indication that Tommy Dobson, founder of the fox hound pack that eventually became the Ennerdale and Eskdale Foxhounds took fell terriers to one Kitchen, a breeder of Bedlington terriers, so that they might be served by one of Kitchen's strain of terriers. Many of Kitchens' dogs were chocolate coloured (indeed there are tales that some were almost a pinkish milk chocolate hue) and that chocolate coloured Kennel Club registered Lakeland terriers are still referred to as Tommy Dobson's chocolates today. Dobson was in no way unique in using Bedlington terrier blood to increase the courage of his fell terriers. The Pools of Glenridding, a longstanding terrier breeding family frequently resorted to this practice and photographs of some of the Pools early terriers show animals with whispy coats not dissimilar to coats found on early Bedlington terriers.

There is no actual evidence to suggest that Border terrier blood was used in the creation of the Kennel Club registered Lakeland terrier, but it seems likely that Border terrier blood may have entered into the fell terrier lines that gave rise to the Lakeland terrier. Certainly there is proof that when fell terriers proved a shade too reckless or foolhardy and sustained damage while working foxes they were sometimes mated to Border terriers. Border terrier blood via a half bred fell/Border terrier owned by Major Burdon certainly entered into the blood of the famous Buck/Breay terrier lines. Likewise John Parkes who continued to breed from this Buck/Breay line also used Border terriers bred by Ray Walker to continue his family of fell terriers. Graham Ward of Durham who breeds typey box-headed dogs descended from the dogs of Harry Hardasty of the Melbreck Foxhounds also used a 'pedigree unknown' Border terrier to produce his strain of terrier. Likewise Richard Bland of Hope Lorton mated his fell terrier strain to an Otterburn bred Border terrier to breed more placid working terriers.

It is certain that small Irish terriers entered into the pedigrees of early Kennel Club registered Lakeland terriers and there is some evidence to suggest that a small Irish terrier was used to breed many of the early Kennel Club registered Lakeland terrier winners. John Winch of Consett, County Durham who is considered by many to be the authority on the lineage of the northern working terrier types believes that long before the Lakeland terrier began to separate from the rough-and-ready indigenous fell terrier types Irish terrier blood was introduced into the native stock, for shortly after the potato famine of 1831 a large Irish population settled in western Cumbria and by the turn of the twentieth century box-headed fell-type terriers had begun to appear at working terrier shows in the Lake District (it is a mistake to believe that working terrier shows began in the 1960s). Certainly certain early Lakeland terriers had a decided Irish terrier appearance. Miss Morris who gave Orgill Copper Coin his first Challenge Certificate was criticised because Copper Coin displayed certain Irish terrier features. Turk the unregistered terrier kennelled at the Melbreck kennels and owned by Harry Hardasty had an Irish terrier head and a coconut-matting type coat: this is associated with Irish terriers.

More interesting still are the white-bodied terriers, both fox terriers and Jack Russell terrier-types that were absorbed by both the Kennel Club registered Lakeland terriers and the local fell terrier strains. Clapham's book *Fox Hunting in the Lakeland Fells* caused renewed interest in fell hunting and both sportsmen and celebrities journeyed north to fell walk and to witness the prowess of the foot packs. There is little doubt that an interchange of dogs started after the publication of Clapham's book for fell terriers started appearing at southern hunt kennels and white-bodied terriers were worked with some of the fell packs. Willie Porter of the Eskdale and Ennerdale Foxhounds wrote to Jocelyn Lucas in 1930 and mentions that he kept a strain of working fox terrier (he goes to some pains to stress that these dogs were 'working' fox terriers – and they were in all probability leggy Jack Russell-type dogs) which he considered to be first rate though not as game as the strain of Lakeland terrier that was kept at the hunt kennels. Winch is, in fact, of the opinion that some of the most typey white-bodied Jack Russell-type terriers were bred in the Lake District during the early 1930s and there is no doubt that these terriers were later absorbed by certain strains of fell terrier.

Later Major Williams brought an extremely typey strain of working fox terrier to the Lake District and these dogs were absorbed by the strains of Lakeland/fell terrier kept by Jim Dalton at the Blencathra Foxhound Kennels. Turk, Daltons most famous and most attractive terrier had a box-headed appearance and was much more typey than even some of the early registered Lakeland terriers.

More important still, at least as far as the development of fell terriers rather than registered Lakeland terriers is concerned, was the contact certain fell pack terrier men made with the badger digging clubs of the south of England. As to whether Arthur Heinemann who inherited terriers from Nicholas Snow, Squire of Oare, sent terriers to the fells has long been debated – and Heinemann certainly visited the Lake District and took part in fell hunting. What is certain and is well recorded is that terriers from the Ilfracombe Badger Digging Club came into the possession of Fred Barker when he hunted the Pennine Foxhound pack at Ousby. This blood too was absorbed by fell terrier strains and caused a considerable change to the fell terrier gene pool.

As it happened, so saturated were the fell terrier strains with white-bodied working terrier bloodlines that many litters of fell terrier produced what were known as 'white Lakeland terriers' from time to time and, as these white Lakelands bred true to type (as far as colour was concerned) and were often extremely good looking and typey terriers they too were absorbed by the Jack Russell terrier stock of the time, but this must be discussed at a later date.

A dichotomy in the fell terrier types began to appear in 1912 when the name Lakeland terrier was given to some of the more typey sorts of fell terrier and in 1921 the Lakeland Terrier Association was formed and Lord Lonsdale asked to be president of the association. It was said that the Lowther family had kept a strain of fell terrier for over seventy years and this fact could be authenticated by records. In passing it is worth noting that Frank Jackson, writing in *Dog World* (1990), mentions that white terriers were also bred by the Lowther family.

It took a further eight years for the breed to be exhibited under Kennel Club rules and in 1928 three Lakeland terriers were exhibited in London all owned by Mr Paisley who kept a box-headed strain of Lakeland terrier that closely resembled early Welsh terriers in type. A further tidying up of the type occured during the 1930s and terriers that resembled Irish terriers, fox terriers and terriers with the deep mahogany tan one associates with Welsh terriers began appearing on the Lakeland terrier benches. For a while it seemed that the true Lakeland terrier would be lost, for according to Geoffrey Sparrow, *A Terrier's Vocation*, it became almost impossible to tell Welsh from Lakeland terriers (it should be added that both types not only shared a common origin but were closely related) and Mrs Spence who showed the great Lady of the Lake wrote in an impassioned manner to request that no further adulteration of Lakeland terrier blood lines should take place lest the true Lakeland terrier be lost. It is worthy of note that while alien terrier types, wire fox terrier, Welsh terrier, Irish terrier blood were commonly mated to the early Lakeland terriers the breed received few infusions of native fell terrier blood during the formative period of the Lakeland terrier.

Yet there were many who swore by the working ability of the improved Lakeland terriers; Winch believes that many of the Lakeland terriers were equally as good at work as the rough less typey fell terriers. Certainly Willie Irving kept Kennel Club registered Lakeland terriers at he Melbreck Foxhound Kennels at Hope Lorton though Joe Armstrong, a close associate of the Irving family, was quick to mention that Willie Irving kept two strains of working terrier, a fell type and Kennel Club registered Lakeland terriers. One peerless worker certainly appeared in the ranks of the newly created Lakeland terriers. During the early 1930s Harrison Tweedie bred a Crufts winning Lakeland terrier which in turn sired a restless, aggressive terrier called Rastus which Tweedie gave to local policeman Harold Watson. Rastus was a bad killer which worried sheep, killed cats and caused mayhem in kennels once he became bored or was kept inactive but he proved a doughty worker to fox and badger and he was mated to many fell terriers from less typey strains.

On the whole the newly created Lakeland terrier was not considered to be a suitable dog for hunt service however. Some had no spirit and daunted once they received a bad drubbing from foxes. Others had too much spirit and became too hard suffering serious damage from foxes and badgers alike. Few Lakeland terriers had the temperament desired by fell hunters though Tommy Coulsen's Lakeland terrier Vic bred from a

Rillington bred bitch mated to Oregill Henchman enjoyed the unique distinction of working seven days with seven different packs of foxhounds.

After the Kennel Club afforded the Lakeland terrier recognition the two-way traffic twixt fell strains and Lakeland terriers ceased abruptly though it became common practice to tidy up fell terrier strains with Kennel Club registered Lakeland terrier blood. This crossing of fell terriers with Lakeland terriers became very common after the 1960s when the craze for working terrier shows began. Nuttall believed that it then became impossible to win at working terrier shows if one's fell terrier stock was not liberally spiked with Lakeland terrier blood, though judges such as Johnny Richardson, huntsman for the Blencathra Foxhounds would not nominate fell terriers with obvious Lakeland terrier ancestry as hunt terrier show winners.

Certainly, many fell terrier breeders used Lakeland terrier stud dogs to breed litters of showy terriers. Ward, whose terriers were descended from Harry Hardastys' fell strains chose to tidy up his dogs with a dash of Lakeland terrier blood as did Ward's close associate John Winch. John Cowen of Bullyhouse Farm, Embleton, succeeded in producing a very typey strain of fell terrier by also blending his Hardasty bred terriers with Lakeland terriers such as Netherfield Newsboy and Alf Johnston's Copper Coin (a Lakeland that features very strongly in many fell terrier pedigrees).

It is a little known fact that the top winning and excellent producer Sid Wilkinson's Rock had a strong trace of Kennel Club registered Lakeland terrier blood in its ancestry. Wilkinson's Rock was bred in the purple and had lines to Bowman's Lil (a white-bodied Jack Russell terrier) Barker's Red Rock and lines to white-bodied terriers dating back to dogs from the Ilfracombe Badger Digging Club. Wilkinson's Rock is a particularly important sire for not only did the dog breed a great many working terrier show fell-class winners – including many of Middletons' dogs and Harold Long's last champion bitch – but because the dog carried so many lines to white-bodied working terriers, the recessive white-bodied offspring thrown by Rock and many of his progeny became much of the foundation stock of the Parson Jack Russell terriers, but this subject will be dealt with more fully at a later date.

However, there were many who avoided the blood of Kennel Club registered Lakeland terriers like the plague for the blood was reputed to produce bad fighters, dogs which were difficult to kennel and terriers with poor noses, though Nuttall of Holmes Chapel believes that the signs of a poor nose manifested by many Lakeland bred fell terriers was simply due to the fact that despite the gassy disposition of the terriers they were reluctant to find their foxes and engage them in combat. Richardson certainly did not favour 'blood terriers' as he referred to dogs with a strong trace of Lakeland terrier blood. Likewise the new Blencathra huntsman Barry Todhunter who had served his apprenticeship with master craftsman Johnny Richardson stayed well clear of dogs which were known to have Kennel Club registered Lakeland terrier in their ancestry.

However, two of the most famous breeders of fell terriers which were free of Lakeland terrier taint were Cyril Breay of Mallerstang and Kirkby Lonsdale and his life-long friend Frank Buck of Leyburn. The strain these breeders created originated from Sealyham terriers kept by Breay in 1925 but when Breay came north he bred more and more fell terrier blood into the stock he kept and worked. During the wartime years Border terrier blood via Major Burdon's half bred Border fell terrier was introduced. From this time forth the Breay Buck line began to throw huge bull terrier headed offspring from time to time though Breay vigorously denied he had introduced bull terrier blood in the creation of his strain. Black terriers began to appear in the early 1950s when Breay bred Gem a prolific bitch who in turn gave rise to Davey, a black harsh-coated fell terrier who together with Wilkinson's Rock and Hardasty's Turk became one of the most important sires in fell terrier history. Davey mated to a local game keeper's dog bred Skiffle, Breays most successful show bitch, that won frequently at Bramham Moor, one of the most prestigious working terrier shows in Britain.

During the early 1960s a distinct strain of fell terrier began to evolve from the smooth-coated bull terrier-headed black terriers derived from Breay's Gem and for some reason it became popular practice to call these terriers Patterdales. This was clearly a misnomer for Patterdale is a village near Ullswater a far cry from Mallerstang, Kirkby Lonsdale and Leyburn where the type had started to evolve. Furthermore the type of terrier bred by Patterdale-based breeders was a strong-headed hard-coated fell terrier quite unlike the descendants of Breay's Gem. The term Patterdale had obviously been coined outside the Lake District for in 1967 when Brockley showed Rusty (a son of Breay's Rusty) at Bramham Moor he was asked by the late Johnny Richardson what this smooth-coated dog was. Brockley replied 'A Patterdale', but Richardson shook his head and added 'A Patterdale is another name for a Lakeland terrier' (at the Keswick meeting where the Lakeland Terrier Association was formed the breed was labelled the Lakeland or Patterdale terrier).

However, it is worthy of note that Breay did not continue to breed this bull-headed type of terrier and neither did he succeed in fixing a type. Photographs of Breay's terriers taken outside Breay's home at Kirkby Lonsdale shortly before he died show rough-coated red fell terriers; leggy, reasonably typey, but a far cry from the black bull terrier-headed fell terriers which were later to be labelled Patterdales.

The task of fixing a type of terrier from this strain fell to Brian Nuttall of Holmes Chapel who has worked as a gamekeeper and terrier man for both fox hound and mink hound packs. Nuttall, considered by many to be the world's most scientific terrier breeder, upgraded his own fell terriers by using Breay's Davey and other stud dogs of the same line and by dint of a judicious breeding programme managed to produce a fairly true breeding strain of black terrier with smooth or harsh coats and scaling in at twelve to thirteen inches at the shoulder. (There have been reports that Nuttall's terriers are getting smaller but Brian denies this and states that his own terriers have stayed the same size, whereas the terriers seen at working terrier shows have become progressively taller.) This may well be true. In the late 1960s Jeff Burman of Louth, Lincolnshire, offered a cup for the 'Best Over Thirteen Inches Terrier' and there were few contenders. Today at the time of writing most terriers seen at hunt and working terrier shows are well above thirteen inches at the shoulder.

To achieve his desired goals Nuttall adopted a breeding programme that was both consistent and scientific. Nuttall adopted the method of line breeding Breay practised at one time mating twice into the line and once outside the bloodline. So consistent has been Nuttall's breeding plan that the majority of black fell terriers – the so-called Patterdales advertised in sporting papers – claim descent from Nuttalls' dogs. From time to time Nuttall has used small amounts of Border terrier blood in the creation of the strain and subsequently hard-type coats have now become fixed in Nuttall's strain of fell terrier.

So distinctive has the strain become, or so different from other fell terriers, that many working terrier shows are contemplating staging separate classes for these black fell/Patterdale terriers. In many ways this is an admirable suggestion for a dichotomy has developed in the fell terrier and two distinct types have emerged – those dogs favouring Lakeland terrier in type, shape and colour and the black fell terriers of the type bred by Nuttall. However few have continued Nuttall's admirable breeding plan and black fells have been subject to much indiscrimate breeding schemes. Intermediate types twixt Lakeland terrier types and Patterdales are legion and to standardise the type created or refined by Nuttall would appear to be a difficult project.

From time to time Nuttall's strain produces chocolate coloured fell terriers in litters born to all black parents. The origin of this strange colour – and chocolate fells have pale eyes and putty-coloured noses – is curious. The dam of Gem, Breay's great brood bitch, was Ruby a rather unsightly chocolate coloured bitch bred from a male from Walter Parkin – the Lunesdale huntsman – and a pedigree unknown fell terrier from Tebay. As to where this colour originated is a mystery. Tale has it that a chocolate coloured field spaniel features in the pedigrees of many fells. Others believe that Tommy Dobson's Bedlington terrier/fell cross introduced the colour into both Lakeland and fell strains. It is worthy of note that Breay once mentioned to Akerigg, a close friend of his, that the chocolate terrier Ruby owed her colour to a field spaniel cross.

The impact of some of Nuttall's stud dogs on the working terrier scene has been terrific. In 1986 Rocky, a black fell terrier very inbred to the Black Davy line was sold to America as a stud-cum-working dog. Later his son Ricky was sold to Judy Umek a California-based terrier enthusiast so the future of this true breeding line of fell terrier in the New World looks secure.

One of the Nuttall bred studs, Flint, was yet another prodigious dog that stood at stud in South Wales before being sold to Lancashire. While at stud in the north Flint produced Hinchcliff's Black Uns, a doughty strain of terrier kept by Nigel Hinchcliffe of the Pennine Hunt Kennels. Such was the dogs worth that he was mated (a little unwisely perhaps) to his daughters' granddaughters and great-granddaughters. Strangely Nuttall placed little value on the dog 'At that time I owned some sixteen terriers and of these Flint was the worst'.

A certain amount of mystery surrounds one of the most famous black fell terriers Smithy. Smithy stood at stud at the kennels of Ken Gould but the origin of the dog is a mystery. Gould bought the dog, pedigree unknown, from a man who had tired of badger digging and Smithy had been worked lightly. He grew into quite a famous fox-digging terrier who proved to be a potent stud force in the type. Didricksen claims to have bred the dog from a Nuttall bred stud dog mated to a bitch from John Cowen of Embleton, a black-and-tan bitch with lines to both Copper Coin and Newsboy, but despite this rather mixed breeding Smithy proved to be a great stud force and many lines were based on this dog. As a result of the presence of Copper Coin close up in Smithy's pedigree; the dog threw a large number of over-sized offspring but breeders who sought to further the bloodline by judicious inbreeding programmes have succeeded in breeding out this tendency to produce over-large terriers and the type bred from Smithy seems to have levelled out at twelve to thirteen inches at the shoulder.

Smithy's line was continued by the Ashford family – Karen and Wayne Ashford – who have, by selective and careful line-breeding, succeeded in producing a family or strain of very typey twelve to thirteen inch hard-coated black terriers with strong (but not over-large) heads and straight fronts. The Ashford's strain has not only proved very satisfactory workers above and below ground, but have won well at working terrier shows throughout Britain. The type is slightly different from the terriers produced by Nuttall and it is fairly obvious some very typey Lakeland-type terriers have been used in the creation of the strain. In all probability the very classy Newsboy and the equally typey Copper Coin have contributed much to the terriers kept by the Ashfords, though the type closely resembles Breay's Skiffle.

Fells and Lakeland-bred fells are well represented at working terrier shows at the time of writing and this popularity seems to be increasing. Many are however too large to work all but the largest earths and some are so stiff in their movements that they would be unsuitable for work under ground. In closing it is worth noting that the idea that many fell huntsmen keep large powerful terriers is a false one. Photographs of Tommy Dobson and his terriers tend to give the impression that Dobson favoured huge terriers. In point of fact Dobsons terriers were thirteen inches tall and some were smaller. Dobson, it should be mentioned, was under five feet tall and hence his terriers always appeared to be much larger than they were.

The Jack Russell Types

It is said that in 1815 John Russell, a student at the University of Oxford, was strolling through the town when he spied a terrier that took his fancy. Davies, the autobiographer of the student, describes the dog as being fourteen inches tall, fourteen pounds in weight and white with tan head markings with a shilling-sized dot near the base of its tail. The dog would today be described as broken-coated rather than rough and was the property of a milkman whose name will never be known. Russell bought the terrier, a bitch he called Trump, and the animal enters history as the *magna mater* of a strain of terrier that became either the wire fox terrier or the Jack Russell terrier, for the student graduated to become a parson, the Reverend Jack Russell, who eventually obtained a living from the parish of Swimbridge in Devon. Story has it, and legends concerning this sporting parson abound, that Russell mated Trump to his father's black-and-tan terrier thereby starting a strain of terrier that he was reputed to have kept through a very long and active sporting life.

Russell hunted regularly; perhaps with the same passion as did Cumbrians of his era.

> We can hunt on Monday
> We can hunt on Wednesday
> But we canna hunt on Tuesday
> As we have to bury mother!

For it was not unusual to find members of the clergy riding to hounds six days a week and appearing in the pulpit for a brief sermon on the Sabbath. Indeed the sporting clerics of Victorian England bore but little resemblance to the effete and obsequious clergy of Trollope. John Froude, a contemporary of Russell (with whom early historians often bracketed Russell), was a villainous bully constantly at war with the Bishop of Exeter and parish alike. Froude too rode to hounds, but also organised a spiteful band of rustic louts who cut the tails from horses and burned barns and ricks at their master's bidding. John Radford, also a contemporary of Russell, brawled his way through Oxford finally taking up a living not too far from Russell's parish where he fought tinkers and gypsies for money and continued to engage in drunken brawls until his dotage. It was said of Radford that it was disturbing to find a drunken brute brawling in Exeter on a Saturday night and even more disturbing to find the same man preaching a sermon in the pulpit on Sunday!

Hence Russell's passion for hounds and terriers was not considered unusual and scarcely worthy of comment from his bishop. The role of the Devonshire parson was a curious one, often midway between that of a squire and that of a parson. Eleanor Kerr describes Russell's role as that of a 'squarson' a man who enjoyed the benefits afforded to both the clergy and the land-owning gentry of the region.

Russell's main passions were for horses and hounds rather than terriers, however, for he hunted both otter and fox with his pack of hounds and probably regarded terriers as merely implements to expel the quarry from its lair so that hounds might pursue it.

Thus Russell required a particular type of dog, a terrier that bolted foxes and otters rather than a dog that lay close to its quarry and tried to thrash it to death. Hence he is said to have avoided breeding from known fox-killing terriers and been shy of using smooth-coated dogs because he believed that the jacket was produced by the bulldog cross and the bulldog ruined the gentlemanly qualities of his strain.

Russell preferred leggy, narrow-fronted terriers; spare of meat but strong enough to withstand a battle with a fox. His terriers were not taken to an earth when hounds marked to ground for his terriers ran with the hounds and while this is not a particularly efficient or sensible practice it does require a leggy, lean and athletic terrier to stay with a pack of foxhounds. It is said Russell required a terrier to resemble a vixen in shape and to be able to follow a fox into any crevice.

It is extremely difficult to determine where truth ends and legend begins when one studies the life of John Russell. Lucas states that Russell would take a terrier, work it to death and if the dog proved to be of the right mettle, breed from its brother! There is however nothing to substantiate Lucas' statement. Likewise Williams of Four Burrows who bred a strain of undocked working fox terriers (Scorrier terriers) stated that Russell was never a serious breeder of terriers but simply bought and sold any terrier he could obtain – Russell according to Williams was that most odious of creatures – a dog dealer.

When John Russell died his terriers and hounds passed to Nicholas Snow, the sporting squire of Oare who apparently worked them to fox but sold some of his young stock to one Arthur Heinemann who lived at that time in Peep Out, Porlock. (Heinemann eventually used the nom de plume Peep Out when he wrote articles for sporting periodicals).

Heinemann was an astounding character and larger than life if stories about him are true. He came from a family of publishers but was never a businessman himself, though Dan Russell, who knew Heinemann well, describes him as having some considerable literary talent. Heinemann was absurdly generous and his generosity made him prey to unscrupulous associates so that it is said Heinemann squandered £70,000 and lived the latter days of his life in penury living on the £6 a week Tim Sedwick, assistant editor of *Shooting Times* paid him to write as hunting editor for the magazine.

Heinemann worked his terriers to a variety of quarry. He served as Master of the Cheriton Otter-hounds from 1902–1905 and worked terriers in conjunction with the pack. Later Heinemann founded a badger digging club and in a manner befitting a latter-day John Tucker Edwardes put out fifty puppies a year 'at walk' with local farmers receiving them back to enter to badger when the terriers were eighteen months of age. However Heinemann achieved no distinction as a trainer of terriers and his terrier pack had a reputation for being rather wild and unbiddable. Dan Russell, who knew Heinemann intimately, tells a tale of how Heinemann mounted on a rather excitable pony had taken a small team of his terriers to Porlock. The pony had an irritating manner of stamping when terriers approached him and the terriers equally irritated by this mannerism attacked the pony which panicked and threw Heinemann onto the railings of Porlock church.

Heinemanns' terriers were very game however and numerous hunt kennels sported terriers given them by Heinemann. A grandson of Heinemann's Pal a famous dog throughout Devonshire was sold by Heinemann to Major K. A. C. Doig who hunted a pack of terriers bred down from dogs from Russell's Tip (there is a question-mark as to whether John Russell bred Tip or whether the dog came from the Scorrier kennels) and of course the founder of Russell's kennels, Trump. Doig hunted a pack of some twelve couple of terriers in East Africa and worked five thousand acres of scrub, hill and forest to antelope, jackal, waterbuck, warthog and even leopard. Leopards are inordinately fond of dog meat and raid villages to kill and eat watch-dogs. However, like all felines when run hard with several dogs they tend to tree and thus afford the hunter a chance to shoot them.

However, when Heinemann died in January 1930 after suffering a chill while out coursing, his terriers were dispersed to the wind. Various breeders continued to breed dogs which were similar in type to some of Heinemanns' terriers – he kept a great variety of dogs varying from ten pound terriers to terriers in excess of seventeen pounds in weight – and there are sporting terrier pedigrees which were said to prove descent from Heinemanns' dogs.

Norman and Vernon Bartlett apparently bred leggy Russells of this kind as did Jeff Burman of Louth, Lincolnshire who during the late 1960s showed a leggy fox terrier-like dog called Link that had a reputation of being an excellent dog to ground.

However the great mass of dogs purporting to be Jack Russell terriers can hardly claim descent from the dogs bred by John Russell. In all probability these dogs are the result of possible white sports bred from black-and-tan terriers or bull terrier black-and-tan hybrids or beagle crosses mingled with other breeds such as Sealyhams, fox terriers and fell types. Most southern and midland hunt kennels kept a motley band of Russell types during the years following World War II though few claimed to own a true breeding strain of white-bodied working terrier. Jack Cobby of the South West Wiltshire was, however, an exception to the rule and at one time kept an extremely typey sort of terrier bred down from Isaac Bell's Pincher. Pincher, who features in Jocelyn Lucas' book *Hunt and Working Terriers*, was not an attractive type of dog though he was reputed to be an excellent worker. Cobby's best, most typey terrier, was Pickaxe a rich tan-headed white-bodied dog that had a reputation for being a great stayer and a good finder above and below ground. As Jack Cobby approached retirement age however he stopped breeding these terriers and began keeping a strain of Border terrier which he claimed were better workers than the Jack Russell-type terriers he kept.

However, during the 1950s two breeders of Jack Russell-type terriers did much to improve the popularity of the type (and in the 1970s the Jack Russell terrier became Britain's most popular breed of dog). The first breeder, Miss Sixton, kept, bred and worked the Breach strain of terrier, dogs which according to Jim Blake of Burnley were some of the most easily entered of all the terriers Blake had kept. Blake obtained two of these terriers from Miss Sixton in the early 1960s, entered them to fox, badger and otter and found them outstanding workers. When Bob Robertson of North Kenton, Newcastle-upon-Tyne – a close friend of Jim Blakes – lost his famous Irish-bred Jack Russell terrier Tinker, Blake put both his Breach-bred terriers to Robertson and despite the fact that the pair were brother and sister Robertson mated them together.

The result of this incestuous union was Penny who was quite a slow starter as a worker – though this may have been due to the fact that Bob Robertson was not a great success at the initial entering of terriers (a point he regularly made in letters to the author of this book) – but a series of accidents and illnesses from which Robertson eventually died prevented Penny from being trained and on Robertson's death she passed to Graham Ward who had just started breeding Hardasty's strain of terrier which he obtained from Cyril Tyson of Egremont. Penny proved to be one of the most important broods in terrier history. She entered into Wards fell terrier strain and produced some first-class fell working dogs that won at every major working terrier show in Great Britain (white-bodied working terriers bred from this fell strain have also been shown as Jack Russell terriers and have won well throughout Britain).

Later Penny bred a litter of puppies for Harry Telfer and one of these puppies mated to a terrier from Malcolm Cox of Luton bred Errol Forsyth's Pip, a cornerstone amongst the working Jack Russell terriers of north eastern England. Forsyth is a fascinating character who had worked aboard a whaler before becoming a part-time gamekeeper and had a great knack of entering terriers. Pip had entered well at slightly

Forsyth's Pip: one of the most influential sires in Jack Russell terrier history

less than a year of age and became a nailer to fox or badger. His nose was outstanding and when he stopped in front of an earth or set and showed an interest in the hole the place was certainly inhabited. He worked ten years before retiring to stud in Sutton Coldfield and Lichfield and he bred a great number of offspring.

One of Pip's most famous sons was Tony Metcalf's Tod, a smaller dog than his sire and a shade more morose but a wonderful worker above and below ground. Tod was a showy dog and in the north-east – a hotbed of good class working terriers – he won repeatedly at hunt and working terrier shows. Tod, who died in January 1991, was a sterling finder, a wonderful stayer and a top class digging dog.

Tony Metcalf continued the line by mating Tod to Velvet, also sired by Forsyth's Pip, and bred Eddie Metcalf's Rocky, a typey game dog and almost a replica of his double grandsire Pip. Rocky, too, has an excellent reputation as a worker and has won at most of the shows in the north-east against some of the hottest competition in Britain.

Rocky continued the bloodlines of the famous Pip by mating Polo, a Hume bred bitch with a strong trace of white Lakeland blood (incidentally Polo was one of the top-winning terriers in Great Britain) and produced an excellent typey worker Gavin Ellis' Gem.

However, an even more important dog produced by Forsyth's Pip was Carl Pollitt's Damien who will be dealt with at a later stage in this book.

To return however to the lady terrier breeders of the 1950s and 1960s. The second breeder of importance was Miss Joan Begbie of Worth Maltravers, Wiltshire who kept a line of terriers inbred to the Vale of the White Horse bred terrier Seale Cottage Welcome, an extremely tough little terrier that used to catch and kill hedgehogs by biting through their spines regardless of the hurt she received in doing so. Miss Begbie added other lines to her original mixture namely those of Jack Cobby's Pickaxe, but despite her occasional outcross bloodlines she continued to inbreed to Seale Cottage Welcome and succeeded in producing some extremely typey and fairly small working terriers many of which are featured in Eleanor Kerr's book *Hunting Parson*.

During the late 1950s there was a revival in interest in shows for working terriers and some of these shows attracted a considerable number of competitors and spectators. Bramham Moor staged truly spectacular shows during that period and a win at this show was regarded as really prestigious.

During this period two of Britains most successful exhibitors came from the tiny Derbyshire village of Etwall. Bill Brockley and Eric Taylor often fielded some of the most spectacular terriers in Britain though they kept terriers which were not related to each other.

Brockley achieved considerable success with his bitch Tussle, a twelve inch tan and white terrier that had a decidedly houndy appearance and critics described her as a short-tailed beagle. This bitch was supposedly bred by horseman Dorian Williams or rather at the stables of Dorian Williams and was an adult when Brockley bought the bitch which was in whelp to an unknown but obvious fell-coloured dog for some of her puppies were self-coloured tans and all of her whelps were far from straight in the leg. Tussle was in fact a remarkably well-made straight-fronted animal, though if Brockley showed her in wet conditions which made her miserable she had an unfortunate manner of tucking up her loins which gave her back a curious, unsightly roached appearance.

When Tussle was a little over the hill as a show dog – Brockley never really knew Tussle's age – he mated her to a fine copper red and white terrier owned by Mary Browning the artist, a dog that Brockley considered to be one of the most typey terriers in Britain. However frequent injections to prevent the bitch coming into season coupled with Tussle's age conspired to make Tussle somewhat less than fecund and the union produced a single puppy Teasle, a dark red and white bitch a shade over ten inches at the shoulder which won a few B.I.S. prizes for Brockley but was not the class of her mother.

As a work dog, Teasle was excellent and Brockley adopted a curious method of using her to extract foxes from the many smooth sided land drains that abound in Derbyshire. Brockley would allow Teasle to listen to the sound of another dog working its fox far up inside the drain and then attach a length of clothes line to the bitch's collar. By now Teasle would be dribbling saliva at the prospect of engaging the fox and the action of Brockley attaching the line to her collar made her squeal with excitement. Teasle seemed to know exactly what was required of her for she flew up the drain and took hold of her fox allowing Brockley to haul both dog and terrier down the drain. She performed this feat so often that she became amazingly dextrous at extracting foxes from such dens despite the fact that Teasle was only twelve pounds in weight.

Some time before Teasle died Brockley obtained a heavily marked copper, tan and white terrier bred at the Fitzwilliam Foxhound Kennels and closely related to Ruth Haw's great show dogs Pedro and Grip – two of the gamest terriers ever to draw breath (Brockley eventually bought Grip, showed her and sold her, in whelp, to a Breay bred terrier). Scamp as the Fitzwilliam bred terrier was called had 'jibbed while working, failed to enter to fox and been passed off as useless.' Brockley kept the dog for two seasons and would probably have been wise to have mated him to Tussle for Scamp threw some excellent lookers and workers. However, in his fourth year Scamp entered to fox and while he never went on to become a great worker he worked a few badgers and foxes in the artificial earths around Etwall.

One of Scamp's progeny, Tarka, was a different kettle of fish however. Tarka was returned to Brockley as a stud puppy in lieu of fee and was out of a typey slightly houndy pedigree unknown bitch also bred in Etwall. Tarka was a demon: he was a copper red, heavily marked dog nearly thirteen inches high with a slightly crowded mouth that was later corrected when he pulled out all his incisors drawing foxes. Brockley would have done well to continue his bloodline but Tarka was mated to unsuitable bitches and hence produced little of any value.

As a worker Tarka had his limitations. He was, according to Jim French, one-time terrier man from the Meynell Foxhounds, far too hard to be of much use as a hunt terrier and this opinion was echoed by Sam Towers of Polesworth, terrier man for the Atherstone Foxhounds, where Tarka obtained a working certificate. Couragewise, Tarka could not be faulted but he was scarcely a clever worker and his only approach seemed to be to attack his quarry, be it fox or badger, head on and to suffer awful punishment without complaint. When hurt, and he frequently was, he attacked his foe with great fury and lay mute for as long as twenty minutes or so and was a fractious, difficult dog to kennel with other terriers. Courageous to a fault he would have been more at home with a fell pack than with a pack such as the Meynell where a dog that slew or damaged foxes was not required.

Driver, Brockleys other successful show dog, had curiously sloped hind-quarters which he passed to his many progeny. Driver had won the Jack Russell class at Bramham Moor and was reserve champion to

Breay's great bitch Skiffle at that show, but Driver became coarse as he grew older and seldom achieved success in the show ring. Driver was a late starter workwise and began entering to fox only at the end of his third year. He achieved some success workwise and eventually obtained a working certificate from the Meynell Foxhounds.

During the late 1960s and early 1970s it was not uncommon to find every honour offered at a working terrier show won by dogs kennelled at Etwall and for many years Eric Taylor shared honours with Brockley. Taylors top winning dog was a tri-colour thirteen inch dog called Badger bred from one of Taylors bitches mated to a Meynell Foxhound terrier called Rocky. Taylor used the dog Rocky when the animal was in its dotage and senile, and it spent its last years blind and infirm content to bark at skulls stripped of their meat by fleshers working at the hunt kennels. In his youth Rocky had been a very typey dog and an excellent worker and although senile produced Taylor's dog Badger, a good worker and a truly beautiful terrier.

At this point it might be wise to refer to the type of terrier winning at most hunt shows during the mid-1960s. The majority of winning Jack Russell terriers were seldom bigger than twelve inches at the shoulder at this time and there were classes at many shows for under ten inch terriers. It is exceedingly difficult to breed tiny good-quality terriers and few specimens of this size were good typey looking terriers though Charley Lewis of Northamptonshire did produce two or three good winning dogs of this size.

In the mid-1960s Jeff Burman of Louth who wrote copiously on the merits of what were then called 'Genuine' Jack Russell terriers (dogs of thirteen to fifteen inches tall and finely built) offered a cup for the best dog over thirteen inches tall. At first the cup attracted some hideous dogs which towered above typey terriers and Burman threatened to withdraw his prize. However, the presence of dogs such as Taylor's Badger in the classes gave Burman's award some credibility and the standard of exhibit improved accordingly and it is likely that the Burman cup and the terrier Badgers' wins brought about a metamorphosis in the working terrier scene for larger, taller more typey terriers began to appear and furthermore began to win at working terrier shows.

Other exhibitors enjoyed great successes. Ted Adsett who worked his terriers with the Chiddingfold and Leconfield Foxhounds at this time won many prizes with a uniform type of terrier and on Adsett's death many of his terriers were bought by Eddie Chapman one of the founders of the Jack Russell Terrier Club of Great Britain. Likewise the Goddard family who hunted hounds for the Chiddingfold and Leconfield Foxhounds showed Scrap and Lady, two magnificent typey terriers.

It is now necessary to mention the incredible Roma Moore, a human dynamo of a woman who in the mid-1960s had started the Midland Working Terrier Club, a club that produced an interesting newsletter and high quality working terrier shows, but when Roma Moore left the Midlands to live in East Africa, the club declined and became relatively unimportant.

However, in 1973 Mrs Moore approached numerous terrier enthusiasts with a view to starting a Jack Russell Terrier Club and in 1974 a meeting was called, a show (judged by Vernon Bartlett) held and a committee for the newly formed club elected. From the outset divisions in the club were all too obvious. Bartlett insisted on judging to the 'one pound to one inch' standard supposedly adopted by John Russell (fourteen pounds to fourteen inches). Hence only large terriers were placed and a very large terrier, Bully, awarded the B.I.S. Many of the exhibitors claimed they had been judged unfairly though to be quite truthful Bartlett judged to type and all his winners were 'Genuine Jack Russells'.

However there was a great deal worse to follow for the early days of the club were turbulent to say the least. At the first meeting a working standard for the breed-type was drawn up on the guide-lines suggested by the author in his book *The Jack Russell: its Training and Entering* and it was decreed that

a. Two types of 'Russell' were to be classified – an eleven inch and over type and an under eleven inch type of terrier.
b. Two types of coat: rough and smooth would be considered.
c. The club was to be referred to as The Jack Russell Club of Great Britain.
d. An advanced register for selected approved dogs was to be started as soon as possible.
e. Brindle markings would make a dog inelegible for the advanced register.

From the very start the advanced register, which was proposed by Mr Johnson of East Anglia, proved a disaster and it was never disclosed why the idea that brindle markings (a motion proposed by Neil Davidson of Penybryn Hall, North Wales) should disbar an exhibit from the advanced register though it is to be assumed that Neil Davidson considered that brindle markings indicated that the terrier had bull terrier blood not too far back in its ancestry and for some reason the committee considered that the very mixed, variable and heterogenous terriers in the club should be kept 'pure'! Later this desire for purity of type was to cause considerable problems.

The advanced register proved to be little short of being a joke for any committee member could nominate a terrier for the register and hideous and unsuitable dogs failed by one member of a committee were passed by another who was better-known to the owner of the terrier. The advanced register became a standard joke and many serious exhibitors and breeders refused to submit their terriers for examination and selection for the advanced register.

However, problems really began when the newly formed club held its first Jack Russell Terrier Club of Great Britain show. That first show was judged according to the recently drawn up club standard by Moses Smith and the Consett-based barrister John Winch and both judges agreed to give the B.I.S. to Derek Hume's dog Grip. Now Grip conformed to the club standard of excellence almost exactly and to all intents and purposes Grip was an ideal Jack Russell terrier. The trouble began when it became known that Hume's dog was bred from a fell terrier!

The subject of white-bodied Lakeland terriers had been touched on in the chapter concerned with fell terriers. To explain the presence of these white terriers simply: when two fell terriers carrying the genes of white-bodied terriers are mated together roughly one quarter of the puppies born to the pair will be white-bodied terriers

Fr Fr

FF Fr Fr rr

FF pure breeding fell
Fr fell coloured but carrying genes for white-bodied terriers
rr white-bodied terrier carrying no genes for fell-coloured terriers

Grip, despite the excellent quality of the dog, was a 'White Lakeland' and strictly speaking, at least according to the purists on the committee, not a Jack Russell terrier despite the fact that the dog would never produce a fell-coloured puppy if mated to Jack Russell-type bitches.

Hume had purchased the dog from Ron McKay of the Morpeth Foxhounds who mentioned that he had a litter of puppies bred from a black fell terrier and out of a wooly coated type of Jack Russell-type bitch. Most of the litter were red or black in colour but the Russell coloured dog was exactly what Derek Hume required.

Even before the dog achieved his controversial win at Stoneleigh he had had an amazing run of show successes. There were few working terrier shows Hume had not won with Grip and the culmination of a very successful show career was Grip's win at the Great Yorkshire Show where the best of Britains' working terriers can be seen. Hume's Grip also won reserve best in show at Yorkshire when the dog was beaten by one of David Jones (Huntsman of the David Davies Foxhounds) rough-coated dogs.

Grip produced several winners when mated to McCance's Sheba, a winner but a shade short-legged for Humes' tastes and one of these puppies, Tango, was kept by Hume. Later the dog mated Frank Clasper's bitch and bred a very fiery beauty that Derek named Gravel, a dog that bore his sire such enmity it was impossible to kennel Gravel near Grip.

Tango was in turn mated by one of Eddie Chapman's Foxwarren terriers Mariner, a heavily marked but well bred terrier which was serving its time at the Braes of Derwent Foxhounds and Hume bred yet another excellent whelp, Gem, by mating Mariner to Tango (Grip-X-Sheba). Grip produced a torrent of winning terriers and according to purists in the Jack Russell Terrier Club of Great Britain 'tainted the Jack Russell terrier blood with the blood of Lakeland terriers'. The fact that the dogs owned by club members were extremely mongrelly and uneven at that time was overlooked by the committee and by this time many of the best dogs owned by club members were related to Grip and thus it was considered expedient to overlook Grip's mixed ancestry!

Two very successful exhibitors appeared in the ranks of the Jack Russell Terrier Club of Great Britain during the next five years – Eddie Chapman and Greg Mousely, both active exhibitors and hunt terrier men for foxhound packs – and it should be borne in mind that at this time the club had been ridiculed as being a 'club for pet terriers' – a rather puzzling criticism perhaps as pet terriers are often excellent workers if given a chance, for with careful and gradual entering most terriers will work.

Eddie Chapman had been a miner by trade but some time in his thirties had decided to give up his lucrative job in the pits and take up full-time hunt terrier work. Eddie had served an excellent apprenticeship with Gerald Jones who wrote under the nom de plume Dan Russell and who had been taught terrier work by Arthur Heinemann. Chapman although quite a small, lightly-built man had become a renowned digger when he worked with the Monmouthshire Foxhounds. Thus Chapman had a great knowledge of terrier work before he became a committee member of the Jack Russell Terrier Club of Great Britain.

Chapman's stock dated back to the terriers of Enid Hosegood and his principal terrier Foxwarren Sinbad was the result of mating a Monmouthshire Foxhound-bred terrier to Exmoor Sinbad, a terrier owned by Gerald Jones and a renowned worker that had seen service with many foxhound packs in and around Devon. Chapman's Sinbad was an excellent digging terrier that had brains and guts aplenty. He was seldom badly scarred despite the fact that when Eddie worked with the Catistock Foxhounds, Sinbad was worked seven days a week. Later after a chance accident had killed Sinbad, Chapman bought the dog Jaws from Ted Adsett – a dog of a different type perhaps but bred back to the famous Rhino and a renowned worker to fox. Chapman now keeps an enormous kennel of Jack Russell terriers.

Mousely who later became chairman of the Jack Russell Terrier Club of Great Britain has had a meteoric rise to fame as a terrier man. His first terrier Rastus was bred by Meynell Foxhound terrier man Malcolm

Pert

Haddock from terriers bred by Barry Dainty (terrier man for the pack at Kineton and kennelman for the Meynell Foxhounds) from a local bred stud dog. Rastus was born at an unfortunate time in Haddock's life when kidney failure caused Haddock to leave hunt service and dispose of many of his very classy terriers. Rastus had an interesting pedigree, was a very classy animal and proved a great asset in setting Mousely on the road to success. The dog was wildly exhuberant begging to be worked and had an excellent nose. Thus it was not surprising that Mousely not only founded a strain on the animal but became a part-time terrier man for the Meynell Foxhounds for Mousely was a successful builder by trade and declined to work at full-time hunt service.

Later Mousely began hunting his own pack of hounds working mink along the rivers of Derbyshire and fielding a pack of otter-hounds that manifested a strong trace of Welsh hound blood in their ancestry. In the meanwhile his terriers were virtually unbeatable at the club and working terrier shows throughout the Midlands and the South. Mouseleys' terriers are perhaps some of the most typey Jack Russells in Britain – twelve to thirteen inches tall, tight broken coats and straight fronts. Mouseley's success has been both justified and hard earned.

To return to the Jack Russell Terrier Club of Great Britain. Movements within the club indicated that a schism was about to occur for Bartlett's idea of establishing a club for what was once referred to as 'Genuine Jack Russells' had taken root. Bartlett's group had the cohesion that the Jack Russell Terrier Club of Great Britain did not have, for the latter club had been plagued with quarrels, disputes and expulsions of various members. Thus early in the 1980s the followers of Vernon Bartlett promptly formed the Parson Jack Russell Terrier Club which once it was consolidated and had drawn up a standard, promptly applied for Kennel Club recognition for the type and in the last year of the decade that recognition was granted.

In the months leading up to the granting of Kennel Club recognition a curious state of affairs existed. The sporting press published letters from owners of Jack Russell terriers which indicated that while the Jack Russell Terrier Club of Great Britain had no wish to obtain Kennel Club recognition, seemingly they did not want the newly formed Parson Jack Russell Club to receive that recognition either. It is fairly easy to see why. Once one type had been recognised by the Kennel Club the other type would be relegated to something second-rate. Yet the Parson Jack Russell Terrier Club had its imperfections: the Parson does not breed true to type. Ken Bowden in *Our Dogs* states that 'entries of this type often resemble a variety class'.

It is interesting to note the attitude of both clubs to that 'nigger in the woodpile' the white Lakeland terrier. From the very start of the Jack Russell Terrier Club of Great Britain the committee seemed opposed to introducing white Lakeland terrier blood into the Jack Russell terrier gene pool, despite the fact that these dogs have done a great deal to tidy up very untidy looking Jack Russell terrier types. However the Parson Jack Russell Club has not been as short sighted for many of the terriers registered by the club have either been white Lakeland terriers or bred from these terriers.

It has been argued by Eddie Chapman that white Lakeland terrier blood has a damaging effect on the Jack Russell terrier. Eddie argues that if these Lakeland terriers are brought into the bloodlines of Jack Russells they will produce terriers which are too hard for hunt service in the South and Midlands where terriers are required to bolt foxes rather than kill them (and Lakeland terriers certainly kill foxes) and that improvement of type should be made by practising a careful eugenic programme using existing stock rather than deliberately out-crossing to alien types of terrier. As it happens the majority of the members of either club are not likely to put terriers to ground anyway and the use of white Lakeland terrier blood certainly improves the quality of Jack Russell terriers and improves it quickly one should add.

Yet another cat is about to be thrown amongst the pigeons however. In 1990 the Australia Jack Russell Club has applied to have its standard considered by the Kennel Club and if one looks at the Australian version of the Jack Russell terrier it becomes apparent that the Australian Russells are very inferior to the stock bred in Britain. The future of the various Jack Russell types looks confused to say the least!

The Sealyham Terrier

A spectator with little or no knowledge of dogs or cynology would, on visiting Crufts for the first time and hearing broadcasters narrate the virtues and qualities of various breeds, be forgiven for thinking that the exhibition craze had done little to reduce the working ability of the breeds exhibited at this show. However, the truth is that the show craze and breeding exclusively for aesthetic appeal has produced non-retrieving retreivers, non-pointing pointers, collies which find the herding of livestock a bewildering activity and terriers that have neither shape nor instinct to enable them to be suitable dogs to work to ground. Sadly one of the breeds that has been most damaged by the whims of breeders seeking to produce animals solely for exhibition has been the Sealyham terrier.

The Sealyham terrier is said to have originated in Pembrokeshire and to have been the production of one of J. O. T. Edwardes, the sporting squire of the estate of Sealy Ham. Edwardes served as a captain in the 23rd Regiment of Foot and later retired from service to manage his estate. R. Booth writing in *Shooting News* (30 November/6 December 1990) believes that it was Edwardes passion for otter hunting that triggered off his desire to produce a new type of terrier, but it is difficult to substantiate Mr Booth's statement for whereas the Sealyham has been used for otter hunting – indeed Lucas ran packs of Sealyham to pursue otters – the shape of the original Sealyham was a shade too low to the ground to give the dog the mobility required to follow hounds in wet conditions and over the obstacles and hazards found on riparian terrain.

Edwardes is said to have conducted his experiments to create a new type of terrier in 1850 though how he undertook his project is the subject of some speculation. Three theories as to the origin of the Sealyham terrier should be considered.

a. The Sealyham is an entirely new breed created from scratch, so to speak, by John Tucker Edwardes.
b. The type is a modification of the old rough-coated black-and-tan English terrier much altered in type and colour.
c. The Sealyham is a relatively pure form of the Flanders and Low Countries hound mentioned by Turbeville in 1575.

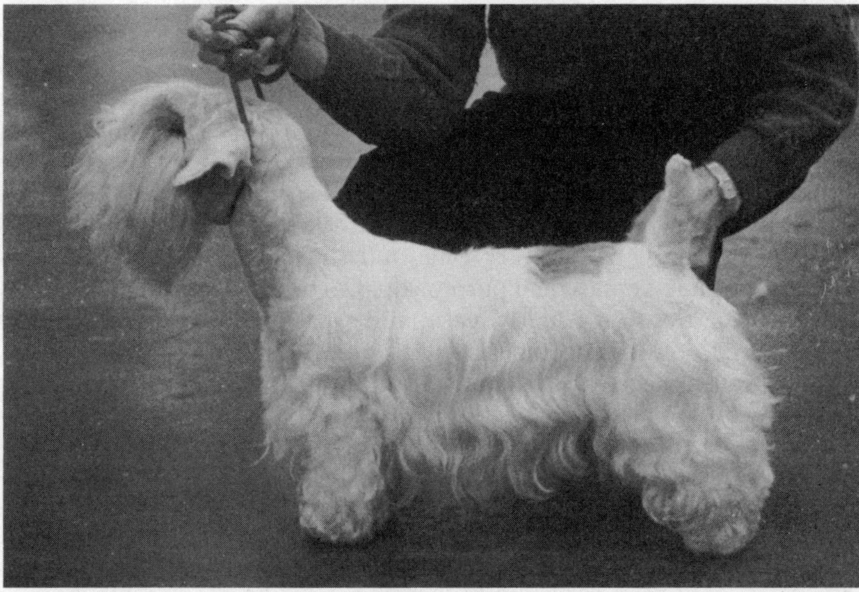

Sealyham terrier

There is little doubt that Pembrokeshire had a native breed of terrier long before John Tucker Edwardes was born and it is likely that these terriers were simply forms of the black-and-tan terriers which gave rise to the Welsh terrier and the unregistered strains and types such as the Ynysfor terriers which until the 1950s were bred at and around the kennels of the Ynysfor otter-hounds. It is possible that John Tucker Edwardes used these dogs as his foundation stock, introduced new blood, kept back white 'sports' that appeared in the litters and produced a relatively true breeding type which became known as the Sealyham terrier. Frankly this is the most logical of the theories concerning the origin of the type, for it is a relatively simple matter to fix a true breeding type similar to that of the Sealyham from black-and-tan terriers carrying the genes that can produce white-bodied terriers. It is worthy of note that in 1891, shortly before the death of John Tucker Edwardes, he is reputed to have offered for sale a Sealyham terrier called Tip 'Pedigree known for 100 years – warranted to go to ground to fox. Price £5'. Clearly these terriers were being bred long before John Tucker Edwardes had been born!

Lucas, however, suggests that Edwardes began from scratch so to speak, mating various types of short-legged terrier together and using breeds such as the Dandie Dinmont terrier, an extinct type of bull terrier known as the Cheshire terrier (small pit-bred strains of bull terrier existed in Cheshire until the 1920s) and possibly some strain of white-bodied fox terrier less leggy than the type bred by John Russell who was a contemporary of Edwardes. Lucas suggests that the corgi may also have been used in the creation of the Sealyham terrier to give the breed strength of bone and to shorten the legs of the type but offers poor evidence to substantiate his theory other than to state that wall-eyes are found in both Sealyhams and Cardigan corgis.

However, it is unwise to dismiss out of hand the notion that corgi blood did play a part in the creation of the Sealyham. Irish terrier breeds – Glen of Imaals, Irish, Kerry Blue and soft-coated Wheaten terriers were at one time kept as dual purpose dogs to destroy vermin and to herd sheep and cattle, so it is fairly reasonable to assume that Welsh farmers too required dogs that could also fulfil more than one function. Lucas suggests that the corgi shows no inclination to go to ground. This simply is not true, for some corgis need to be tethered to prevent them becoming a nuisance because of their desire to run to ground.

There is little evidence to suggest that the hounds of the Low Countries were the ancestors of the Sealyham other than the fact that when the purges of the Huguenots followed the St Bartholomew Day massacre, many Flemish Huguenots came to settle in Pembrokeshire, but there is no evidence that small hounds with a tendency to run to ground came with these refugees. It would be just as logical to assume that at the time of writing America is overrun by pot-bellied pigs for the United States absorbed many refugees of the Vietnam war.

Likewise, tales of how Tucker Edwardes made selections amongst the puppies he put out to walk with tenant farmers are not only legion but probably apocryphal. Tale has it that Tucker Edwardes would approach these puppies, gun in hand, and if the whelps showed the slightest fear or apprehension he shot them. Those that passed this test were subjected to an even more gruelling ordeal before they were even a year old for Edwardes would order gamekeepers to set traps for polecats, fierce hard-biting ancestors of ferrets, and encourage the puppies to rush into the cage-traps and draw out the furious and foul-smelling creatures. Those who failed to perform this task no doubt followed the route taken by the more timid puppies! There is also a tale that one of the terriers which failed the polecat test was pardoned because a local farmer begged the whelp's life, and the terrier went on to become the most famous badger hunting terrier in Pembrokeshire. It is indeed difficult to tell where fact and fantasy begin and end where nineteenth century terrier enthusiasts are concerned.

However what is obvious is that Tucker Edwardes set out to produce a fairly short-legged chunky sort of terrier which was capable of going to ground on fox, badger or otter with bone and substance enough to withstand the rough and tumble meted out by such foes and strength of jaw enough to punish its enemies. Edwardes seemed to have sought to breed a white-bodied terrier easily identified by hounds one supposes, though hounds are a great deal more perspicacious than casual observers might imagine, weighing twelve to fourteen pounds in weight and capable of following most quarry below ground.

It was an ideal standard of excellence for a working terrier and many sought to maintain this type of dog. Gladdish Hulkes, a New Forest hunter, once kept a small pack of these terriers, bred from stock he obtained from a Pembrokeshire butcher who knew the then aging Edwardes well. Hulkes kept up to ten couple of these terriers described by him as 'weasel-bodied dogs' and on his death-bed willed them to Lucas rather than sell them to 'fanciers' for the breed was attracting some considerable attention from the 'show bench' fraternity. Sausage, a diminutive Sealyham terrier mentioned by Lucas when he wrote for *Field* under the *nom de plume* 'The Lad' was scarcely nine pounds in weight and was bred from the dogs Lucas obtained from Gladdish Hulkes.

Sir Jocelyn Lucas began his interest in Sealyham terriers shortly after World War I in which Lucas had won a Military Cross for gallantry and had amputated two of his own toes when they became gangrenous after his capture by the Germans! Lucas had served his apprenticeship by hunting a pack of fox terriers to rabbit, rat or w.h.y. (what have you) as Lucas stated in a letter to the author.

It is worthy of note that Lucas adopted a curious method of working a pack of terriers – though he hunted a pack efficiently and kept good order amongst the terriers, which are the most difficult of dogs to control in a pack situation. It was Lucas' custom to run young unentered terrier puppies with beagles to encourage the terriers to hunt and to give tongue while hunting. Lucas devised this technique when he was putting together a pack of trencher-fed terriers owned by local fox terrier keepers and contined to use beagles in the pack long after he obtained his Sealyham. In passing it is worth noting that the running of hounds of any sort in conjunction with a terrier pack is a practice that can be ruinous, though this statement will be explained at a later date.

Lucas made an incredible name for his pack of Sealyhams during the 1920s, though he had many critics, for terriers seem to attract the spiteful and the vicious elements of human society, but later in the decade he published a challenge to any kennel of any breed of terrier to compete against his Sealyhams in the field, and not surprisingly he had no takers and the spiteful criticism of Lucas abated even though it did not cease.

It would be difficult to imagine more versatile terriers than those bred by Lucas, for he ratted the pack, hunted them to otter both in conjunction with otter-hounds and simply as a terrier pack and dug badger with these terriers. On badger digs he took several diggers with him and many of these diggers were military personnel willing to give up their free time to accompany Lucas for Lucas had incredible charisma that did not diminish when he became an elderly gentleman. He became an M.P. in his middle years and apparently one of the only questions he asked of the House of Commons was whether it was legal to have a type of terrier named after him, for Lucas had become aware that the Sealyham terrier was becoming too heavy and cloddy to wrok and too much emphasis was being placed on producing a coat that could be trimmed to hide certain defects.

When Lucas wrote for *Field* using the nom de plume 'The Lad' he attracted a large readership, but also a large number of critics particularly when he wrote of having some thirteen terriers to ground in the same set. Terrier locators were not invented until the 1960s so the muffled baying of dogs being pushed into badgers by enthusiastic terriers working behind them must have made digging to these Sealyham terriers particularly difficult in a large badger set. He received a spate of rather poisonous mail after publishing this article, but terrier men seem to have always been vitriolic in their criticism of others in the sport.

The Sealyham terrier now embraced by the Kennel Club was undergoing a considerable metamorphosis however. Larger terriers were being bred, more typey perhaps but too large to get to ground in tight places and too cloddy to be mobile. Giants had begun to appear at Lucas Ilmer Kennels. Ilmer Jack was twenty-four pounds in weight but held an M.F.H. certificate and somehow invariably got to his foxes, though the dog was at its best during a badger dig where his strength and courage made him a valuable asset to any team, but Jack was by no means a large dog compared to some of the Sealyham terriers that were being shown at the time. Tom Horner *Terriers of the World* states that Huntsman and Peer Gynt, two magnificent terriers illustrated in Lucas book *The Sealyham Terrier* were twenty-four and twenty-seven pounds respectively and this huge increase in size, though corrected in later years, was the death knell for the Sealyham as a working terrier.

Lucas was not the only person to lament the passing of the old type of Sealyham terrier. In the 1950s Dr Frantisek Horak, a Czechoslovakian dog enthusiast embarked on a somewhat curious breeding project which was said to be inspired by his discontent with the shape and coat of the typical Sealyham terrier. Horner *Terriers of the World* states that Horak mated his Sealyham terrier to a Dandie Dinmont terrier, but there is much evidence to suggest Horner is correct, though there is little doubt that Dandie Dinmont terriers featured in Horak's later breeding programme.

The breed booklet *This is the Cesky Terrier* written by Mr Filip Johnnson of Sweden, states Horak simply mated a Scottish terrier bitch Scotch Rose to a Sealyham terrier dog Buganier Urquell and produced the desired product, though there is little doubt that Dandie Dinmont terrier blood was used to refine the cross-bred stock. At the time of writing the Cesky terrier is of very variable type and two distinct sorts of Cesky terrier may well be produced in the next decade or so. The Cesky is a shade too heavy-coated to be an ideal working terrier unless it is clipped prior to entering it for coats of this type 'ball up' in clay or snow. Apparently the Cesky is regularly worked to fox by Polish and Czechoslovakian hunters but at the time of writing only one British breeder, Liz Gay of Gamston, has bred this unusual terrier and put them out to working terrier enthusiasts.

The Cesky is a well-formed terrier, ten to fourteen inches at the shoulder and thirteen to twenty pounds in weight. The Cesky's head is powerful and strong enough to give a good account of itself below ground. The muzzle is a little long compared to the Sealyham of the 1920s but with this length goes a powerful bite. The breed is however sometimes subject to a peculiarity known as Scotty cramp that is peculiar to Scottish terriers and has been offered as proof of the Cesky's Scottish terrier origins.

An equally interesting and very attractive type of dog that owes its origins to the Sealyham terrier is the Lucas terrier. Basically the Lucas terrier is a cross between the Norfolk terrier and the Sealyham. Indeed pedigrees of Lucas terriers sometimes indicate that the dogs are first cross Sealyham-X-Norfolk terriers.

It is said that the Lucas terrier was the result of an accidental union between the two types of terrier, but this seems to be extremely unlikely. Lucas had a considerable interest in the Norfolk terrier long before he began to consider breeding the Lucas terrier. In his masterly book *Hunt and Working Terriers* (1931) he includes a large and fairly explicit chapter on the type that was later to stratify into the Norfolk and Norwich terriers though he refers to the type as the Norwich or Trumpington terrier. Lucas takes some considerable effort to explain how neatly constructed and small of size the Norwich or Trumpington terrier actually was and to stress that few were heavier than ten pounds in weight (the standard of excellence for the Norfolk or Norwich terriers makes no mention of weight but suggests ten inches at the shoulder should be an ideal height). Lucas does however mention that the type was inclined to be a fighter 'I gather Norwich terriers scrap a bit sometimes' and this was a quality Lucas certainly did not admire for Lucas once said that a bad fighter in kennels was 'as much use as a sore head'. It becomes fairly obvious as one researches Lucas, his writings and his kennel policies that his interest in the type was far from casual and that he deliberately experimented with the type to produce the Lucas terrier – he obviously intended to produce a small agile Sealyham typed and coloured terrier from the union of Norwich and Sealyham terrier.

Hybrids between Sealyham and Norfolk and Norwich terriers can be very variable however. First cross hybrids are invariably either brown, tan, cream, wheaten, black-and-tan or any other colour type found among Norwich or Norfolk terriers (Norwich terriers which are a prick-eared form of the common stock that spawned both Norfolk and

Norwich terriers are seldom used in the creation of Lucas terriers for prick ears are considered undesirable in these hybrids). Second cross hybrids between F1 Norfolk Sealyham hybrids produce roughly twenty-five per cent Sealyham coloured or white-bodied offspring

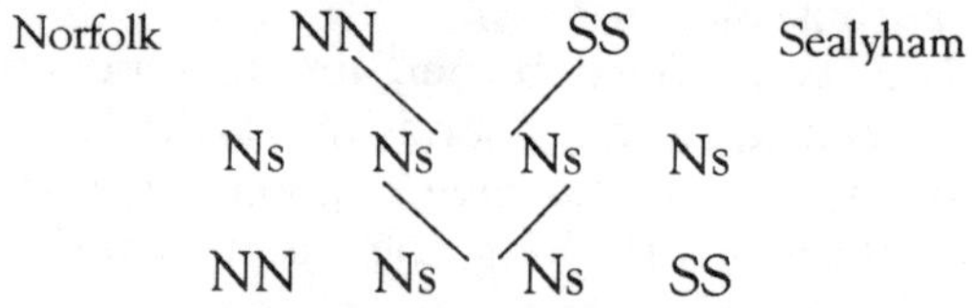

NN Norfolk parent and pure Norfolk coloured hybrid
SS Sealyham and Sealyham coloured hybrids
Ns Norfolk coloured hybrids carrying Sealyham coloured genes

In 1988 the Lucas terrier club published a working standard, but it was far too vague and indecisive to be a useful guideline for future breeding projects.

Characteristics

The Lucas (*sic*) should be a good-natured cheerful friendly and sporting little dog. A keen hunter and an enthusiast. Most people who have owned one find them enchanting characters. I think this is because they are less aggressive, softer and more affectionate than one would expect and more solid of character than some small dogs. Most have a wonderful temperament.

Conformation

The Lucas should be a compact dog and although small should have strong shoulders and hind-quarters, not too long in the leg. Average bitch about ten to twelve inches tall at the shoulder and proportionately quite a broad chest. Head smaller than a Sealyham. Ears small and dropped. Eyes dark. Mouth true not undershot – if they are it would be advisable not to breed. Nose should be black. Back straight and not too long. Tail is traditionally docked though some are left these days and look attractive either way – it is a matter of personal taste. Movement should be free and lively.

Coat

Rough. Does not moult; needs to be stripped or groomed and tidied up regularly or both.

Colour

Anything from almost white, wheaten-and-white to almost black.

Weight

Bitches twelve to fifteen pounds. Dogs sometimes slightly more.

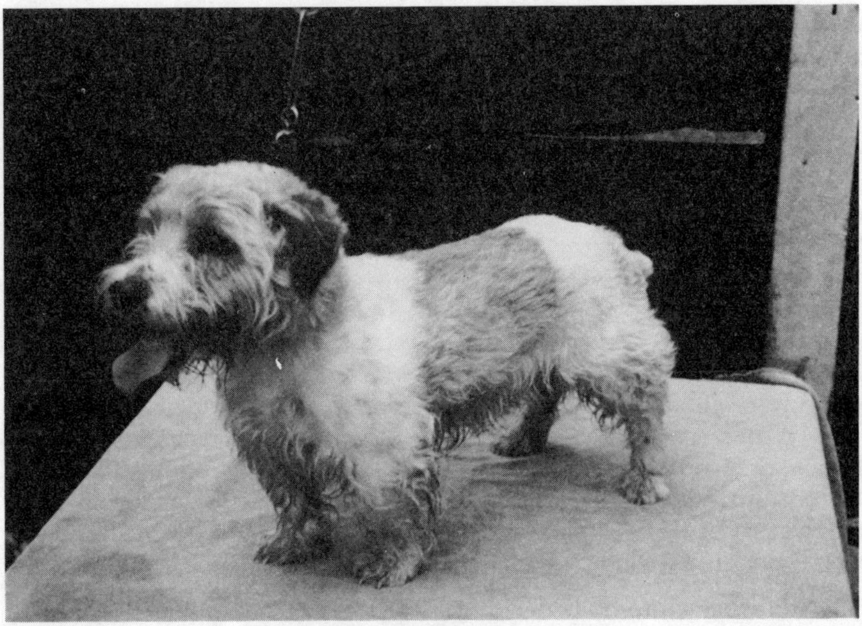

Jason Barnes' Polo: a Lucas terrier

At the time of writing the breed type has a very small gene pool and in 1987 only three litters were born, all sired by Jason Barnes dog Polo an attractive tan-and-white box-headed dog, but it was planned to breed two litters of F1 Lucas terriers by mating small Sealyham terriers to Nan Fan bred Norfolk terriers, but the gene pool of the type is still pitifully small. Frank Jackson writing in *Our Dogs* (1990) mentions that if the type could be produced commercially there would be a tremendous market for the stock in America.

The type is obviously ideally suited for work below ground and a properly conditioned Lucas terrier weighing in at twelve pounds or perhaps a shade more would be able to negotiate any earth and find foxes. However it should be pointed out that despite the fact the dog is purpose bred for work (it has a Sealyham colour and head but is of Norfolk terrier size, few of the forty-two members of the club seem to want to work their dogs. Barnes of Essex is an exception to the rule so it appears. He came by the dog Polo when the dog was upwards of two years of age: it was whelped on the sixth of June 1985 and had seen no conventional work. Barnes obtained the dog simply because Polo was unhappy with children. As a working dog Barnes seems pleased with Polo, with some reservations that is, for initial entering had obviously been omitted and the dog was jack-knifed from pet to working dog without preliminary training. Hence the dog has proved not as useful as some of Barnes' fell-type terriers nor as versatile as the Lucas-X-fell hybrids Barnes has bred from the dog. It is worthy of note that the Lucas-X-fell hybrids sired by Polo are wheaten in colour but still retain the Sealyham shape or rather a shape more akin to the early Sealyham terriers.

The Lucas terrier is an interesting type of dog that would be an excellent prospect for serious terrier breeder to keep and breed. There is clearly a market for this neat and attractive workmanlike terrier and it would take merely a few generations of selective breeding to produce a dog with both the working qualities and type of the old-fashioned Sealyham terrier.

On the subject of the old-fashioned Sealyham – the type bred in 1920–1930 – a letter from Bob Lawrence to *Sporting Dog* asking if anyone bred this old-fashioned type attracted a large number of letters which were published in both *Shooting News* and *Sporting Dog* in 1990. Clearly there are many ways of recreating the old type Sealyham – though octogenarian Alf Rhodes who knew Lucas and who entered Ilmer strain Sealyham to both fox and badger believes it would be a lengthy process. Suggestions as to how the type could be created have been legion and include

a. Refining white-bodied F_2 Lucas terriers.
b. Breeding from white sports that appear from time to time in certain strains of Cesky terrier – these white sports would breed true if mated together.
c. Mating F_2 Lucas terriers to Cesky terriers and mating F_2 Cesky Lucas terriers together

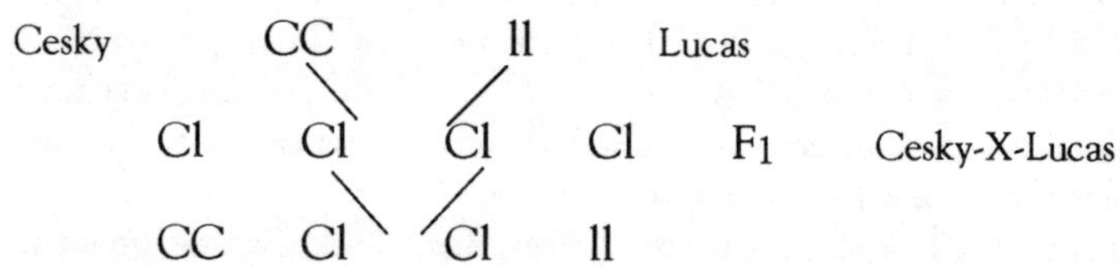

CC Cesky parent and Cesky coloured hybrid
Cl Cesky Lucas hybrids
ll Lucas parent and hybrid with Lucas terrier colour, but with stronger head

d. Mating Sealyhams to Russell-types (suggested by Bob Lawrence) and breeding from Sealyham-type progeny.
e. Mating rough-coated fell-X-Plummer hybrids to Lucas terriers and breeding out the blanket-marked-bodied terriers.

Clearly there is still considerable interest in the working Sealyham-type and it is hoped the real working Sealyham-type will be revived in the near future.

The Bedlington Terrier

In the years between the world wars it was almost a custom for each and every handbook of dogs to describe the Bedlington terrier as 'the dog with the looks of a lamb and the courage of a lion' and at one time this epigram contained more than a modicum of truth.

The Bedlington terrier, and its near relative the Dandie Dinmont terrier, owes its origin to an area around Rothbury Forest, a tract of land that straddled the border between Scotland and England. Suggestions as to the origin of these unusual types are legion and include

a. Hybrids between some type of hound and some long extinct terrier.
b. Matings between rough-coated black-and-tan and Scottish terriers.
c. A distinct type of dog that, by dint of inbreeding of the original native stock, produced the highly unusual common stock that in turn gave rise to both the Bedlington and Dandie Dinmont terriers.

The stud book mentioned by Redmarshall in his book *The Bedlington Terrier* suggests that the breed can trace its ancestry to at least 1782 when Old Flint, the foundation stud dog of the breed type, was supposedly born, but it was not until 1820 when a Mr J. Howe of Alnwick (reputedly Britain's most superstitious town) visited the tiny mining village of Bedlington (which gave its name to the breed) bringing with him a terrier called Phoebe for hitherto the type had been bred around Rothbury or Framlington and Longhorsly. Joseph Ainsley, who lived in the village of Bedlington is therefore credited with being the father of the breed-type for the bitch Phoebe was passed to Ainsley who continued the line of terriers by mating her to a similar sort of terrier, Anderson's Piper. Phoebe's colour was a black or black/blue and she had a light coloured silky tuft of hair on her head. She was about thirteen inches high and weighed fourteen pounds.

Piper, which was related to Phoebe through a dog called Old Peachem (a popular name for terriers along the border country and a corruption of impeach – to charge or to indict) was 'a dog of slender build about fifteen inches high and fifteen pounds in weight. He was a liver colour,

Bedlington terrier

the hair being a sort of hard wooly lint, his ear was large, hung close to the cheek and was slightly feathered at the tip'.

The result of the union between Piper and Phoebe was Young Piper (because of this lack of originality in naming dogs a great many Bedlingtons were called Piper as many fell terriers are called Turk). Young Piper is always referred to as Ainsley's Piper. Indeed Redmarshall labels the various Pipers, Phoebes and Peachems in the pedigree of the Bedlington terrier thus: Piper R15, Peachem R13, Phoebe R12 (to prevent confusion) and Ainsley's Piper (Piper R16) was probably the first dog to be referred to as a Bedlington terrier.

Other blood may have entered into the pedigrees of these unique sporting terriers. Red Marshall quotes a letter in the *Field* in 1869 signed 'A', the writer of which states that 'at the time when Edward Donkin kept his kennels at Flotterton a colony of sporting nailers then flourished at Bedlington and these nailers were noted for their plucky breed of terrier.' Likewise Hugh Dalziel *British Dogs* (1888) quotes a letter to the *Newcastle Chronicle* in 1872 which states that 'it is not at all unlikely that the Staffordshire nail-makers, who some eighty or ninety years ago were brought from the south and employed at Bedlington, crossed the pure bred native terrier with some of the stock they brought with them having probably fighting purposes in view.' It should be added that such notions are the result of pure supposition for there is not the slightest proof that bulldog blood or the bull terriers bred in Staffordshire either entered into the bloodlines of the Bedlington terrier or for that matter were brought north by these nail-makers. It is indeed illogical to assume that because a band of Staffordshire nailers came to Bedlington that they brought with them pit bull dogs. Not every nail-maker kept bull terriers or had an interest in dog fighting. Winch (1979) is however of the opinion that Northumberland and Durham produced types of fighting dog in the late 1800s and that these were quite distinct from the pit dogs of the rest of Britain for many had rough or broken coats. It is also worthy of note that at the cessation of World War II a popular badger digging-type of terrier in South Wales was the Bedlington terrier mated to a Staffordshire bull terrier – particularly Staffords bred from the rather unfashionable but still utterly game J lines, pure specimens of which were available until the early 1950s. These cross-breds were extremely game, inclined to be mute perhaps, and extremely ugly (particularly as many of these dogs were prone to follicular mange infections which stripped the dogs of hair) but resembled early Dandie Dinmont terriers in type and temperament. It is possible, but no more than possible one should add, that if the nail-makers from Staffordshire brought pit bulldogs with them, and if these pit bulldogs entered into the gene pool of local terriers bred in and around Bedlington the cross may have facilitated the schism that produced Dandie Dinmont and Bedlington terriers from the native stock that spawned both breeds. However this statement is also pure speculation and cannot be substantiated with hard historical fact.

However, whether or not Ainsley's Piper had bulldog ancestors is disputed – what is not disputed is that the dog had great courage. The animal was worked to badger, otter, fox and polecat by Ainsley who was a stone mason by trade and later when the dog was almost geriatric it turned back an angry sow that was in the process of attacking a child – or so legend relates!

Tales of the courage of the Bedlington terriers bred at the turn of the century are also legion. Rawden Lee *Modern Dogs* (1894) mentions the tale of an American buyer who wished for a very game fox terrier to be sent to him. The dealer the American had approached sent him a very game dog and added that this was the gamest fox terrier he could find and if this dog was not suitable the American should buy a Bedlington terrier.

It is worth noting that when breeders in the south wished to endow a strain of terrier with great courage they resorted to crossing the terriers with bulldog or bull terrier blood. Northern breeders however pepped up flagging strains of terrier with Bedlington terrier crosses. Tommy Dobson of the Eskdale and Ennerdale Foxhounds used Bedlington terriers from the Kitchen family to 'soup up' his strain of fell terrier, and produced untypey but utterly game dogs. Kitchens' best dogs were predominantly chocolate in colour and hence the fell strains bred from Tommy Dobson stock which later contributed to the Kennel Club registered Lakeland terrier gene pool often threw chocolate coloured terriers. In fact when chocolate-coloured Kennel Club registered Lakeland terrier puppies are born they are often referred to as 'Tommy Dobsons' Chocolates'.

Tommy Easy, the horseman and horse dealer of Durham, once bred a very hard loose-coated strain of fox terrier by crossing fox terriers with Bedlington terriers, though Easy went to an Alnwick breeder of Bedlingtons to secure the Bedlington terriers he required. Easy's first-cross hybrids were blue/black, linty-coated dogs but threw white-bodied terriers when these F_1 hybrids were mated together. Easy's Trip was sent to America when a buyer requested an iron-hard terrier capable of tackling skunk and many of the working terrier strains bred by Cape Foxhound packs were bred from Easy's strain of Bedlington-X-Fox terrier hybrids.

Lucas mentions a Mr Hanson of Yorkshire who swore by a working terrier with a dash of Bedlington terrier blood – he was sent one such terrier by Tom Easy one should add. Hanson believed that a dash of Bedlington blood of the right strain – and there is evidence to suggest that Hanson had difficulty finding the right strain – produced the best terriers for badger digging and Hanson had a formidable reputation as a badger digger in the north of England.

Lucas also mentions a Mr John Robinson of Cumberland who also obtained some of his terriers from Tom Easy. Robinson worked the Melbreck country, some of the roughest terrain in the Lake District, and mentions that Bedlington crosses are often easy starters and that his Bedlington fox terrier hybrids sometimes bolted foxes when the terriers were eight months of age and the same terrier went to ground in an old badger set, killed a fox and fought a badger until it became dark and Robinson called the dog out. Robinson later sold the terrier to the West Norfolk hunt kennels.

Braithwaite Wilson of the Ullswater Foxhounds was of the opinion that the Bedlington terrier cross did litle to improve strains of fell terrier. At that time, 1920–1930, John Pool of Glenridding had quite a lot of very hard tough Bedlington-bred fell terriers that had an excellent reputation amongst Lake District hunters. Wilson did not like these dogs as he considered that the loose coat of the Bedlington hybrid made the dog sensitive to the cold and wet weather one encounters in the Ullswater hunt country. Eddie Pool, son of John Pool, repudiates this statement however and states that the terriers bred by his father at that time were much prized not only for their courage but also for their hardiness.

Lucas also mentioned the dogs of Sir Thomas Ainsworth, Master of the Tipperary Foxhounds, who worked fox terriers (in all probability these dogs would be called Parson Jack Russell terriers today) which were white Lakeland-bred though the original Lakeland terrier had a dash of Bedlington terrier blood (Ainsworth states half-Bedlington, half-Lakeland terrier). Ainsworth's original terrier was probably bred by

Wiseman a terrier breeder from near Leeds who sent quite a lot of terriers to the Tipperary hounds during the 1920s and it is worth noting that the coffles of terriers brought in by Cartwright of Gloucester in the late 1930s not only sometimes came from Tipperary but had linty coats not dissimilar to the dogs bred by Tom Easy.

However, while it is obvious that Bedlington cross-bred terriers found favour with hunters and badger diggers it is worthy of note that few pure-bred Bedlington terriers were used at hunt service and while this could be attributed to the fact that the long legs of the Bedlington terrier and the deep, often unspanable, chest of the bench-bred Bedlington terrier did not find favour with many diggers there is considerable evidence to suggest that much of the fire one associates with the Bedlington terrier of the 1900s had been bred out even by the 1930s though pure-bred Bedlington terriers were worked by many south Welsh badger diggers at that time and the photograph of the now famous Salter's Wood badger dig of 1917 shows an old-fashioned Bedlington terrier owned by Rawlinson (a dog which died after a mauling by a badger in 1918).

There is some evidence that whippet blood was added to the Bedlington terrier gene pool to breed a more typey leggy roach-backed terrier, but this whippet blood would have done little to quench the fire of the Bedlington terrier. Early whippets, rag dogs, rabbit-coursing dogs and race dogs alike were often some of the very bravest animals imaginable. Likewise it has been said that lurcher blood may have also been mated to the early Bedlington terriers – though the purpose of this breeding is debateable (certainly there may have been many Bedlington lurchers bred in the early part of this century and Brian Vesey Fitzgerald *It's My Delight* suggests that the lurcher of the northern tinker and Romany clans, the Faas, the Angusons and the Stewarts with whom Vesey Fitzgerald travelled, were Bedlington rather than collie-bred). However the decline of the working qualities of the Bedlington terrier was according to Margaret Williamson, breeder of the Gutch Common strain of Bedlington terrier due to crosses with miniature poodles which were used to breed in a more easily trimmed coat in the bench-bred Bedlington.

Interest in the working qualities of the Bedlington terrier plummeted after World War II. George Newcombe, breeder of the Rillington strain of Bedlington terrier started his kennels with a purchase made from the £5 'Welcome Home' money he obtained from locals when he returned home from World War II. His first purchase was a terrier he bought from Mr Hammond of Kirkby Moorside and from this purchase he bred the famous Rillington strain of Bedlington terrier. Newcombe is an expert terrier man by any standards – Winch once described him as one of the last great terrier men – and in his hands the puppy he purchased became an excellent worker. At first Newcombe hunted badger regularly but after a while he became aware of the terrible damage these animals could inflict on a hard type of terrier and henceforth ceased to hunt badgers. His terriers became a familiar sight at meets of the terrier packs around the Dales and his Bedlington terriers saw service with the Farndale, the Glasedale, Salter's Gate, Sinnington and Wensleydale Hunts.

However, Newcombe noticed that it was becoming increasingly difficult to find suitable working terriers to use to outcross with his Rillington strain Bedlington terriers and observed that fewer and fewer owners wanted to exploit the working capabilities of the Bedlington terrier. Thus when the Working Bedlington Terrier Club was formed Newcombe joined and because of his enormous experience of working Bedlington terriers to ground he seemed an automatic choice for the post of chairman of the club. The purpose of the club was to maintain and improve on the working qualities of the Bedlington terrier, but it became apparent to Newcombe that the pure-bred Bedlington terrier was far too far gone to revive as a working terrier breed. Unlike other breeders who opted for a process of slow eugenic advancement of the working Bedlington terrier Newcombe – always with a reputation for being a working terrier heretic with highly original views – opted to outcross with other types to breed his now improved working Bedlington terrier. Newcombe chose to outcross with the dogs of John Cowen – fell terriers with a strong trace of Kennel Club registered Lakeland terrier (Netherfield Newsboy and Orgill Copper Coin) and he awaited the results of his breeding plan with some trepidation. To Newcombe's surprise the hybrids resembled primitive Bedlington terriers (not dissimilar to the dog owned by Rawlinson and featured in the photographs of the Salters Hall Wood badger dig of 1917 – though Rawlinson's dog was a pure-bred Bedlington terrier) possibly because many strains of fell terrier have traces of Bedlington terrier blood not too far back in their pedigrees. Reports concerning the working ability of these hybrids seems to be excellent. The majority are not oversized and give tongue freely and well when below ground. Newcombe has now bred several of these crossbreds (wrongly referred to as Rillington strain Bedlington terriers by those who own them, for the term Rillington strain Bedlington terriers would be best kept for the pure-bred Kennel Club registered stock Newcombe once owned, worked and bred).

What is more interesting still is the fact that these cross-bred Bedlington terriers have been used to mate to greyhounds to breed lurchers and the progeny from these matings have proved very successful as workers to rabbit and hare and are frequently advertised in sporting papers.

Not every breeder of working Bedlington terriers seemed dissatisfied with the working instinct of pure-bred Bedlington terriers however. The late Margaret Williamson bred the famous Gutch Common strain of Bedlington terrier for many years and many working terrier owners swear by these pure-bred terriers. The strain produces animals which are smaller than the usual bench-bred Bedlington terriers and many of these dogs are easily spanned and hence capable of getting to ground in fairly tight places. Still many working terrier enthusiasts fight shy of owning Bedlington terriers simply because of the reportedly high failure rate of these terriers. Despite the attempts of the very short-lived Working Bedlington Terrier Club the Bedlington terrier is a far cry from the tigerish terriers described by Rawden Lee or the do-or-die terriers bred by Ainsley.

However, a far more serious problem than absence of true grit has begun to affect the Bedlington terrier. Some years ago it was noticed that many apparently normal Bedlington terriers took sick and died before they were two years old. Others bloated badly and were ill for several years before expiring. Similar symptoms occurred from time to time in breeds such as Dobermanns, Skyes and West Highland white terriers and it was ascertained that these peculiarities were due to the fact that certain dogs displayed an inherited disposition to develop livers which tend to accumulate copper salts. Copper retention disease, or copper-toxicosis is rampant amongst Bedlington terriers at the time of writing and as many as sixty per cent of all Bedlington terriers carry the genes that produce this rather frightening disorder. Research into copper-toxicosis is progressing rapidly however and lists of tested 'free of copper-toxicosis' sires and dams are available to anyone who is contemplating buying a Bedlington terrier. If breeders are truthful about the puppies they breed 'carriers' of this unfortunate malaise can be identified and copper-toxicosis erradicated or at least its incidence much reduced. Contrary to the rubbish uttered by owners of supposedly working Bedlington terriers, both workers and bench-bred Bedlington terrier strains produce puppies displaying this unpleasant abnormality.

Thus the present state of play of the modern working Bedlington terrier and the pros and cons of working such a breed.

The Norwich/Norfolk Terrier

Both the Norwich and the Norfolk terrier –they are simply prick-and-drop eared forms of the same breed type – are interesting little dogs. These are possibly the smallest of the true working terriers and this small size and the incredible vivacity of the breed makes them interesting dogs to own and work. To watch a small team of Norwich or Norfolk terriers busily working a rat out of a pile of twigs or a rabbit from a patch of rushes is a delight to anyone who has an eye for a good sporting terrier. The enthusiasm of the type is in fact reminiscent of the keeness displayed by some strains of short-legged Jack Russell types that were once part and parcel of every hunt kennel, but began to die out when working terrier shows became popular.

The origin of the breed-type is a little hazy despite the fact the Norwich and Norfolk terriers seem to be a relatively modern creation. On first impressions the breed appears to be very closely related to certain Scottish breeds – breeders of the prick-eared types often mention that their terriers are mistaken for Cairn terriers from time to time, but there is every possibility that the original terriers were fairly pure forms of the Old English rough-coated black-and-tan terriers. The Old Adam of the breed type was said to be a terrier called Rags owned by one Jack Cooke of Brooks Lodge near Norwich at the start of the twentieth century who employed a horse breaker called Frank Jones; who became better known as Roughrider Jones after the fame of the Roughriders during the Spanish/American war.

Jones later moved to Market Harborough in Northamptonshire to work for a horse dealer called Stokes and Roughrider Jones supplemented his income by selling these tiny terriers, some of which he supposedly bred and others which he bought from friends in Norfolk. Supplemented seems hardly an appropriate word, for Jones is reputed to have sold terriers for as muuch as £25, six times the wage a horse breaker and groom might have expected at that time.

That the type was already breeding fairly true to type in Norfolk is borne out by the fact that one R. J. Read of Hapton Hall, Norwich who bred the Horstead strain of Norwich terrier during the early 1920s bought the stud dog Aylsham by dint of driving through the village of the same name and seeing the dog (pedigree unknown) running in the streets of the village. Likewise, there are tales of similar type dogs being

Norwich terrier

bought in the market of Kings Lynn earlier in the century and of dogs of a similar type kept by rodent operatives during the Boer War. There is little doubt that these early Norfolk-bred terriers were in fact fairly pure forms of the Old English rough-coated black-and-tan terrier and were breeding fairly true to type long before the Norwich and the Norfolk terrier became popular.

It is said that the terrier Rags was given to Mr Cooke by his breeder, a Mr E. Jodrell Hopkins, who owned a livery stable in Trumpington Street, Cambridge and bred a type similar to the Norwich and Norfolk terriers which he called Trumpington terriers which apparently had an excellent name as ratting and rabbiting terriers in and around Cambridge.

Marjorie Bunting in her book *The Norwich Terrier* (1980) states that tale has it the dam of Rags was a brindle Aberdeen-type terrier (Scottish terrier) and was sold to Jodrell Hopkins by an army reservist who was called up to serve in the Boer war. However what is certain is that Hopkins sought out one Doggy Lawrence, a Cambridge dog dealer, and mated his bitch to an unknown stud dog kept by Lawrence. Lawrence, like Jones, had a thriving trade in providing small red terriers for undergraduates who had an interest in ratting (the tales of sporting undergraduates who whiled away their days at Cambridge ratting, dog fighting and cocking are legion), and it should be mentioned that the all-embracing 1911 Protection of Animals Act which effectively outlawed the rat pits had yet to be passed! It is said that Lawrence bred a strain of terrier by crossing small Irish terriers with Yorkshire terriers, but this story is supposition and it seems more likely that Lawrence too simply acquired a type of Old English rough-coated black-and-tan terrier that bred relatively true to type. Later Rags, the result of the union between Hopkins bitch and the stud dog kept by Doggy Lawrence, mated a variety of bitches including a black-and-tan terrier brought back from Ireland by Jones, a fox terrier, a Trumpington terrier, a small Glen of Imaal (for some reason cynologists with an interest in the Norwich/Norfolk type seem eager to stress the types Irish terrier ancestry) and a prick-eared terrier called Ninety owned by Podge Low of Norwich. Low's father was a vet (F. Low – a great horseman and hound afficionado) and the bitch Ninety had been brought in to be destroyed. Low however liked her 'expression' and kept her.

Ninety's ancestry is a bit of a puzzle. She would have passed as a prick-eared Russell type at one time, or may have been one of the last of the Old English white terriers that became extinct shortly after the turn of the century. Likewise Ninety could well have been a small bull terrier-type similar perhaps to the Cheshire terriers described by Lucas which were blended with native terriers to produce the Sealyham. Whatever Ninety's breeding – and there is a photograph of her still in existence – she was mated to Rags and produced a litter which gave rise to the terriers kept by Jack Read who bred the Horstead strain of Norwich terrier but on Read's return from World War I he found his strain had all but died out except for two bitches who were well past their prime. He is reputed to have mated one of them to a Bedlington terrier he kept. A puppy from this union (Bedlington Norwich) was reputedly mated to a Staffordshire bull terrier kept by the Countess of Kimberley, a whelp from which was in turn mated to a small Irish terrier and a puppy of this union mated back to one of Jack Cookes' strain (Cooke, Master of the Norwich Staghounds, owned Rags the sire of many of Roughrider Jones terriers). Later Aylsham, the terrier Read had seen running in the streets of that village, was used to breed Jack Read's Horstead Mick – a prepotent sire in the breed at that time.

Lucas knew Read quite well – he mentions Read in *Hunt and Working Terriers* (1931) – and was particularly interested when he realised Reads' dogs seldom scaled in at above ten pounds but were 'dead game' despite their small size. One of Reads' dogs, Tango (an elderly dog by the time Lucas interviewed Read) had the distinction of drawing a fox terrier from a drain when the hunt terrier was engaging a fox (a good reason for not putting two hunt terriers to ground in the same earth).

Reads' terriers were bad fighters and had a reputation for being quarrelsome. He told Lucas that once when he rode to a friend's house he took two bitches with him, kennelling them in a stable while he spent the evening with his friend. When Read returned he found both terriers

Norfolk terrier

had fought a jaw-to-jaw battle and were nearly dead. Lucas noted that Read adopted a peculiar method of separating two terriers which were locked in conbat with neither wishing to release a hold; Read carried both antagonists by their tails and hung them over a stable door – one inside the other outside until they decided to release their holds. Lucas who detested kennel fighters – he gave scrappers away to pet homes – was intrigued to see the way Read dealt with very aggressive terriers that fought silently (Lucas believed this was due to their bull terrier ancestry) and it is obvious that he considered producing Lucas terriers from these Norwich terriers as early as 1920. It is interesting to note that Lucas often referred to the Norwich/Norfolk type as Trumpington terriers (one of the early breeders, a Mr Hodgeson of Cowford, Sussex, had brought his terriers from Hopkins of Trumpington, Cambridge) long after the expression had fallen into disuse in the dog world.

It is also interesting to note that Lucas goes to some considerable effort to expound on the virtues of the Norwich/Norfolk as a ratting or rabbiting terrier. He makes no mention of the prowess of the breed below ground. Lucas is not alone in his lack of praise for the terriers ability to work to fox and badger however. Mrs Molly Richardson writing in the Norwich Terrier Club Bulletin 1955 says 'If the description "working terrier" is meant only to apply to fox and badger, I do not personally think Norwich terriers fill the bill as an ideal. If by working terriers is meant as applied to rats, moles and rabbits etc. then I personally believe the Norwich terrier is unsurpassed and the fulfilment of a farmer's and countryman's dream.'

'Taking just the case of fox and badger – the average Norwich terrier is too small, his head and neck built for one quick snap rather than a prolonged struggle underground. Compare the shape of the jaw of the ideal hunt terrier. Secondly his (the Norwich terrier) similar shape and colour to a fox are a great disadvantage when bolting them. I have twice experienced very narrow escapes for my Norwich terriers mistaken for a fox, in one instance by the whipper-in and in the other by a very hot-blooded pack of hounds. Some people I know will tell you this is nonsense, but I hunt three days a week and I can assure you it is not.'

Marjorie Bunting also goes to some length to assure would-by buyers that the Norwich is not suitable for fox or badger digging. In her chapter 'The Norwich and Norfolk Terrier' in *Terriers of the World* (1984) she states 'There is substantial evidence to suggest that these breeds do not have any great prowess as workers to fox and badger. Indeed, some who have bought them for that purpose have been disappointed, but it must be remembered that Norfolk is an arable shooting area rather than a grassy hunting country and small ratting terriers were needed to work in or under stables and farm buildings and in farmyards and hedgerows to help control rats and rabbits which ruined the crops.'

However, one questions why breeders are quite so adamant why a particular breed is not at its best working quarry below ground, particularly as there is ample evidence to suggest otherwise. It is worthy of note that Mrs Bunting in her excellent book *The Norwich Terrier* mentions the dogs of Mrs Sheila Monckton, author of the booklet *The Norwich Terrier* (published privately) who owned two dogs, Jericho Topper and Jericho Red Mischief, which regularly went to ground and worked fox and Red Mischief earned a working certificate for his pains though Mrs Monckton too expressed fears about the dogs being mistaken for foxes.

Mischief also worked badger (at that time it was perfectly legal to work badger with terriers) and Mrs Monckton recalls the time a badger was drawn with her Norwich terrier still attached to the badger's tail.

A curious tale is also told of Miss Eleanor Johnson's Ch. Whinlater Cain. The local pack of foxhounds had run a fox to ground and a terrier was needed to bolt the fox. When Miss Johnson offered the use of her dog the hunt servants politely refused saying that he would not do, but the dog ran to ground and bolted the fox.

Likewise Mrs Fagan who owned a very successful strain of Norwich terrier mentions that her foundation bitch Brownie was very keen on hunting badger and 'lived down a badger warran (sic)'. Mrs Fagan sold several of her terriers to MFHs in England and Ireland who wished for small terrier capable of working in tight places.

Likewise the Farndon strain of Norwich terrier owned by Mrs West boasted several dogs which had MFH working certificates and there is a tale that in 1936 Ch. Farndon Red Dog ran a fox to ground and had to be dug out of the earth into which he had followed the fox. The following day the dog won a Challenge Certificate at Crufts!

Tobit, a popular sire prior to World War II, not only sired a drop-eared champion but was said to be a noted worker to badger and held a MFHs certificate.

More interesting and perhaps more controversial still is the statement made by R. C. Bayldon who had some knowledge of Norwich terriers and considerable knowledge of working terriers generally. In the 1950s *Field* published numerous articles concerning the working ability of Norwich/Norfolk-type terriers and in October 1951 Bayldon stated 'Of the few terriers now left to us that really look like good workers, the Norwich is a predominant example . . . the image of an ultra varmint, stout, rough-and-tumble little terrier.' Readers may wish to note the contrast between the opinions voiced by R. C. Bayldon and that of Molly Richardson some four years later!

However, yet another reason for Molly Richardson's statement and the opinion of Marjorie Bunting might be offered. During the 1950s working terrier shows became popular and a great many hunt and working terriers went on display. Many of these terriers were proudly exhibited by their owners despite the fact that some of these dogs were hideously disfigured by encounters with both foxes and particularly badgers. It did in fact become the mark of a true terrier man to display badly mutilated dogs that would have been best left at home. It is not unreasonable to assume that many breeders of Norwich/Norfolk terriers were reluctant to have the puppies they sold mutilated in the way hunt terriers often appeared to be despite the assurance given by R. C. Bayldon that the Norwich looked the part of the good worker.

Furthermore, hand-in-hand with the popularity of the working terrier came the appearance of the dog dealer often as not men who were purveyors of canine misery and despite the connections the breed had with Doggy Lawrence – a famous Cambridge dog dealer it may be that breeders were reluctant to see their puppies traded, bartered, swopped and sold by less caring terrier owners – and at the time of writing the lot of many working terriers in the hands of dog dealers is worthy of investigation by the R.S.P.C.A. It is peculiar how many breeders of this very attractive terrier-type went to some pains to explain how their dogs were unsuitable for fox and badger digging yet Jocelyn Lucas, an ardent and enthusiastic badger digger, had few qualms about breeding a new type of sporting terrier from the Norwich/Norfolk terrier. It is also worthy of noting that during the early 1960s hunt and working terrier shows often staged classes for under ten inch working terriers, both coloured and Jack Russell-type terriers. Many of these terriers – far from being pet-stock terriers – an opinion proffered by Jeff Burman in *The Midland Working Terrier Newsletter* from time to time – were excellent working dogs. In fact at one show staged in Peterborough in the late 1960s five of these diminutive terriers were shown in the 'working certificate class'. Ruth Haw mentions that one extremely typey smooth-coated brown terrier – similar to the brown terriers bred from Breay's fell terrier Rusty was in point of fact twenty-five per cent Norfolk bred and some very classy Jack Russell-type terriers of this era owed their origins to Norfolk terriers. Lucas also mentions a twelve pound terrier bred by American hunt packs to flush foxes from tiny earths in the Shelburn Foxhound country. These terriers were apparently bred by crossing a small Sealyham terrier bitch with a champion fox terrier and mating the progeny to a Norfolk/Norwich terrier called Willum Jones imported from Jones a Leicestershire breeder. Later West Highland white blood was added to the mix and more Sealyham blood to increase head size in the terrier. The type is still kept by a few breeders but is not a popular type of terrier even in the Shelburn Hunt country.

The breeders of Norfolk/Norwich-type terriers do however go to considerable pains to show how efficient the type is as a rabbiting and ratting terrier.

Lucas, *Hunt and Working Terriers*, makes mention of a Mrs Garden Duff of Hatton Castle, Terriff, Aberdeen who owned these terriers that killed over 400 rabbits on their own. They were not used to shooting over them and Lucas mentions that they were gun-shy.

Marjorie Bunting mentions the ratting ability of the Colonsay terriers bred by Miss Macfie who sold dogs to local farmers in Suffolk to keep down rats while Molly Richardson, who was so much against the type being used for fox and badger digging (reference her letter in 1955 edition of *The Norfolk Terrier Club Bulletin*) bred the Quartzhill terriers and mentions that her bitch Thistle killed twenty-one rats in twenty minutes. Thistle often worked with ferrets and nailed rats as they emerged from the holes thereby affording them little chance to escape.

Rags, a Foxybrooks-bred dog, killed 80 out of the 132 rats killed while rick threshing – ricks were at one time enclosed by a length of fine guage wire netting through which rats could not escape when the threshing began and huge hauls of rats were taken during this time for it was customary to place terriers within the enclosure so that they might catch the rats as they left the ricks.

Victor Page, who bred the Waveney Valley strain of drop-eared terrier, tells the tale of how some customers had come from the Midlands to buy some sheds from him. As the buyers turned over the sections of the sheds rats exploded from the sanctuary and were killed instantly by the Norfolk terriers.

Mrs Bunting also records that one bitch in Scotland killed 300 rats and a wild cat in a fortnight – and wild cats which sometimes scale in at up to twenty-five pounds in weight (a twenty-five pound cat was killed at Ham Estate, Caithness in 1984) are no mean opponents for a terrier which is seldom more than twelve pounds in weight.

Also a sporting terrier, a terrier which is capable of working a variety of quarry in a variety of situations, the Norfolk/Norwich-type (after 1957 drop-eared terriers were called Norfolks and prick-eared dogs Norwich terriers and the dichotemy between the types has widened still further since that time) seems to be ideal though modern breeders tend to be reluctant to allow their dogs to hunt fox. In closing it is well to remember the advice offered by Molly Richardson in *The Norwich Terrier Club Bulletin* (1955) 'I suggest we leave the fox and badger to hunt terriers and concentrate on producing a Norwich terrier who can and will deal with every other sort of vermin that worries a farmer and one who is also the most active, intelligent and charming companion and assistant to the countryman and his family.'

The Dandie Dinmont Terrier

In 1814 Sir Walter Scott, then a penniless clerk to the court, hurriedly penned the draft of his novel *Guy Mannering*, a hastily written pot boiler written anonymously for he believed the role of a novelist to be beneath the dignity of a clerk to the court. Guy Mannering, a student with the gift of seersight, predicts a series of catastrophes while staying at the home of the Laird of Ellangowan and the plot, brimming with contrived coincidences, tumbles to an untidy conclusion introducing colourful characters such as Meg Merrilies along the way. One of the other characters to emerge from the pages of the novel is a sporting squire, a rustic Border farmer called Dandie Dinmont who kept a team of sporting terriers which he carefully entered to quarry via rats, stoats, tods (foxes) and brocks (badgers) until 'they fear nothing wi' hair on it'. Later the name Dandie Dinmont was applied to a type of terrier bred along the borderland twixt England and Scotland, though long before the birth of Walter Scott the terrier was breeding relatively true to type.

Several, often fanciful, theories are offered as to the origin of the Dandie Dinmont terrier.

a. Northumberland is the meeting point for Scottish and English-type terriers and the Dandie could therefore be a hybrid form of these Scottish and Old English rough-coated black-and-tan terriers.
b. The breed is a result of mingling some form of terrier with the blood of some kind of rough-coated hound.
c. The breed could have developed independently of any other type of terrier due to the insularity Northumberland and Roxburghshire enjoyed until the nineteenth century.

On the surface of it the theory that the Dandie is simply a hybrid form created by mating Scottish and English terriers together seems a fairly logical one. The itinerant breeders who were said to have first bred the type crossed back and fore across the Borders without restriction, though they were known as muggers in Scotland (they soldered and repaired tin mugs) and potters (they also repaired tin pots, pans and plates) in England. There is in fact a tale concerning one breeder, a Godless hard-drinking, hard-swearing, piping tinker called Piper Allen who

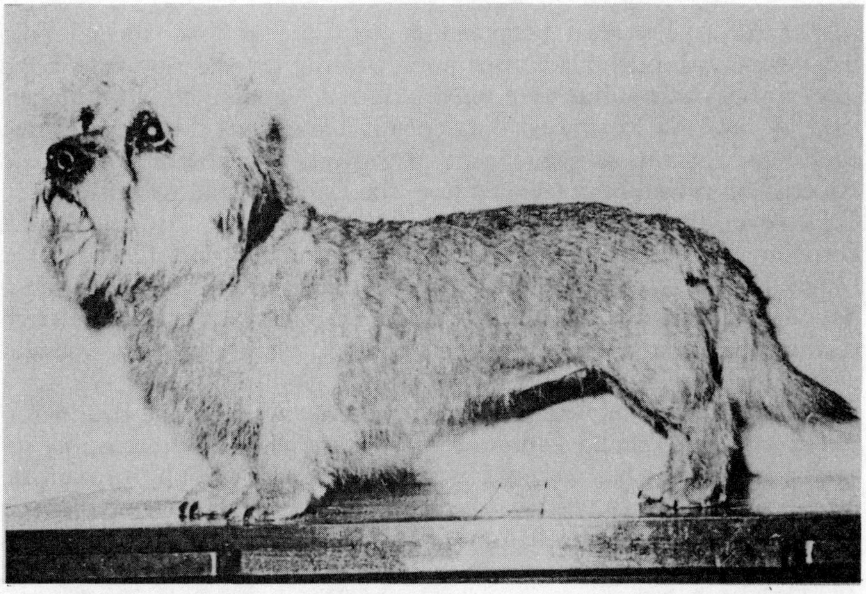

Dandie Dinmont terrier: E. A. Oldham's Ch. Warkworth Waverack

owned an outstanding terrier that would 'face a foumart (polecat) bang a tod (fox) or bang a brock within its hame' (punish a badger deep in its set). Allen was offered the tenancy of a farm in exchange for the dog by the Duke of Northumberland but replied 'I wouldna take yer whole grund fer him' adding 'What use a ferm for a piper', when politely declining the offer.

Scott certainly modelled his sporting squire Dandie Dinmont on sporting landowners of the Border country though James Davidson of Hindlee on whom Dandie Dinmont was supposedly modelled was not known to Scott under after *Guy Mannering* was published. Davidson certainly kept terriers of the sort described in the book (briefly one should add, for Dandie Dinmont is not important to the highly convoluted plot of the book and neither are his terriers) and though he died in 1820 some six years after the publication of *Guy Mannering* he profited by breeding these terriers during the last years of his life.

J. H. Walsh who wrote copiously under the nom de plume 'Stonehenge' believed that the Dandie was in fact the result of mating a dachshund to some form of rough-coated terrier and his book *Dogs of the British Isles* (4th edition published 1888) was criticised because of his heretical theories concerning this Borderland terrier. Whinstone, D. J. Thompson Gray, author of *Dogs of Scotland* (1891) supports Walsh's theory adding that the eye of the dachshund is similar to that of the Dandie and the ears of both breeds are also nearly identical. It is however possible that a type similar to the dachshund and the turnspit, dogs that manifest shortened limbs similar to those of Texel sheep, could have existed throughout Europe and certainly there is no evidence to suggest that dachshunds were imported from Germany to Northumberland by sporting itinerants. It is equally likely that the rough-coated dachshund, strains of which are still worked in both Britain and America, may well be descended from the Dandie Dinmont terrier.

However, there is considerable evidence to suggest that the Dandie Dinmont is related to some sort of rough-coated hound. Gordon, *The Dandie Dinmont Terrier* (1972), compares Garrick's etching of the otter-hound Stanley with an illustration of Dr Brown's Puck and Rough (Dandie Dinmonts) and there is a striking similarity in both type and coat.

It has also been argued that the dichotemy between the Bedlington terrier and the Dandie Dinmont (they were at one time possibly regarded as the same breed) could have been brought about by introducing otter-hound blood to produce the leggier houndier modern Bedlington terrier. Winch, in his article in the *Fell and Moorland Yearbook*, describes the Dandie as the *crème de la crème* of working terriers and mentions that the Earl of Antrim once won both the Dandie and the Bedlington classes at a certain show with dogs of the same breeding. Vero Shaw also classed the Dandie and the Bedlington terrier as the same breed in his book *The Illustrated Book of the Dog* (1879–1881).

It is however likely that a breed-type quite distinct from any other terrier existed in the Border districts and because the possibility of obtaining fresh terrier blood was remote in the Borders a type of terrier that was quite distinct from any other terrier may have evolved by dint of inbreeding to certain prepotent sires.

Dogs of great courage were always prized in the north of England and Scotland where foxes were regarded as vermin rather than sporting quarry. Thus a hard-biting type of dog capable of dispatching a fox quickly and efficiently rather than bolting it was required. Tom Horner comments on a curious custom supposedly adopted by old-time breeders of matching a dog against two badgers – and if he attacked one badger while the other still seized him he was deemed game! Game indeed would such a dog need to be, for the damage wrought by any adult badger is terrifying as anyone who has had a dog trapped between a sow and a boar badger can attest.

Early breeders and those who worked the type endeavoured to breed a small terrier possibly only ten to eleven inches at the shoulder and weighing thirteen to eighteen pounds in weight for such an animal would be an all-round working terrier, small enough to get to a fox and strong enough to withstand the rush of a badger but Nettle bred by Davidson of Hindlee, supposedly a very aggressive dog, scaled eleven pounds in weight though she 'was never tried at large vermin'. An eleven pound terrier would probably fair quite well even against a large

Westmorland fox, but would be a shade overmatched by a badger and the ideal weight for a Dandie Dinmont is now considered to be around eighteen pounds in weight though bitches may be a shade lighter.

What is peculiar about the Dandie Dinmont is the incredible power of the jaws and the large teeth which seem more in keeping with a dog the size of an Airedale rather than a dog scaling eleven inches at the shoulder. It has been argued that these teeth and the huge masseter muscles that can clamp such a jaw together is an indication of bull terrier blood in the not too distant ancestry of the Dandie, but this is far from the truth. The majority of the pit dogs fought by Black Country dog fighters had quite small teeth though the masseter muscles that operated the jaws of these fighting dogs were large and powerful.

The head size, the strength of jaw, the structure of the teeth of the Dandie Dinmont terrier have certainly been appreciated by working terrier breeders of the past. Captain Jack Howell, MFH, who achieved Kennel Club recognition for the Sealyham terrier, once told Lucas that Tucker Edwardes had certainly used Dandie Dinmont terrier blood in his creation of the Sealyham terrier and that some years before *Hunt and Working Terriers* (1931) had been written Sealyhams with the tufted top-knots of the Dandie Dinmont were commonly seen in badger digging teams in Pembrokeshire. Howell remarked, a little unscientifically perhaps, that these tufted top-knots together with the large eyes Dandies possess always went with a dog possessed of great courage. It is interesting to note that breeders of wire-haired dachshunds also equate a large prominant eye with a dog of great courage.

There is some slight doubt as to whether Frantisek Horak used Dandie Dinmont blood in the creation of the Cesky terrier. Breed handbooks attribute the Cesky's origin to a cross between a Scottish terrier and a Sealyham terrier, but Horner is adamant the breed is simply a cross-bred between a Dandie Dinmont and a Sealyham terrier. The tail carriage of some Cesky terriers together with the raised rumps of supposedly untypical specimens is an indication perhaps that some Dandie Dinmont blood was used in their creation. In passing it is worthy of noting that the working terrier races that are so popular today are by no means new. Dandie Dinmont racing was a popular field event during the 1930s.

Few hunters seem to work Dandie Dinmont terriers today though the breed clearly still retains some of its previous sporting potential. For a brief period of time a Miss Nightingale of Rutland who was said to be able to claim descent from Piper Allen did show her dogs in the working terrier shows of the 1960s and put dogs out to gamekeepers so that her stock could be worked to badger. Tale has it that some of these dogs were inordinately good stayers below ground though they were often a shade too hard. Miss Nightingale also stated that her terriers had excellent noses and found well even in the deepest sets in Lincolnshire – a county famous for its deep badger sets some of which were so complex and ancient that both Lucas and Cartwright of Gloucester fought shy of them. However since the early 1960s few breeders of Dandie Dinmont seem to wish for their wards to compete in working terrier shows and hence the dichotemy between the working terrier scene and the show bench has widened considerably where Dandies are concerned.

Alf Rhodes, an octogenarian with considerable expertise with both Dandie Dinmonts and Sealyham terriers, and one who visited Lucas on numerous occasions, is of the opinion that the Dandie Dinmont still has a lot of, albeit unexploited, working qualities and many would still work well if given a chance to do so. It is in fact a pity that nobody is prepared to exploit the working qualities of the Dandie Dinmont for the type is still ideal for working below ground.

The Manchester Terrier

This is a tall elegant terrier which at a distance has been confused with a young Dobermann for in many ways the Manchester resembles a miniature Dobermann both in colour and outline.

There is little doubt that the Manchester terrier is simply a much-tidied stream-lined smooth-coated edition of the Old English black-and-tan terrier. It is likely that the type was once worked to fox, badger, otter and required to go to ground in the manner of its relative, the fell terrier. However this terrier became urbanised so to speak and hence was bred to work quarry found within the confines of large towns – namely the brown rat, *rattus norvigicus*. Rats live in some horrendous habitats and often feed on putrid filth, hence a rough-coated dog whose fur would often be caked in dirt after ratting forays was not required. Thus a process of selection was evolved to produce a dog with a very tight smooth coat that would not ball or cake with filth.

For some curious reason the sport of ratting is not held in high regard by many terrier men, but the process of hunting rats requires a very special type of dog with very special physical and mental qualities. It is also a fact that many terriers that will lie close to and bay at a fox are shy of biting and killing rats, particularly when the dog has been badly bitten and the wounds have started to smart. Rats move at a great speed over the short distance twixt feeding ground and warren, particularly if they are surprised or frightened.

A quick or nippy dog rather than a dog with the devastatingly furious speed of the greyhound is required for ratting, a dog that can snatch and kill rats as they flash from place of cover to place of cover across runs scarcely a foot long. Coupled with this the dog must have instant reactions and must galvanise into action in a split second reacting instinctively to movement yet sensible enough to determine friend from foe – chicken, duck or ferret from rat. Whippets often make incredibly good ratting dogs but few are tough enough to endure the bites several dozen rats may bring and the force with which a rat can bite has to be experienced to be appreciated.

An agile dog is always desirable for ratting dogs must snatch and bite at obscene angles to prevent a rat escaping. Furthermore rats enjoy living in tangles of rubbish into which a dog must thrust its head to snatch, or jump to catch a bolter. Good ratting dogs are often the

Manchester terrier

acrobats of the canine world and the terrier with the dull dogged persistance of a badger-digger's terrier is seldom agile enough to be a first-rate ratter.

Furthermore a ratter, a terrier which is required to work regularly and kill a large number of rats performing nightly or several times a week needs a high pain resistance. Rat bites often cause the dog's muzzle to swell and bites inflicted on a still swollen muzzle are excruciatingly painful. Buyers out to procure a dog suitable for training for the highly competitive rat pits were sure to test a dog by working a freshly bitten terrier that had been rested long enough to allow its face to swell, on a crop of fresh rats. Many good dogs, quite game animals, jib when subjected to this sort of treatment, so a pain resistant dog, a dog that could soak up punishment like a sponge, makes the ideal ratter. It is worthy of note that most breeders of the very hardest fell terriers tell tales of ratting trips when their dogs were over-matched by an over abundance of fresh hard-biting adult rats. It is a fact that many badly bitten terriers will allow large vigorous rats to escape yet snap up grey immature rats that are unlikely to be hard biters. Ratting terriers need to be a special kind of dog if they are to be worked regularly to rat.

Nose is an under-rated quality amongst terriers these days, but the age-old dictum – no nose, no find; no catch, no kill – certainly does apply to dogs that are required to hunt rat. Rats are pungent animals yet often live in even more pungent surroundings nesting in banks of manure, offal, rotting vegetation, dragging often putrid viands into their lairs. It requires a dog with an excellent nose to detect the inhabited lairs of rats in such conditions. So strong is the scent of rats that dogs frequently false-mark freshly vacated warrens. Thus top-grade ratting dogs need to have discerning noses to find warrens that still house rats. Dogs which will mark and always mark accurately in all conditions are highly prized amongst all rat hunters – and ratting is a pursuit that is as addictive as an opiate to both man and dog one should add.

What is not often realised is that a dog that is required to work, catch and kill many rats several times a week needs to be of a phlegmatic disposition. An excitable dog makes mistakes and a dog that regularly misses rats becomes even more excitable. Hysteria is not uncommon amongst unsuccessful quick-silver excitable dogs that are ratted. Excitable dogs, no matter how agile they are, no matter how impervious to pain they seem, never become top-class ratting dogs. The majority of top-class ratting dogs worked in Victorian rat pits were bull terrier bred for the cross gave not only courage and tenacity, but lent a phlegmatic disposition to the terrier allowing it to catch and kill systematically with a stoical indifference to both the pain it was suffering and the cries of the audience watching the carnage taking place within the pit.

Thus the Old English black-and-tan terrier was crossed with small agile pit bull terriers to give the breed a disposition that made it impervious to rat bites and a phlegmatic disposition with possibly whippet or Italian greyhound blood to give the terrier the ability to make a fast and decisive bite at its rats. Horner *Terriers of the World* suggests that the credit for hybridising terriers with small greyhounds or whippets to refine the Manchester terrier should be given to one John Hulme and the cross gave the resulting terrier speed enough to be used as a rabbit courser as well as to be an efficient rat killer. Furthermore the new type of terrier took on a smarter neater more streamlined appearance because of its sighthound blood.

It now becomes expedient to explain and describe those most bizarre of English sports – rabbit coursing and the slaughter of rats in the rat pits – and when one examines the finer points of both activities one begins to realise why the rest of the world considers the British stark staring mad!

Rabbit coursing is best described as an activity that somehow or other skirted the regulations imposed by the all embracing 1911 Protection of Animals Act but encroached on human decency. It was certainly not hunting in the conventional sense of the word and to all intents and purposes it was an epic of brutality and futility.

Some thirty-one rabbits were ferreted, netted and taken to the venue where the rabbit coursing meet was to be conducted. It is interesting to note that during the infamous Walters v. Meaken case of 1912, a case that effectively made rabbit coursing the object of such public disgust that the activity ceased forthwith, some fifty-five rabbits were coursed or simply slaughtered by dogs. Each rabbit was given some sixty yards start or law and a pair of dogs slipped on the rabbit. Rabbits taken and released off country seldom run far and bewildered by the experience, terrified by the shouting of the spectators, run blindly or simply crouch to await capture. Hence a dog would need to run perhaps a hundred or so yards to catch its rabbit. This poses no hard task for an average dog, but after several runs dogs begin to tire and muscles start to ache and some dogs will quit cold long before fifteen or sixteen runs have been made. A fairly fast but extremely tenacious dog would be best employed at such a task and it appears that the winners of early rabbit coursing meets would have been terriers of some sort. Gradually a special sort of dog was developed to compete in these meets. Vero Shaw writing in 1879 states 'Rabbit coursing, once so popular a sport, has gradually waned. Some ten or twenty years ago it was all the rage with that class with which the whippet is so closely associated. The dogs then used were of an entirely different stamp to the dogs of the present day, in fact they were terriers proper. The predominating colours were red, wheaten, many too were blue with tan markings. With the gradual decay of rabbit coursing and the introduction of straight-out running has disappeared the type of terrier formerly used. Now speed is the main object sought for; the main consideration is to get the greatest amount of speed into the least possible size. Hence to obtain speed those interested in the breed have resorted to Italian and English greyhound crosses. Many are so finely bred that they strike the observant eye as being nothing more than diminutive greyhounds.' If Vero Shaw is correct and he has a reputation for being so, then the terrier may well be the ancestor of the whippet and the Manchester terrier may well have been a spin-off by-product as the terrier metamorphosed into whippet.

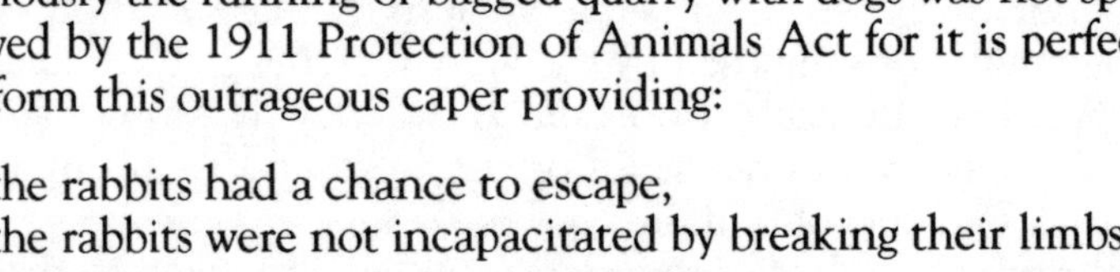

Curiously the running of bagged quarry with dogs was not specifically outlawed by the 1911 Protection of Animals Act for it is perfectly legal to perform this outrageous caper providing:

a. the rabbits had a chance to escape,
b. the rabbits were not incapacitated by breaking their limbs etc.

If the rabbits were released in an enclosed space however the Act would have been contravened, and fear of prosecution probably deterred organisers staging further rabbit coursing meets.

The self-same Act brought about the end of that exclusively British sporting event – the rat pits. This sport certainly did contravene the 1911 Protection of Animals Act and was the first Act of Parliament to ever give some protection to the rat. Prints of Tiny, a diminutive Manchester terrier-type animal, slaying huge rats almost the size of the dog attacking them in a pit the size of a ballroom give a woefully inaccurate picture of the event. Most rat pits were scarcely more than six feet in diameter with smooth walls some three feet high surrounding the enclosure. There are some instances of dogs killing a thousand rats in such an enclosure but such spectacles would have been extremely rare and furthermore costly to stage for rats were often caught by professional rat catchers who sold them to the rat pit owner for two shillings and sixpence a dozen for poor grade mangy sewer rats and farm raised rats which were relatively free of mange fetched nearly three times that price. Few major events fielded more than a hundred rats for a single dog to kill though a black-and-tan terrier called Billy (Billy was one of the stream-lined bull terriers that may have been used in the creation of the Manchester terrier) was able to slay 100 rats in six minutes and thirteen seconds in a pit slightly more than six feet in diameter.

The British must have appeared absolutely absurd in the eyes of the rest of the world for we find it essential that the most barbaric and bloody of spectacles are often governed by the most stringent rules imaginable. 'Ratting' as the slaying of captive rats within an enclosure was called, was governed and regulated by strict rules. The rats were tipped into the pit from large bags or crates and time allowed for the rats to settle. When the rats had huddled in a pile against the walls of the pit (most pits were circular in shape – pits such as were depicted in the engraving of Tiny killing rats against the clock would never have been used to stage such a spectacle) a dog was placed gently on the floor of the pit and the clock started. No rat was allowed to move more than twice its length after being bitten or the match was lost (Horner *Terriers of the World*) and rats suspected of playing possum amidst such hellish carnage were given a sharp crack on the tail with a heavy stick to discourage them from playing dead. Clearly the spectacle contravened not only human decency but also the 1911 Protection of Animals Act and the Act closed down such performances for ever. In 1912 the owner of a notorious Leicester rat pit was prosecuted, fined and made to give a promise 'that he would never again promote such a spectacle'. His defence had been that he had used the rat pits to train dogs to kill rats – but the court did not accept this defence.

Such were the barbaric events that guided the evolution of the Manchester terrier.

However the breed was in a state of decline since the abolition of ear-cropping. Ear-cropping consisted of cutting and trimming the ears of a dog so that the ears adopted an upright carriage and gave the dog an

Tiny

The Wonder, weighing only 5½lbs.

Pedigree by Old Dick out of Old Nell.

The property of James Shaw, Blue Anchor, Bonhill Row, St. Luke's.

This extraordinary little Black and Tan has won 50 interesting events, including the following matches: 2 matches of 6 rats when he weighed 4½lbs.; 20 matches of 12 rats at 5lbs. weight; 15 matches of 20 rats at 5lbs. weight; 1 match of 50 rats; 1 match of a 100 rats in 34 minutes 40 seconds on Tuesday, March 30th, 1847. Beat Summertown bitch "Crack" of 8lbs., 12 rats each, September 14th. Beat the dog "Twig" at 6½lbs. on November 7th, and on Tuesday, March 28th, 1848, he was matched to kill 300 rats in 3 hours; he accomplished the unprecedented test in 54 minutes 50 seconds, which took place in the presence of a crowded audience at the above house. May 2nd—killed 20 rats in 8 minutes; May 23rd—won a match of 50 rats against Mr. Batty's bitch "Fun", 8lbs.; August 15th—won a match against "Jim", 50 rats; September 5th—won a match of 12 rats, 2 minutes 30 seconds; October 24th—won a match of 50 rats, time of killing 20 minutes 10 seconds; November 4th—won a match of 100 rats, 30 minutes 5 seconds; January 31st, 1849—won a match of 100 rats, 20 minutes 5 seconds; March 27th—killed 200 rats, 59 minutes 58 seconds. The above extraordinary feats were accomplished without either taking dogs or rats out of the pit.

Tiny killing rats in a pit

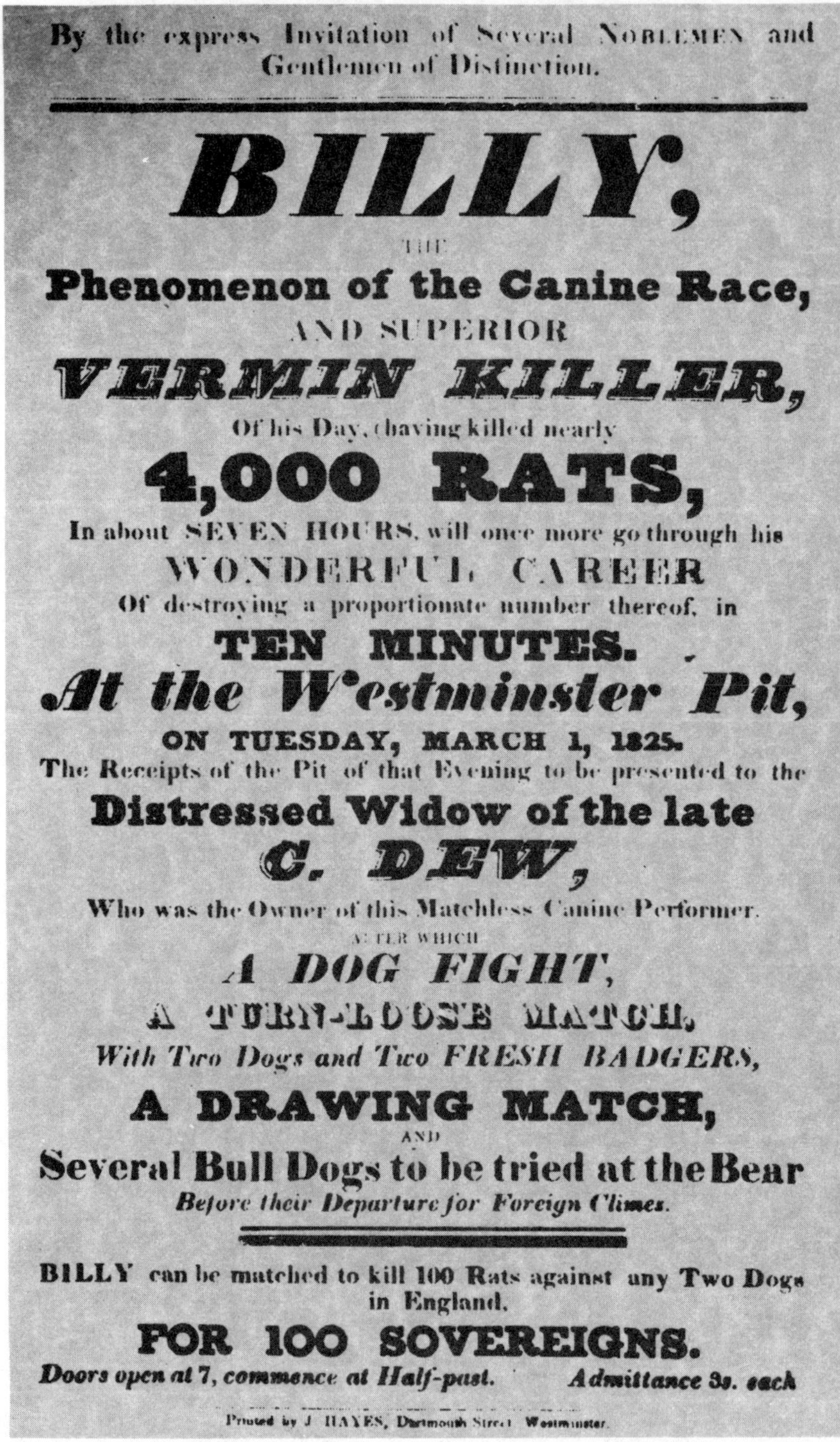

By the express Invitation of Several NOBLEMEN and Gentlemen of Distinction.

BILLY,

THE

Phenomenon of the Canine Race,

AND SUPERIOR

VERMIN KILLER,

Of his Day, (having killed nearly

4,000 RATS,

In about SEVEN HOURS, will once more go through his

WONDERFUL CAREER

Of destroying a proportionate number thereof, in

TEN MINUTES.

At the Westminster Pit,

ON TUESDAY, MARCH 1, 1825.

The Receipts of the Pit of that Evening to be presented to the

Distressed Widow of the late

C. DEW,

Who was the Owner of this Matchless Canine Performer.

AFTER WHICH

A DOG FIGHT,

A TURN-LOOSE MATCH,

With Two Dogs and Two FRESH BADGERS,

A DRAWING MATCH,

AND

Several Bull Dogs to be tried at the Bear

Before their Departure for Foreign Climes.

BILLY can be matched to kill 100 Rats against any Two Dogs in England,

FOR 100 SOVEREIGNS.

Doors open at 7, commence at Half-past. *Admittance 3s. each*

Printed by J. HAYES, Dartmouth Street, Westminster.

alert expression. In the 1880s numerous letters decrying the cropping of ears appeared in the national press and King Edward VII was lobbied to bring about a cessation of the practice. In 1898 ear-cropping was made illegal and as the Manchester terrier had always been cropped before this date (and breeders had deliberately bred dogs with thick leathery ears which facilitated the process of cropping) the breed lost many of its supporters. It is interesting to note that in 1987 advertisements for cropped-eared Dobermanns appeared in *Exchange and Mart.* The breeder had bred the puppies in England and taken them to Eire to have them cropped for the 1898 Act does not apply to Southern Ireland. It is worthy of mention that in 1974 the Manchester Terrier Club passed a resolution that in future club members could not sell their puppies to countries where ear-cropping was still practised.

William Drury in his book *British Dogs* (1903) expresses his alarm at the malpractices that were used to produce a winner from a poor-grade show animal. Not only was dyeing commonly practised (Perkins Aniline Dyes made this process feasible though extremely painful as the dyes work on furs and hair only when the solution is hot) but the heads of puppies were tightly bandaged to ensure the adult animal had a long slender head and flat cheeks.

It is extremely difficult to find Manchester terriers that are worked to any sort of quarry which is a pity as a sixteen inch dog would still be suitable for working rats and would certainly not tower over modern working terrier show winners for dogs of this size are frequently among the winners at certain shows in the north of England. Neil Davidson of Penybryn Hall, North Wales, who not only bred Manchester terriers but also worked many breeds of terrier to rat, fox and badger believed that the working instinct had been totally bred out of the breed and that Manchester terriers showed little inclination to work rat let alone go to ground to face fox. If this is so it is a tragedy for once working instinct is bred out of a breed of dog it is nearly impossible to rekindle it in that breed without resorting to out-crosses with other types of terrier.

In closing it is worth noting that the resemblance of the Manchester terrier to the Dobermann is not accidental. It is said that when Louis Dobermann of Apolda began creating his new breed of dog many were coarse of type and resembled hybrid Dobermann-X-Rottweiler crosses. To refine the Dobermann, breeders were said to have used Manchester terrier crosses which gave the Dobermann its streamlined attractive appearance.

The Welsh Terrier

The Welsh terrier together with its close relative the Lakeland terrier represents the purest form of the Old English rough-coated black-and-tan terrier described by Horner as the Old Adam of the British working terrier. It seems likely that when the black-and-tan terrier fell into disfavour with Southern and Midland Fox and Otter-hound Kennels – they were replaced by classy white-bodied working terriers either fox terrier-types or the multitude of white-bodied terrier types that gave rise to the breed-type known as the Jack Russell terrier – many Welsh and Lakeland foxhound packs still kept strains of black-and-tan hunt terriers which worked fox and sometimes badger.

Horner states that as early as 1450 there was a Welsh poem – a poem that obviously relied on repeated assonance (the repetition of the syllables of coch-red) to enhance the flow of the poem 'a black red-bellied terrier bitch to throttle a polecat and tear up a red fox' and such a description obviously describes a black-and-tan terrier of the type kept by many foxhound and otter-hound kennels throughout Wales. As late as 1950 Tom Evans of Blaengarw, a famous breeder of working terriers and springers believed that strains of Welsh terrier quite distinct from the Kennel Club registered Welsh terriers existed in Cardiganshire and Pembrokeshire and that these terriers were simply relatives of the black-and-tan terriers that Edwardes used to create the Sealyham terrier. Black-and-tan terriers are still popular amongst working terrier *aficionados* in West Wales though many of these terriers are simply fell or Border/Lakeland hybrids and the pure-blooded black-and-tan terrier native to West Wales has now been much diluted with imported fell hybrids which have been found to be superior at both finding and staying to the original black-and-tan Welsh-type terriers.

Until the 1950s two kennels bred Welsh black-and-tan working terriers – the Ynysfor Otter-hound Kennels owned and hunted by the Jones family of Ynysfor and founded around 1760 and the Glasnevin Foxhound Kennels founded in or around 1720 though it is said that a pack of Welsh hounds which were probably used to hunt wolves hunted the Glasnevin hunt country in the time of King John

The Ynysfor hunt terriers were kept free of Kennel Club registered Welsh terrier blood and were smaller box-headed black-and-tan terriers which weighed in at fourteen pounds and were seldom more than

Welsh terrier: Kingpin

thirteen inches at the shoulder. There is some doubt as to the purity of this strain however for in the 1950s Major Roche, master of the Ynysfor Otter-hounds, sent a terrier to Harry Smith, huntsman for the Kendal and District Otter-hounds. The terrier was almost identical to local fell terrier-types (indeed it was absorbed into the gene pool of the local fell terriers). As to the breeding of this dog it seems likely that the dam line was pure Ynysfor-bred and could trace its pedigree back to 1800 but the sire of this dog was said to be a Coniston-bred hunt terrier. In type there was little or no difference between fell and Ynysfor terriers and there is a likelihood that over the years there has been an interchange of terrier blood twixt the Lake District and Wales.

There is some, albeit scant, evidence that Welsh terrier blood was also used to improve and tidy up Lakeland terrier stock – indeed Geoffrey Sparrow *A Terrier's Vocation* makes reference to a story related to him by a huntsman who decided to stop using Lakeland terriers at his hunt kennels when he found it difficult to tell the difference between Lakeland and Welsh terriers. Miss Morris, breeder of the Kelda strain of Lakeland terrier, believes that shortly after World War II a Welsh terrier-type of Lakeland began appearing in the show ring, better in type, slightly taller with the facial markings she associated with Welsh terriers. Furthermore the dull tan of the typical pre-war black-and-tan Lakeland terrier began to be replaced by the fiery red-tan of the typical Welsh terrier. Whether or not this infusion of Welsh terrier blood did anything to damage the working ability of the Kennel Club registered Lakeland terrier is questionable. It is sufficient to say that by the early 1950s a dichotemy had already begun to appear in the fell and Lakeland terrier types and few fell packs huntsmen (the Irving family – Willie and Arthur – were exceptions) kept Kennel Club registered Lakelands at hunt kennels. It should also be pointed out that infusing working terrier strains with Kennel Club registered Lakeland blood to tidy up the appearance of the fell terriers so that they might win at working terrier shows is a relatively modern practice that many believe has ruined the working ability of the fell strains.

However, in recent years the height of the winning terriers at hunt terrier shows has increased dramatically and whereas some twenty-five years ago a fourteen inch terrier would have been considered oversized at these shows today many of the winning terriers dwarf these fourteen inch terriers of yesteryear. In recent years the dull tan one associates with fell-bred Lakeland terriers has given way to a fiery red-tan which is typical of many Welsh terriers. Whether this colouration has appeared as a result of

a. crossing fell terriers with pure-bred Welsh terriers or
b. crossing fell terriers with Lakeland terriers with Welsh terrier blood or
c. the deliberate selective breeding of fell/Lakeland strains to produce specimens with this attractive colouration

is open to question.

Few Kennel Club Welsh terriers are worked today simply because the breed is not as popular as it once was and hence Welsh terrier puppies are not as freely available to hunters and also because the Welsh terrier is a shade too large to work in most fox earths in the South and Midlands – though huge terriers are often seen at Lakeland terrier classes in northern working terrier shows. (Welsh terriers are sometimes in excess of fifteen and a half inches at the shoulder and weigh twenty pounds or so).

However the history and development of the breed is fascinating. Terriers were often dyed and faked before showing and Tom Evans of Blaengarw often told the tale of one Welsh terrier breeder who produced a spate of terriers which were sent to America. A successful Kennel Club winner eventually found its way to the USA and won everywhere it was shown. One day the dog needed to be bathed and the soap and water washed out the dye to reveal a black and grizzle dog with a white front. Caveat Emptor perhaps!

Cledwyn Owen was quite a famous breeder of Welsh terriers in the early part of this century and Horner states that when he saw a particular fault developing in the terriers of the town where he lived (Owen lived in Pwllheli) he bought up a dog that was free of that fault and allowed it the freedom of the streets in the hope that it would stamp its type on the local terrier bitches.

Mr Walter Glyn described by some as 'the architect of the breed' once told Lucas a story of a stud dog known as the Blind Dog kept by Cledwyn Owens. The Blind Dog was one of a litter bred from the bitch Dewran who lost an eye while in whelp and Lucas attributes the fact that all the puppies were born blind to pre-natal influence. Clearly the bitch carried the genes for some abnormality of eyesight – for acquired characteristics cannot be inherited.

The Airedale Terrier

If the definition of a terrier is 'a dog that is required to go to ground and face down or flush fox and badger' then the Airedale, which measures twenty-two to twenty-four inches at the shoulder with weight commensurate with height and type, is far too large an animal to qualify for the title 'terrier'.

Why such a large dog, albeit a large dog bred on terrier-like lines, should have been bred at all is something of a mystery and explanations of its origin are seemingly offered by those who have precious little knowledge of the tasks a working terrier is required to do. It is said that sporting miners living in the valley of the river Aire – a river which flows through the industrial towns of Leeds and Bradford, bred such terriers to work rat on the banks of the Aire and its tributary the river Wharfe as well as to work small game that also lived on the banks of these rivers.

Anyone who has worked rat even in riparian conditions will realise that a smaller more agile dog is a more suitable ratter in any conditions and agility far more than size is an all-important quality in a rat dog. However it must be conceded that ratting dogs of all breeds display a peculiarity when ratting in deep water. Dogs which are swimming while carrying rats seldom shake and kill rats while still treading water – rats that are brought out of the water stone-dead have either died from the excessive pressure exerted by the dogs carrying them or have expired from fright. Dogs of all sorts will not, and probably cannot, shake water-caught rats to death until they find solid earth or rock beneath their feet. This fact, and this fact alone, may have prompted breeders to produce leggier, bigger terriers but this explanation too seems unlikely. When one explores the origin of the Airedale and examines the literature concerning the breed it becomes patently obvious that those who have penned articles about this breed have been concerned only with the aesthetic qualities of the type and have never ever ratted along river banks!

What is to follow is a heretical view that will certainly not find favour amongst purists and modern Airedale enthusiasts. It is likely that the original Airedale was simply a large all purpose crossbred dog of dubious breeding, a sporting companion dog that breeders later decided to breed on terrier-like lines to produce a large edition of the box-headed black-

Airedale terrier: Mrs J. Averis' Ch. Turith Adonis

and-tan terriers of the time. That some of these dogs were used as ratters is probably true – most breeds of dog show at least some animosity towards and some propensity to kill rats. That the Airedale was bred specifically to kill rats is patently hogwash as any serious hunter of rats will attest. The type is simply too big to be a competitive or sporting rat killer.

Lucas is very specific as to the origin of the Airedale – too specific in fact to be considered as an accurate source of information. Lucas states quite categorically that during the time when Barney Ottershaw (a singularly appropriate name) was Master of Otter-hounds, a sportsman with a bull terrier bitch conceived the idea of mating his bitch to an otter-hound to produce a dog that would be more at home hunting rats in water. Thus, according to Lucas the sportsman lay in wait while the pack came along the banks of the Aire to draw for otter and allowed a hound called Thunder to mate his bitch. It should be added that such a glib explanation of the origin of the Airedale should cast doubt on the authenticity of the rest of Lucas' historical research into the history of terriers.

Lucas continues even more exactly by stating that the bitches from this union were mated to a Gordon setter (the cross was used to breed in the black-and-tan colour no doubt!) owned by a Bradford butcher though Irish terrier blood had also been added to the mixture before this cross was made. Lucas also believed that a Scottish collie and a curly-coated retriever also mated to the progeny of the terrier/otter-hound/Irish terrier Gordon setter cross to breed a dog that was good in the water (one would question why Scottish collie was used) and to have a good nose that was capable of finding any quarry. Lucas whose fluid style of writing was seldom marred by serious research certainly goes overboard in his explanation as to how the Airedale was bred.

Horner *Terriers of the World* mentions 'it will never be known exactly how the Airedale was fashioned but he was certainly improved faster than any other breed.' This improvement was almost certainly wrought by crossing the rough-coated mongrelly black-and-tan terriers with Irish terriers – a cross that would have certainly imparted the box-like head so beloved by many breeders of English rough-coated terriers until the Airedale resembled a large edition of the rough-coated black-and-tan terrier, the Welsh and later the Lakeland terrier. C. H. Lane *All About Dogs* (1900) states that he does not believe the Airedale should have been classed as a terrier and that it would have been better grouped amongst the crossbreds or the hound group. Holland Buckley *The Airedale Terrier* (*Our Dogs*) adds further that the early litters of Airedale often produced dogs that were clearly quite good examples of Old English terrier (black-and-tan), Airedale, otter-hound and Welsh terrier and that one litter produced terriers which won prizes as a Welsh or Old English terrier despite the fact the parents of the dog were supposedly pure Airedale terriers.

Yet for all its mixed and mysterious origins the Airedale was considered one of the most versatile of dogs. In Lucas, *Pedigree Dog Breeding* (first published in 1925), there appears an amazing advertisement which describes the versatility of this dog.

> Burglar-proof Airedales Always For Sale. Metcalf, the original breeder of this famous breed has several well-trained Dogs to offer, over distemper, not quarrelsome, used to children and livestock and specially trained so that ladies can manage them. They are brimful of intelligence, almost human, obedient and safer than safe. Also some holy terrors that will face sticks and bricks, can smell tramps a mile off, down intruders, but love, honour and obey their owner. Mr Loader of 18 Bridge Street, Old Tredegar, Mon., writes this day (27th) I received Jack all right, and he is a Jack and find him just as you say and just what I asked for. I am very pleased with your terms of sale of dogs which shows your honest dealings but I knew who I was sending to, as I have handled some of your dogs before and I knew I would get a straight deal and satisfaction (Nuff said). Satisfaction and qualification guaranteed at ordinary prices. State requirements. Write Metcalf, The Northern Government Contractor for Dogs, Airedale House, 196 Harbottle Street, Newcastle Upon Tyne. All breeds catered for, satisfaction guaranteed. For Show, Sport or Companion.

A curious advertisement by any standard, slightly demeaning to ladies perhaps by today's notions and sure to cause offence to those who tend to support minority groups but a fair indication of the qualities at least some of the early Airedale terriers possessed. It should be noted that dogs were sold for 'Show, Sport and Companions'.

In the same issue of the book Lieutenant Colonel Richardson of Surrey advertises 'Airedales the best watch-dogs – pedigree, specifically trained for house protection against burglars, best guards for ladies living or walking alone, safe with children not quarrelsome.' It is also interesting to note that Richardson had penned a fairly lengthy tome entitled *Watch Dogs – their training and management* which sold for eight shillings and he had devised and marketed a skin cure for mange and eczema.

Likewise, Miss Turner, 10 Argyle Street, Reading, 'Breeder of Pedigree Airedale Dogs for showing and all purposes'. Clearly the breed was considered as one of the most versatile types of dog despite its large size which prevented its use as a true working terrier.

Horner, *Terriers of the World*, mentions that during the Russo-Japanese war, an event that jack-knifed Japan into the twentieth century, several Airedales were sent to Japan and used for various purposes (messenger dogs, guard dogs) and used to seek out the wounded. Unfortunately for the Japanese at least, the Airedales were said to prefer the scent of the white-skinned Russians. It is also worthy of note that Horner mentions Col Richardson who during World War I supplied Airedales to the British Armed Forces. Airedales were used as messenger dogs running the gauntlet of machine fire to take messages between the trenches and also dogs that occupied the role the German shepherd dog occupied in the trenches of the Axies.

Further proof of the versatility of the type was offered by one Henry Lewis, a lurcher breeder, from Swansea who in the early 1900s sold many Airedale greyhound lurchers which were famed for their versatility and found a market amongst warreners (the most conservative of lurcher owners) and poachers throughout Britain. Lurchers bred by Lewis were frequently advertised in *Exchange and Mart* as Lewis-bred lurchers in the same way as Hancock-bred lurchers are sold today.

However, despite the fact that many of the early breeders fought their dogs against not only other Airedales but also against bull terriers, the absence of large predators and suitable quarry offered little chance for British Airedales to show their mettle in the field, and it was in America that the courage and versatility of the Airedale terrier was tested. The most famous strain of Airedale worked in the USA was the Oorang strain bred from the stud dog King Oorang, mated to several bitches some of which were bred from Richardson's strain of Airedale. The strain was utterly game and faced puma, bears, both grizzly and black, jaguar and timber wolves as well as elk, deer and moose. The casualty rate amongst packs of Airedales used to hunt large quarry, particularly against feral pig and Prussian boar, was high for terrier courage is increased ten-fold if the dogs are aided and abetted by other game dogs. Ben Lilly who accompanied Theodore Roosevelt on his famous 'Teddy Bear hunt' was asked by his biographer why he declined to use Airedales to bring large predators to bay. Lilly is reputed to have said that these dogs came to grief in scrimmages because they were too plucky for their own good.

Australia too provides good sporting quarry to test the mettle of the Airedale. The native marsupials are usually slow-moving and with the exception of the now-extinct thylacine or Tasmanian wolf and the badger sized Tasmanian Devil, scarcely testing quarry for highly plucked dogs. However E. M. Pullar in his paper 'The Wild (feral) Pigs of Australia: their Origin, Distribution and Economic Importance' (1953), drew the public's attention to the huge number of wild or feral pigs living in Australia. These pigs, descendants of primitive breeds such as Tamworths and Berkshire pigs taken to Australia in 1788, were left to feed around settlements in much the same manner as did their medieval ancestors. Pigs were deliberately introduced to the Bass Islands by escaped convicts while the large herds of feral swine on Kangaroo Island are the result of a spiritual revival at the turn of the twentieth century which taught its converts that the dietary code of Leviticus XI should be practised and pigs must be regarded as unclean. Settlers who were converted to this faith simply turned loose their pigs which, in a country where the only predators were dingoes and wedge-tailed eagles, bred excessively.

It is a mistake to confuse these feral pigs with the fat pink pigs of TV commercials. In the late eighteenth century the pigs imported to Australia were descendants of primitive types of pig that still had the propensity to grow the knife-like tusks of their wild ancestors. Feral specimens are often lean slab-sided animals that are known as razor backs by those who still hunt them and while many are multi-coloured animals some have reverted to the colour of the wild boar that begat the species. The feral pigs head is much more developed than that of its tame counterpart – Clive Roots *Animal Invaders* (1976) attributes this to the fact that feral pigs are continuously employed rooting for grubs and edible plant roots – and the tusks, the lower canines of the feral pig, grow to almost twelve inches long and are terrible weapons. These pigs are now considered as pests as not only do they prey on ground-nesting birds but in some areas slay twenty-five per cent of the lambs born. However, in Queensland which is the most heavily infested state bonuses were actually paid to farmers who did not actively welcome pigs on their properties for many considered the lean musky tasting meat of the razor-back to be a bonus and turned loose domesticated pigs to swell the herds which congregated around the water-holes in certain areas. It should also be pointed out that since the pig was officially gazetted as vermin 25,000 pigs have been killed annually and in 1961–62, 54,000 were killed by bounty hunters.

The Australian film *Razor-back*, which starred the comic-turned-straight-actor, Bill Kerr, was clearly ludicrous for it depicted a homicidal pig the size of a rhinoceros, but the courage of a razor-back or even a domesticated swine must not be underestimated. The name Eberhard means 'brave as a boar' and both Hellenic and Germanic legends are pock-marked with tales of the fighting prowess of the wild pig, and the account of the horde which hunted the boar in the Mabigion tale Culuwch and Olwen is both entertaining and exciting.

It was not unnatural or unusual that bounty hunters hunting down these razor-backs turned to terrier breeds to bring these pigs to bay so that they might be shot. Irish terriers, a shade too small to be intimidating to the pig were used but the Airedale proved a larger and more useful type of terrier. During the 1960s when pig hunting was both popular and profitable teams of Airedales were hunted to wild or feral pig but the popularity of this terrier was short-lived for it was found that the hybrids twixt shepherding dogs and pit bull terriers or Staffordshire bull terriers were not only more easily obtained but more suitable for pig hunting – the collie brain gave the hybrids sense while the bull terrier blood provided courage.

Lucas however liked the Airedale terrier and when he was unable to obtain pure-bred rough-coated otter-hounds he produced a near replica of the breed by mating Airedales with bloodhounds and stated that the crossbreds fought like Welsh otter-hounds.

Clearly the Airedale is too large to be of much use at hunting the fox, the last available medium sized predator that the British can legally hunt, but there are many who still swear by the courage and guarding instincts of this attractive and apparently very versatile terrier type.

The Fox Terrier

There is little doubt that the fox terrier and that ill-assorted group of terriers collectively known as Jack Russell terriers are closely related and derived from the same stock. In fact when Lucas compiled his masterly *Hunt and Working Terriers* (1931), he included two chapters, 'In My Experience' and 'More Opinions and Yarns', in which he relied on letters he received from many contributors as a basis for his research. Many of these contributors stated that they worked fox terriers which Lucas may have taken to mean the Kennel Club registered smooth or wire-haired fox terriers whereas in point of fact these contributors were referring to types of dog that would be referred to as Jack Russell terriers today. Nimrod Capell, Isaac Bell and that great raconteur Captain T. Holland Hibbert certainly kept what they referred to as fox terriers but they obviously meant that they kept terriers which were worked to fox and not the classy bench terriers known as fox terriers. In fact Corbett in his masterly book *Man Eaters of Kumaon* relates that he seldom ventured out without the company of his diminutive fox terrier – though in point of fact photographs taken of Corbett with his terrier show a smooth-coated Parson Jack Russell terrier.

The subject of the origin of white-bodied terriers has been dealt with earlier in the book and it is sufficient to say that three theories concerning the origin of these terriers can be considered.

a. The terriers were simply 'sports' found in a black-and-tan terrier litter.
b. Beagle blood brought about the creation of the type.
c. Bulldog or bull terrier blood introduced the white colouration.
d. A combination of a, b, c contributed to produce both the fox terrier and the unrefined types known as Jack Russell terriers.

It is worthy of note that while Sydney Castle, *A Monograph of the Fox Terrier* (6th edition), goes to some pains to state that the type is not the result of mongrelising or crossing certain breeds 'the breed has been of the terrier order for centuries' he gives no explanation of the origin of the breed type. J. A. Doyle, author of *The Book of the Dog,* is a little less pedantic however, 'The antiquity and the precise origin of the modern fox terrier is involved in considerable obscurity. It is probably true that some of them were not wholly free from alien crosses of Beagle and Bull

Smooth-haired fox terrier: Mollie Harmworth's
Ch. Bengal Ashgate Quadrille. (Photo Lionel Young)

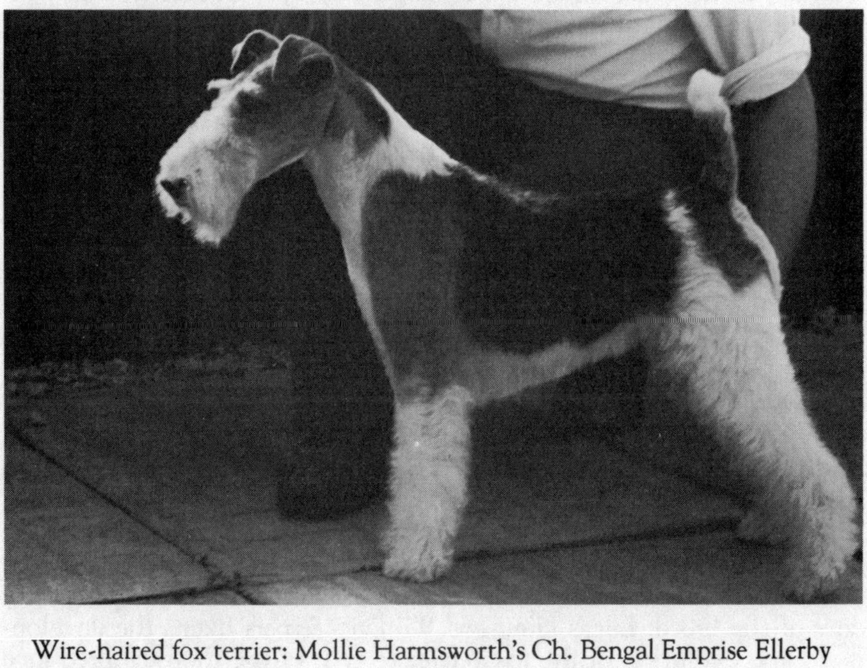

Wire-haired fox terrier: Mollie Harmsworth's Ch. Bengal Emprise Ellerby

terrier, but I feel sure that a careful analysis and investigation of pedigrees would prove that the best fox terriers were those that for many generations had been bred from dogs of one definite type and in whose pedigree there is as little alloy as possible.' In short both Castle and J. A. Doyle believed that the fox terrier-type, whatever its origins, had existed in its pure breeding form for centuries.

Two types of fox terrier exist – the wire and the smooth-coated types – and it is more than just possible that both types share a common origin. Certainly certain specific dogs appear in the pedigrees of both types of fox terrier.

The evolution of conventional fox hunting techniques contributed much to the development of the fox terrier. Prior to the mid-seventeenth century foxes were regarded as vermin, as nuisances that were best killed and killed quickly lest they caused more damage to stock. However, once the conventional fox hunting with 'horse and hound' had become popular the death of the fox was not the ultimate goal of those who hunted it. Indeed once a fox had run to ground evading the efforts of the hounds and the care of the earth stopper it was sometimes considered expedient to leave the fox to ground. These 'leave 'em alone' tactics were not adopted by many fox hound packs however, and the majority of 'hunts' employed hunt terriers. Outside the Lake District and certain districts in Wales, foxes were afforded some scant protection as they provided great sports for those who wished to ride to hounds. Landowners who shot or dug foxes were in fact treated with some distain by hunt followers some of whom were known to paint signs such as 'This man shot a fox' outside the houses of people they considered to be 'unsporting'.

Thus terriers which would bolt a fox without killing or hurting it were prized by huntsmen who organised the sport for mounted packs. Holland Hibbert did not like a dog that was too hard – 'No one wants a half-dead fox' he told Lucas and for this reason he kept white terriers as Borders and fell-types damaged a fox too badly to allow it to afford a lengthy run for the hounds.

John Russell is said to have kept only rough-coated terriers – though there is no evidence to substantiate this belief one should add – for he was said to believe smooth-coated terriers had too much bull terrier in their make-up and this bull terrier blood ruined 'the gentlemanly nature' of the terrier. J. H. Walsh (Stonehenge) shared Russell's opinion and deplored the infusions of bull terrier blood that were being bred into strains of fox terrier. Yet at the turn of the century Carson Ritchie, *The British Dog*, states that the smooth fox terrier was Britain's most popular breed of dog.

The fox hound kennels bred the very best fox terriers during the early days of the breed. Lucas *Hunt and Working Terriers* likens the development and evolution of the fox terrier to that of the thoroughbred race horse and equates the Byerly Turk, the Godolphin Arab and the Darley Arabian to Old Jock bred in the Rufford kennels in 1859. Old Trap bred by Mr Arkwright, Master of the Oakley Foxhounds and the fabulous Grove Nettle 1862 bred at a foxhound kennels that was later to amalgamate with the Rufford Foxhounds.

Whether or not these classy hunt terriers were exposed to the same degree of work as were their less fashionable relatives is questionable. The craze for showing terriers began when W. R. Pape staged the first dog show in Newcastle-upon-Tyne in 1859 and some forty years later classes for fox terriers were staged at Peterborough Hound Show in much the same manner as fell packs stage classes for 'in service terriers' at Rydal.

Classy, typey terriers were valuable – there are tales of working fox terriers changing hands for £450 in 1900 – and hence the more typey dogs, the classier fox terriers were not subjected to any work that might cause them injury or bring about their deaths and within a matter of twenty years after Pape's first dog show a division had begun to appear in the ranks of the fox terrier – a classy type kept at hunt kennels but seldom worked and a stronger-jawed animal, less attractive perhaps but capable of hard-biting and with strength of jaw enough for the muzzle not to crumple when bitten badly by a fox. Lucas comments that he did not consider the heads of even the best working fox terriers strong enough to withstand the bite of the badger and it is worth noting that Larcombe who was a great badger digger regularly brought bull terrier-bred fox terrier blood into his strain to maintain head size in his terriers. Geoffrey Sparrow, author of *A Terrier's Vocation* obtained two such bull terrier-bred fox terriers from Larcombes' strains and stated that every ten generations fox terriers benefitted from infusions of bulldog or bull terrier blood to increase head size.

Lucas was in fact convinced that only the tendency of breeders to produce long elegant heads in their terriers prevented the fox terrier from being one of the most versatile breeds of working terrier in the world and he was convinced that the type should not have been altered after the type illustrated by the 'Totteridge Eleven' had been arrived at – for the painting illustrates some eleven terriers which could have given a good account of themselves at any quarry.

Leggy fox terriers are a relatively modern type of terrier. Daniel *Rural Sports* (1760) (Horner refers to this epic as 'Field Sports') believed that speed was not a quality he associated with the make-up of terriers but that a terrier should possess the ability to keep up the same pace all day while hunting. Rawden Lee, 1894, states that the leggy terriers which were becoming popular even in his day were the result of breeders introducing the blood of small greyhounds to produce a terrier suitable for rabbit coursing though Carson Ritchie *The British Dog* (1981) mentions that as early as 1794 a terrier had run a mile in two minutes and six miles in thirty-two minutes!

Smooth-haired fox terrier: Ch. Riber Mint Imperial
Rotur Rowanberry

The dichotomy between the working fox terrier and the Kennel Club registered wire and smooth fox terriers widened by the year however and it became a novelty to see a typical fox terrier at a hunt kennel and more of a novelty still to see such a dog worked in the field.

However, fox terriers are sometimes still used by fox hunters. In 1974 John Winch of County Durham caused an uproar when he placed a small Kennel Club registered smooth fox terrier at the working terrier show in Llangollen. Winch defended his decision 'It was the most typey terrier in the class and it bore the marks of having been worked. It was neither too big to get to ground nor was the muzzle too weak to allow it to work. It was certainly the best terrier in the class.'

Cross-bred fox terriers are certainly often seen in working terrier shows. In 1988 Nuttall, a highly scientific fell terrier breeder and a much respected hunt terrier show judge, stated 'It is nearly impossible for any terrier that is not Lakeland or fox terrier-bred to win at a working terrier show today. Certainly the days of small working terriers winning at these shows is a thing of the past – many of the show winners are almost replicas of the fox terriers of the early 1900s and this metamorphosis has almost certainly been wrought by infusions of pure fox terrier or pure-bred Lakeland terrier blood.

It is also interesting to note that in the 1980s the Shifnal based terrier man Bert Gripton sold many terriers to America, terriers which buyers referred to as Gripton terriers. These terriers were, according to Gripton, bred by mating a smooth fox terrier stud dog to Jack Russell-type bitches.

Few Kennel Club registered fox terriers are worked at the time of writing, but it seems likely that as the size of working terrier show winners grows larger and larger more and more fox terrier blood may well be introduced into the working terrier gene pool until pure fox terriers of fourteen and a half inches and above may be worked to fox and small quarry once again.

The Bull Terrier

No breed of dog boasts the strange blood-soaked ancestry as does the bull terrier. Its very history, written as it is in agony and gore, is macabre, bizarre and yet so totally captivating that it is impossible to own a bull terrier of any sort without absorbing at least some of the curious ethos that surrounds the type. Anecdotes concerning bull terriers are legion. Poetry, particularly Black Country poetry describing the prowess of great fighting dogs, is both colourful and plentiful and historical hard, factual evidence concerning the breed has often to be unravelled from mythical sagas so outrageous as to be scarcely believable yet inextricably interwoven with the truth.

Tale has it that in 1209 William, Earl Warrenne witnessed the spectacle of two bulls fighting and a mob urging a band of dogs on to the antagonists. The sight so fascinated the Earl that he decreed that some six weeks before Christmas an aged crotchety bull should be baited to death by dogs and the flesh of the bull given to the poor of the town. Henceforth, dogs were specifically bred to bait these bulls, but the stock that spawned these dogs was already in existence long before Warrenne made his decree. Mastiffs, dogs game unto death, had been bred since pre-Roman times and band dogs, dogs which had so savage a disposition that they needed to be restricted by a band or chain (hence band or chained dogs), which were simply types of mastiff, were the ideal dog to be used by these bull baiters and these small or degenerate mastiffs were the dogs that Blome suggested were possibly the ancestors of the terrier (Blome believed that terriers could be created by mating beagles with mastiffs).

A process of selective breeding followed the start of the bull bait and smaller neater mastiffs, dogs which had the ability to withstand tremendous pain yet still maintain a deadly grip, began to be developed. The nose of these mastiff types was supposedly placed back on the face rather than at the extremity of the muzzle as this curious deformity was said to allow the dog to continue to breath while it increased its vice-like grip on its unfortunate adversary. The very nature of this vice-like grip coupled with the dogs ability to withstand horrific pain has given rise to a series of tales which any thinking, caring person would hope were not true. It is said that a Midlands butcher owned an extremely game bitch which was almost impervious to pain and had the devil's own grip. One day when she was engaging a bull the butcher boasted of the terrible courage and grip of his dog stating that she would as soon lose a limb as release her grip. He was taken to task for his statement and thus he set about sawing the legs from his hapless dog but the hideously deformed torso of the beast maintained its grip on the bull. It is to be hoped that the tale has no substance, but stories of this nature are common.

The continentals have always regarded the British as a race apart to be viewed with wonder and sometimes revulsion, but preferably from a distance. It is believed that it was the Swiss naturalist Conrad Gesner's interest in that most typically British of dogs the degenerite mastiff – it was to be described in print as the bulldog in 1632 but not before – that prompted Gesner to write to the scholar John Keyes and Keyes (who later latinised his name to Caius) reply to Gesner was later to be translated by Fleming and published as *De Canibus Britannicus* in 1576.

Later, Europe was to import these degenerate mastiffs – some of which were later to emerge as the Boxer and also to copy and ape the British quasi-sport of bull-baiting but it should be pointed out that the British bulldog was a far cry from the hideous deformed creature seen on the benches today. In all probability the British bulldog of Caius' day closely resembled both the American pit bull and the Boxer in conformation and general appearance.

Bulls were not the only victims of these ferocious mastiff types. Brown bears ixported from the continent, tortured beyond belief until the already furious ursine disposition was made doubly savage were also deemed suitable adversaries whose teeth and dagger-like claws created mayhem on the dogs that attacked them. Shakespeare, a truly British bard, delighted in the bear baits conducted at the Southwark Gardens where years after the closure of the pavilions it was reputed that the night was still rent with the ghostly screams of stricken beasts that had expired in floods of entrail and gore!

The boar, bravest of beasts, and most terrible of adversaries, was infrequently seen in the 'pits' of Britain, but only because the scarcity of the real article made it difficult to obtain a specimen. Before Shakespeares' days the boar had been hunted to the point where it was considered all but extinct and what specimens remained were kept as park animals, their movements restricted by stout stone walls and their diet supplemented by brewer's waste tipped into bins known as 'franks'. Shakespeare *Henry IV* (part II) enquires of Falstaff whose moustachioed face resembled that of a boar 'Doth the old boar feed in the old Frank'.

However, on the continent where the boar was more readily available it was baited without mercy by the dog bred down from mastiffs imported from Britain. Dr Charles Burney, who visited Austria in 1722, was visibly upset when he witnessed a horrendous eight day bait the centre of attraction of which was 'Will appear a fierce old boar just caught which will now be baited with dogs defended in armour'. It should be added that the continentals, ever enthusiastic about improving on that most peculiarly British of sports, filled the anus of the boar with straw and fireworks and set fire to these inflammables as the bait began. Burney wrote of his experiences with horror in his book *Continental Travels* and vilified the continentals for their interests but was clearly unaware that the baiting of dangerous beasts was an activity that had started in Britain.

Burney's indignation does however act as a weathervane to show how the British had come to regard the spectacle of bull and bear baits during the eighteenth century. Ecclesiastic debate had yet to determine as to whether animals possessed souls, but the rapidly growing towns spawned by the industrial revolution certainly did not welcome the hordes of thugs, villains, whores and pimps that were attracted to urban districts by the bull baits. When a Midland town staged a bull bait and the bull had somehow died before the bait could begin the mob began to wreck the town until the mayor, terrified by the prospect of a riot, secured an elderly horse to be dismembered by bulldogs to please the 'bonny baiting boys who came to bait the bonny bull'.

It seems likely that had not legislation been passed to outlaw baiting and dog fighting the sport would have died a natural death. Public opinion was decidedly against these activities and both sports were generally considered to be a recreation for the base and more degraded members of society: 'Surely diversions of this sort, if we may give them such an appellation are not only a reproach to human nature, but a disgrace to very Christian country' (*Gentleman's Magazine*). However, early in the Napoleonic wars a Quaker, one Mr Pease, became interested in the plight of the wretched victims of baits and brought about a bill which suggested outlawing the various types of bait that were by now relatively uncommon events in Britain, but somehow mention of the bull, the most commonly baited animal, was excluded from the 1802 Bill and the spectacle continued in such towns as Tutbury in Staffordshire and Stamford, Lincolnshire, allegedly the home of the bull bait.

Britain, plagued by 'a fear of the Corsican tyrant' had little time to contemplate the fate of unfortunate bulls, but in 1835 an Act of Parliament was passed – under pressure from the newly formed 'Society for the Prevention of Cruelty to Animals' – which effectively attempted to abolish all forms of baiting.

'Any persons keeping or using any house, room, pit, ground, or other place for running, baiting or fighting any bull, bear, dog or other animal shall be liable to a penalty of £5 for every day he shall so keep and use the same.' The Act carried a more savage sting when it was amended to three months imprisonment as an alternative to the £5 fine!

It is said that the death knell of the bull bait was sounded in 1837 when such a spectacle was held in Stamford and a troop of cavalry and a draft of police was sent to stop the bait. A bill for £600 to cover the cost of sending police and cavalry was sent to the mayor and henceforth the bull bait of Stamford came to an end.

Come on you bonny baiting boys
Who love to bait the bonny bull
Come all those who love to make a noise
For you shall have your belly full

In point of fact bull baits were staged at Tipton Wake in 1837 and Bilston in 1838. It is recorded that the last bull bait – a rather sombre bait in which a very old feeble bull expired in a matter of minutes – was staged in West Derby, Liverpool, and such was the publicity the spectacle received that no further bull baits were staged in England.

It is extremely difficult to conceal the presence of a bait where a bull roaring in agony expires in floods of blood and entrails but baits of smaller less vociferous animals continued for long after the 1835 Act was passed. Dog fighting too had been criticised by articles in the *Gentleman's Companion* and made illegal by the 1835 Act, yet the cessation of the bull bait gave a new lease of life to the minor league baits and dog fights.

Dog fighting had been practised long before William, Earl Warrenne had decreed that a bull should be provided to bait some six weeks before Christmas but it seems likely that if the 1835 Act had not been passed dog fighting too would have died a natural death. However, the British are a perverse race and once the bull bait became a thing of the past, dog fighting once again became popular.

Whether or not the cessation of the bull bait precipitated a change in the development of the pit bull dog is open to question for it is likely that long before 1835 strains of bulldog had been bred exclusively for dog fighting, though the bulldog bred for work against the bull would have been little different in type from the typical fighting dog. Both types would have been fast, hard biting, tenacious and extemely courageous.

It is also worthy of note that a wide variety of types of bulldog were matched in the pits. In Scotland a larger powerful type found favour, slower but stronger than its southern counterparts and weighing in at perhaps sixty pounds or more. In and around London a type of dog that weighed forty pounds was more favoured while in Staffordshire a slightly smaller dog was fought. It is said that a twelve to fourteen pound grappler existed north of the Potteries and this diminutive grappler, the Cheshire terrier, was used by John Tucker Edwardes in his creation of the Sealyham terrier.

Certain pits became famous for the events staged in these places and the more famous pits were seldom raided by the police. One such pit – the Cock Pit, Duck Lane, Westminster, later to be known as The

Westminster Pit – even acquired a certain dubious respectability for only the very gamest of pit dogs were fought in the Cock Pit. In fact it is worthy of noting that long after 1835 high class newspapers carried public challenges and results of dog fights and undergraduates at Oxford and Cambridge kept fighting dogs in their rooms. Alys Serrell, *Hound and Terrier in the Field*, records a dog fight that took place in Cambridge University as late as 1880 and refers to Jack, a much knocked about fighting dog, that had been bred in the Potteries and had fought and killed a giant Newfoundland dog. Large bets were placed on the outcome of these events and possibly because of these large bets, and the inclination of poor losers to report further dog fights to the police, dog fighting became less popular in London and it was the prerogative of the Midlands to produce specific types of fighting dog. Whether the original fighting dogs of the Midlands were simply the bulldogs of old bred in a more streamlined form to perform against other dogs or whether terrier blood had speeded the metamorphosis is open to question. Sufficient to say that by the start of the twentieth century a fast, agile, lightly built form of the old pit bulldog had begun to appear; a type bred almost exclusively for the ignoble sport of dog fighting.

It is impossible to understand the ethos that exists in the Black Country without actually experiencing it. Dieter Fleig *The Staffordshire Bull Terrier* gives no indication of the curious sub-culture that exists in and around Walsall. That dog fighting continued to be popular in such districts long after it was effectively stamped out in the rest of Britain is only understandable if one experiences the curious bonhomie that exists in some of the less salubrious districts of that town. It was said that a rent collector lived in deadly peril when he knocked on the doors of Lower Rushall Street, Walsall, yet a murderer on the run from the police might easily find refuge there. Police informers were *rara aves* in such places and most of the surrounding towns boasted similar 'rookeries' where similar codes of conduct were practised.

Drabble in his *Of Pedigree Unknown* mentions the town of Bloxwich now a suburb of Walsall and a place where dog fighting was still popular until World War II (though the activity is seldom heard of in Walsall in recent years) but Bilston, Darlaston, Wedsnesbury, Dudley and some parts of Birmingham also produced more than their share of those who actually fought their dogs in organised dog fights. Dogs of like weight were pitted against each other and certain families: the Arblasters, the Grundys and the Dunns were famous for their ability to get dogs 'ready' for these mains. The mains were surprisingly well organised and bets were limited to certain amounts so that there was little chance of a poor loser wishing to report his losses to the police – a practice that is also followed in the cock fights that still take place in the Midlands. Tales of chain makers, nail makers and casters betting hundreds of pounds on the outcome of dog fights should be disregarded. Such sums were usually beyond the means of most industrial workers and wagers of this size were sure to produce poor losers who might be tempted to report future dog fights to the authorities.

Battles took place in regulation sized pits – though there were some pits that were reputedly of smaller or larger sizes than usual. The pit used by the Blacks of Lower Rushall Street was reputedly a room in one of the houses of that street, but a line was drawn across the pit and the rules of combat roughly those observed by bare-knuckle pugilists. Each dog was in turn required to cross that line to take the battle to its opponent. It was a bone of contention between Yorkshire and Staffordshire dog fighters that under such rules a dead or dying dog might win a fight if its opponent refused to cross the line to attack the cadaver.

Trainers of note could produce a super fit dog for the mains and it was possible to get a dog exactly ready on the day of the match. Walsall dog fighters fed slop with meat juices to dogs that were out of training and increased the protein content of the diet (together with increased exercise) as the date of the battle approached. It is said that the terraced houses that adjoined the Walsall Arboretum often stank of boiling sheeps heads and the smell of burning bones that had been stripped of meat.

Each dog trainer used special recipes for conditioning a pit dog – ale, cider and linseed was often added to the feeds, but flesh was the ration advocated for the dog about to be pitted. Sheep heads, boiled so that the meat and the brains left the bone, was a common feed for both dogs and children at the turn of the century though it was common practice to feed children meat only when they began work.

Tales of certain pit dogs are still told today. One dog a large putty nosed brown dog called the Bomber had beaten all in his weight group from Birmingham to Cannock. His owner intoxicated by a mixture of ale and success boasted his dog could beat all comers. All agreed this was true, whereupon the owner boasted the dog, even when muzzled, could beat any dog in Bloxwich. This ridiculous boast was seized on and the luckless dog was fought with its jaws bound. The result was obvious and its drunken owner is reputed to have drowned the wretched creature in a well in Great Wyrley.

Another pied dog is reputed to have met its death when it was pitted against two dogs, one straight after the other so that the pied was not allowed to 'so much as catch its breath', but most matches were fought under conventional rules.

Prior to World War II there was always a market for live badgers in Bloxwich and Walsall for owners of Staffordshire bull terriers to test their dogs. Few dogs, not even the gamest of Staffords, will overcome a fresh, healthy badger that has not suffered injury during the 'dig' that secured it. Badgers bite furiously and with great force and it is doubtful if any Stafford ever got the better of a fresh badger – though the majority of old dog fighters claim that such dogs were bred from time to time. Sufficient to say the bite of an adult badger is hard enough to deter even the most persistent dog.

Badgers, to provide these tests, were dug on nearby Cannock Chase or towards Lichfield and sold for £1–2 a piece to owners of pit dogs. Desperate battles are often described by now elderly dog fighters and it is likely that the badgers such people state were killed by dogs had been baited so badly and so often that they would have expired whether or not they had been fought again. Badgers which are fought often and denied freedom pine and fade badly (they seldom refuse food even when in a state of decline, it must be added) and in the latter stages of this state of decline simply curl up and allow a dog to drag them around the pit.

However, badgers were not the only creatures to have been pitted against these lightly built pit bulldogs or bull and terriers: bull terriers as they later became known. Numerous public houses called *The Dog and Monkey* occur throughout the Midlands and the South – a relic of the days when dogs were matched against large monkeys or small apes. One such ape, a Barbary ape called Jacko Maccaco, regularly did battle with light-weight bull terriers and was said to have fought while chained to a doll's house and to have used an iron bar to inflict damage on its opponents.

More bizarre still was the spectacle of duck baiting, the popularity of which is attested by the numerous public houses that bear the title *The Dog and Duck*. Inn signs for these public houses usually depict a spaniel or retriever returning with a mallard, for the duck bait was too gruesome a sight to depict on an inn sign. Duck baiting consisted of tethering a pinioned duck to a pole in the centre of a large pond or small lake. The dog, a bull terrier of the Staffordshire type according to Homan *The Staffordshire Bull Terrier in History and Sport* was allowed to chase and if possible to catch the terrified duck which dived and outswam the dog until exhaustion on the part of dog or duck brought an end to the contest. By definition the 1835 Act should have brought an end to this degrading and pointless spectacle but it was left to the 1911 Protection of Animals Act to bring an end to such degradation.

Yet no more degrading spectacle than the Dog v. Man contests ever existed. Battles twixt bestiarii (fighters of animals) and beasts were described by the Roman historian Martial, but these battles had a certain dignity, albeit a death or glory, about them. The Hanley battle between the dwarf Brummy and the bulldog Physic had no such dignity and would have disgusted even Martial who enjoyed a feast of gore. A deformed dwarf who bore the nickname of Brummy who tradition has it had earned his backers a considerable sum of money when the dwarf had eaten a live cat, agreed to fight a local bred pit bulldog called Physic. Both dog and man were secured by a short chain which allowed neither to escape the attentions of the other. Brummy, wearing only a pair of trousers, pounded his victim sensless. The dwarf punched the dog's head to a pulp and had his arms terribly lacerated by Physic. The Daily Telegraph reported this contest:

> The bulldog came on fresh and foaming with aweful persistance of fury, but with desperate strength the dwarf dealt him a tremendous blow under the chin and with such effect that the dog was dashed against the wall where, despite all its master could do for it, for the space of one minute it lay still and the wretch who had so disgraced what aspect of humanity was in him was declared the winner.

However, in 1859 a sporting gun maker called W. R. Pape in order to sell his wares staged a dog show at Newcastle-upon-Tyne giving shotguns to winners of the classes. The show which was limited to pointers and setters was a huge success and the following year the hastily formed Birmingham Dog Show Society staged a show for many breeds of dog and one of the exhibitors was a dog and wild animal dealer called James Hinks who in his youth had been a noted trapper of goldfinches and linnets in and around the now heavily built up district called Aston.

Hinks won first in the class for bulldogs – a strong class, for dog fighting was a popular sport in Birmingham – but also won first prize with a white English terrier, a breed which because of genetic problems and inherent weaknesses became extinct during the early years of the twentieth century. At this time Hinks, who was not averse to a spot of dog fighting, bred a type of dog which was similar if not identical to the Staffordshire bull terrier – but Hinks found the type with its wide fronts, its often bandy legs and undershot mouth unattractive and hence even before the advent of dog showing had begun to experiment in breeding a new more attractive type of bull terrier. It is worthy of note that a similar unrefined type of bulldog or bull terrier existed from Lands End to Northumberland and that the breed type was certainly not confined to Staffordshire and Birmingham.

Hinks kept a fairly large kennel of dogs at Worcester Lane, Birmingham, where he began experimenting to produce a new improved bull terrier-type which he intended to have an elegant shape with a head devoid of the ugly bull terrier stops which were typical of the Midland bulldog strains.

In 1862 Hinks produced the result of his experiments which incidentally had begun in the early 1850s and exhibited a bitch called Puss, a white bitch with a fairly long strong elegant muzzle. Puss won her class easily for she was far more attractive than her opposition. It is said Hinks was accused of producing only showy dogs which were incapable of working in the pits in the manner of the local bull terriers (bad losers were as common then as now perhaps). Hinks accepted the challenge

Early bull and terrier hybrid

and supposedly fought Puss in Tappers Yard, Longacre against a bull terrier of the old type for a wager of £5 and a crate of champagne. Tale has it Puss took half an hour to kill her foe and returned to the show to win her class – and despite the gruelling battle she had just fought won a prize for the best conditioned dog in the show.

Hinks called his bew breed 'the bull terrier'; hitherto, since as early as 1818, the breed-type of unrefined dog had been referred to as the 'bull and terrier' rather than the bulldog.

It is worth noting that white bull terriers were not uncommon, indeed the famous Paddington White, the property of an unknown anonymous nobleman, is reputed to have produced a strain of white bull terriers which had a tendency to deafness. Likewise the Freeborn family of Oxford (grandfather, father and son) had produced many good white terriers but these were of a type similar to that of the Staffordshire bull terrier but reputedly somewhat smaller.

As yet no standard for the breed type had been drawn up and Rawden Lee reports having visited a show at Laycocks Yard, London and having seen bull terriers that weighed as little as four pounds. Hinks however favoured the larger type of bull terrier – though today's standard states 'There are neither weight nor height limits but there should be the impression of the maximum of substance to the size of the dog'.

The bull terrier bred by Hinks was simply an improved type of bull terrier and still much regarded by sportsmen. G. R. Jesse *Researches Into the British Dog* (1866) states 'Most of the old bull baiters have become extinct and their breed of dog also'. Carson Ritchie *The British Dog* adds 'By contrast the bull terrier always remained a working dog, not just a triumph of inbreeding. It was kept by all classes not just by dog fighters and was a ladies dog as well'. Agnes Weston, the philanthropist, wished she brought her bull terrier with her when she opened one of her Royal Sailors' Homes for she found a rat eating her breakfast in the derelict building she intended to open as a 'home'.

It is also worthy of note that the custom of pinning rosettes on winning dogs is in fact a relic of the time when bull baiting dogs of old were decked with rosettes of coloured ribbon fastened to the dogs by a dab of tar. The dog was supposed to have done battle particularly well if the rosette transferred itself from the dog to the bull!

However, to return to Hink's new improved bulldog or bull terrier. There are no records of James Hinks, breeding programme or formal evidence as to how Hinks produced his bull terrier. It is likely that he mated Staffordshire bull and terrier type stock with that effete sensitive and fortunately extinct Old English white terrier and that perhaps he introduced Dalmatian blood to give the new type better coat and conformation. Various other breeds may have been introduced into the stock by later breeders. Some suggest foxhound blood, borzoi, collie and greyhounds were introduced to improve general type and shape of head.

Yet the improved bull terrier bred by Hinks had a reputation for being desperately game having the devil's own courage and a great propensity to fight when roused. At first only white specimens were considered acceptable and it was reported that Hinks deliberately mated mother to son, father to daughter not to breed coloured specimens into the breed. However old beliefs die hard in the world of fighting dogs and one of those beliefs was that brindle bull terriers were more vigorous and sometimes more game. To create coloured bull terriers, breeders of the 1930s are said to have mated six Staffordshire bull terriers and one Manchester terrier crossed with a bulldog with the white bull terriers and it is worth noting that for some reason coloured bull terriers are usually solid coloured with white markings, coloured in much the same way are Boston terriers – close relatives of the bull terriers.

Bull terriers have a limited use as working terriers in Britain. At one time they were popularly used as Caesar dogs at the end of a badger dig – a dog that had strength and courage enough to hold a badger and prevent it bolting – but since badger digging has been made illegal bull terriers are seldom used as working terriers.

As ratters the breed has a very limited use for despite the claims of breeders – many of whom have obviously never hunted rats – few bull terriers are agile enough to kill rats with any dexterity. Most are too large to work places where rats are likely to frequent and whereas rats die quickly when they come within reach of these massive jaws, rats have to be caught before they can be killed!

However, bull terriers have been worked satisfactorily to larger quarry in Africa, America and Australia. One excellent account of the worth of a good bull terrier is found in Sir Percy Fitzpatrick's book *Jock of the Bushveld* though Lucas states that he was told by Major Court Treatt that Fitzpatrick bred cross-bred bull terriers and did not work or keep pure-bred dogs. Jock, according to Treatt, was a cross-bred not a pure bull terrier as Fitzpatrick implies in his book. It is worthy of note that it was Sir Percy Fitzpatrick who originated the custom of two minutes silence on Armistice Day.

Jock was given to Fitzpatrick by a fellow adventurer and far from being the runt of the litter Jock grows into a superb hunter capable of pulling down wounded buck and becoming a magnificent catch dog. The battle between Jock and Seedling's vicious baboon is both exciting and well written though much of the book is ruined because of needless euphuistic descriptions.

Lucas mentions a Mr L. A. Francis, a lieutenant in the Indian Medical Department, who owned a particularly good Kennel Club registered bull terrier called Lillington Sunstorm that would seek out deer and work a drove of pigs. The dog reputedly drove off a black bear that was attacking his owner.

The breed experienced some popularity as a pig hunting dog in Queensland during the 1960s when the feral pig population of Queensland experienced a boom and it became policy to pay bounty to hunters who were prepared to hunt these razor-back swine. At first Airedales were used but found wanting, later bull terrier hybrids became popular bull terrier/collie or bull terrier cattle dogs or kelpie hybrids found a ready market amongst the bounty hunters. However, more popular, more suitable hybrids have been produced by mating collies, kelpies or cattle dogs with American pit bull terriers.

Bull terrier *aficionados* still continued to breed the unrefined types of bull terrier in the Midlands and Birmingham, however, and nowhere was there greater enthusiasm for the type than in Cradley Heath. In the Cross Guns Inn at the said town there was great interest in the breed, its illegal use and tales of derring-do concerning bull and terrier dogs.

Staffordshire bull terrier

Dennis Abbot, an avid collector of Black Country tales and prints, once joked 'Men were asked to leave the Cross Guns for talking about politics or religion. Come to think of it they were asked to leave if they talked about anything other than bull terriers – though Joe (Mallen the landlord) would tolerate chat about good black reds (game cocks)'

Mallen had bred pit dogs – bull terriers of the Staffordshire type – for over forty years and because of his expertise and his gift as a raconteur he attracted a host of dog fanciers to the Cross Guns and thus the public house became a focal point for bull terrier enthusiasts throughout Britain. Abbot states that Mallen acted as a human stud register for in the years between the World Wars Mallen knew just about every typey bull terrier between Cradley Heath and Walsall – and knew the pedigrees of these dogs as well. There is little doubt that pit dogs were fought in these Black Country towns though it would be a falsehood to state that 'every other household was owned by a Stafford'. Even in its heyday dog fighting was an esoteric interest that never met with the approval of the rest of the population and it would be fairly accurate to state that the Black Country produced more bird catchers and finch breeders than it did dog fighters. In fact the Dunn family who had a great reputation for breeding fighting dogs had an even greater reputation for breeding and trapping what is referred to as the 'seven coloured linnet' (the goldfinch). It would give a totally false impression to assume that the Black Country swarmed with owners of pit dogs for even during the heyday of the Stafford, 1918–1939, the dog fighter was regarded as a bit of an oddity by his neighbours. It would in fact be extremely difficult to find a man who fought his Staffords or any other breed of bull terrier in Bloxwich, Leamore, Blakenhall and Ryecroft today, but breeders of British birds still abound in these districts.

Many dog books tend to give a romantic illusion of the Midland dog fighter and the men who simply owned these pit dogs. It is a totally false picture of the Black Country. Dog fighters were a novelty in the Black Country and viewed not only with curiosity but with some contempt by the majority of the population. The American Steve Eltinge who sees 'the position of Staffords in English society in the industrial revolution as something of a class symbol: coal miners, foundry workers and blacksmiths chose the bull and terrier as a companion – a dog they could identify with' (Dieter Fleig *The Staffordshire Bull Terrier* (1990)) is totally wrong about his conceptions of the Black Country. The most popular dogs of the Black Country were whippets and dog racing was always more in vogue than dog fighting even amongst the chain makers, coal miners, foundry workers and blacksmiths.

Drabble, in his *Of Pedigree Unknown*, gives a colourful though not particularly accurate picture of the curious sub-culture of the dog fighters prior to World War II. Organised rat killing events were things of the past by this time though ratting with bull terriers and bull terrier crossbreeds was always a popular activity in the Black Country. Drabble states that Walsall Darlaston and Wednesbury produced distinct types of fighting dog some districts favouring the squat huge headed type; others a faster more terrierish pit dog. Abbott who collects much data concerning the Black Country believes this was not the case and stated in August 1983 'If a dog was winning well in the mains it was used at stud and people would travel great distances to mate bitches to a really good scrapper. The type of dog changed from year to year. Sometimes low to the ground types appeared sometimes leggier dogs. It all depended on the shape of the most popular stud dog of the time. It is no distance from Walsall to Cradley Heath on the bus and it was the same distance even before the war. People in Bloxwich would think nothing of going to Cradley Heath to buy a goldfinch let alone to mate a dog.'

It is well worth mentioning some of Abbotts' theories on the relationship between running and fighting dogs. Abbott is of the opinion that when the rabbit coursing meets were in vogue in the Black Country the most successful competition dogs were composites of whippet and pit dog for the hybrid type inherited speed from its whippet parentage and grit and tenacity from the bull terrier. Abbott is of the opinion that many of the pale fawns found in Staffords today can be traced back to some of these whippet/pit dog hybrids many of which were the selfsame silvery fawn colour.

However, in 1935 one Joe Dunn, who had written copiously on the bull terrier-types bred in the Black Country decided to found the Staffordshire Bull Terrier Club and the headquarters of the club was the Cross Guns Hotel in Cradley Heath whose landlord Joe Mallen owned one of the great milestones of the Staffordshire bull terrier breed Gentleman Jim – a nickname that had been afforded Jim Corbett, conqueror of John L. Sullivan the Boston Strong Boy some thirty or so years previous.

Breeders such as John F. Gordon whose kennels carried the prefix Bandits (the famous Bandits Fearless Red was a template for the early type) did much to popularise the breed and by dint of his books (and Gordon was a truly prolific writer) did much to allow the public to understand the Stafford temperament.

Abbott says of the early shows staged by the club 'Apparently they were fairly hairy (hair raising) events. Many of the dogs that were shown in 1935 had known work (had actually been fought) and the bringing together of hot fast dogs convinced the animals that they were about to be fought again. Some bad scraps took place at certain shows and some people avoided attending shows if they knew So-and-So was bringing his dog. Some of the dogs would ignore other breeds of dog benched near them but would go berserk when they saw another Stafford. Some of Mallens' dogs were supposed to be wicked and it soon became obvious that they were not suitable for the show ring as they causd a lot of trouble when they met other pit dogs. It's strange that they never or hardly ever attacked other dogs though.'

It soon became obvious that while fast dogs (dogs which fought as soon as real or imagined insult was shown by another dog) were essential for the pits the quality made them less desirable 'on the bench'. It was realised that really aggressive dogs were not only difficult to control but absolute pests when they were taken into the show ring and while the sight of a dog lunging at other exhibits may look impressive to the casual observers stationed around the ring such behaviour often made the exhibits difficult to show and even more difficult for a judge to handle. Early exhibitors and often early judges sometimes adopted the 'no fight, no show' attitude and rarely placed a dog that did not manifest ferocious aggression to other exhibits, but this attitude was both short sighted and fortunately short-lived and a more sensible attitude towards exhibiting soon followed. Less gassy, less aggressive dogs began to be bred and because such exhibits were more easily managed they were more successful than the more unruly dogs. It followed that less aggressive dogs began to be bred and while it could be said that such dogs would have been less than useful as fighting dogs – this point is made by Drabble in his *Of Pedigree Unknown* – it should be pointed out that dog fighting had been made illegal exactly a century before the Staffordshire bull terrier found its way to the show benches.

Drabble makes mention of the two Staffords he once owned in his book *Of Pedigree Unknown* – a dog and a bitch called Grip and Rebel – and states that they were the best rat killing terriers he ever saw. One must assume that Drabble had seen very few top flight rat hunting dogs, for despite the fact that Staffords like all bull terrier types have tremendous punishing bites which kill rats easily and efficiently the Stafford is seldom agile and nimble enough to equal the lighter more agile working terriers at the sport of rat catching. In the rat pits where a thousand rats might huddle against the smooth sided walls of the pit, the Stafford would be hard to better as a rat killer. Working amongst wire, rubbish and knee-deep in mud – and most ratting terriers must work in such conditions while ratting – the average Stafford is far too cumbersome and bulky to be a truly outstanding rat killing dog. However it is equally true that many great ratting terriers have a dash of bull terrier in their ancestry, for the strong jaws and grit conferred by a dash of bull terrier blood allow a terrier to complete its tasks as will as any breed of dog.

As true working terriers Staffordshire bull terriers have enjoyed a somewhat chequered career. Few are narrow fronted enough to work foxes except if these are to be found in smooth-sided large diameter drains. Bull terriers invariably have a tendency to be mute below ground and while they often tackle their quarry with great gusto they perpetrate their deeds in almost total silence. While some Staffords can be taught to give tongue below ground – if dogs encounter badgers during their early ventures to ground they are sometimes bitten so badly that they give tongue quite freely rather than attack their prey silently.

However, while it can be said that mute, silent dogs are seldom terriers which can be easily found by the digger since the advent of the locator there has been a tendency to pay less attention to the breeding of more vocal terriers. A mute dog fitted with a locator can now be found and hence dug with considerably more ease than such a dog could be if it was not fitted with a terrier locator. At one time mute dogs were given away by hunt kennels as a vociferous terrier is not only more likely to bolt a fox, to be more easily dug if it could not bolt the fox, but was less likely to be badly mauled by a fox than would a mute terrier that simply went to ground, took hold and set about its fox.

During the 1970s it was therefore quite a common sight to find bull terriers at working terrier shows for such dogs fitted with locators were commonly used by badger diggers. However the 1973 Badger Protection Act and the 1981 Wildlife and Countryside Act followed by the curious and perhaps unjust 1985 ammendment to the 1981 Act has now effectively outlawed the sport of badger digging and there is little reason to consider the Stafford as a true working terrier. A curious and somewhat disgusting incident did in fact cause many organisers of working terrier shows to state that bull terriers were not to be catered for at some of the better known county shows. A spate of idiots and hooligans encouraging Staffords to attack smaller working terriers had caused a great deal of bad feeling among the working terrier fraternity and these attacks certainly gave ample ammunition to those who were antipathetic to terrier work. Hence certain show organisers instructed officials not to allow bull terrier-toting dog owners on to the show grounds unless they were prepared to leave their bull terriers behind in their vehicles. However, during the early 1980s the sport of working terriers below ground had attracted some of the most unpleasant and perhaps disturbed people to its folds and many of these undesirables owned bull terriers which they insisted on taking to working terrier shows and sometimes setting them on true working terriers. One show official who attempted to bar the owner of a bull terrier entering a show with his Staffords was set upon by the owner of the Stafford and had his nose literally bitten off by the near lunatic dog owner. The incident brought great and bad publicity for the working terrier fraternity and bull terriers were seldom welcomed at working terrier shows henceforth. It is also worth noting that the 'gates' at these shows dropped dramatically in the days following the reports of the prosecution of the idiot who perpetrated the incident. It was unfortunate for the majority of owners of Staffords are sane and sensible people but the action of one or two criminally disturbed louts brought the Staffordshire bull terrier fraternity into great disrepute for a while.

On the subject of bringing the working terrier into disrepute it would be unfair to leave the subject of Staffordshire bull terriers without mentioning what are euphemistically referred to as the Irish terrier trials. Fleig, *The Staffordshire Bull Terrier*, mentions that some very game strains of Stafford are still bred in Ireland and this brings us quite neatly to the accounts of the trials mentioned in *The Working Terrier Year Book* in the early 1980s. These trials were a far cry from the legitimate and legal Teastas Mor trials organised by the Irish Working Terrier Association and consisted of putting a badger at the end of a blind tunnel from where it could not escape and trialling dogs on the live badger, some of which were required to bay at the badger while the Staffords together with Kerry Blues, Wheatens and large crossbreds were required to fight the badger. The contributor who obviously wished to be anonymous stated the trials 'are not exactly legal but not exactly illegal'. The writer is quite wrong: placing any animal in a position from which it is impossible for the beast to escape and thence setting dogs on the said animal constitutes baiting and contravenes not only the 1835 Act but also several clauses contained in the 1911 Prevention of Cruelty to Animals Act and such organisers and spectators who frequent such spectacles are in great danger of being prosecuted. The article or letter was to say the least 'ill advised' and its publication a clear indication of a rather less than sensitive publisher.

During the late 1960s the national press occasionally made mention of the dog fighters of America who bred, fought and above all conditioned fighting dogs called American pit bull terriers. Fighting dogs need special conditioning to get them fit and are given adrenalin-based chemicals to prevent them dying of shock both during and after a main. These articles although quite interesting were woefully inaccurate and probably stimulated a revival of interest in the sport of dog fighting rather than bringing the activity into further disrepute.

The origin of the American pit bull terrier is interesting but obscure. The breed, which is larger, taller and more athletically built than the Staffordshire bull terrier, is constructed more on the lines of a boxer than the typical bull terrier. Suggestions as to the origin of the type are both legion and varied. The American pit bull terrier may well be:

a. A pure bred Staffordshire bull terrier-type bred to be taller and faster than conventionally bred British Staffords.
b. A combination of Staffordshire bull terrier-types and larger British types of bull terrier such as the Blue Paul.
c. A combination of unknown mastiff types mingled with conventional types of bull terrier.

Many credit the dog fighter Cockney Charlie Lloyd with being the father of the American pit bull terrier though M. Homan *The Staffordshire Bull Terrier in History and Sport* states 'Freeman Lloyd, a leading canine authority and journalist tells that on a visit to America during the early 1900s he met a resident of Alabama who was a descendant of a famous Scottish family noted for its leadership in old-time Border cattle raids in the time of Johnny Armstrong. Lloyd asked which Armstrong was the first dogman of his people. Robert Keith Armstrong replied that when bull baiting was made illegal in 1853 the natural sport for men to turn to was dog fighting. He explained that the same breeds were employed for both pastimes. Mr Armstrong continued by saying 'The baiting and fighting dogs had longer muzzles than the fancy bulldogs of the present time.'

Charlie Lloyd was the owner of a gambling emporium on Fifth Street, New York and came by the funds to finance his venture by fighting certain bull terriers that he imported from Britain. His most famous dog Pilot was bought from John Holden who owned a public house called the Red Lion Inn in Park Street, Walsall. Holden was an associate of the Blacks who lived in nearby Lower Rushall Street and Pilot was sired by Robert Small of Sedgeley's dog Billy (proof of Abbott's theory that breeders would travel some distance to mate bitches). Pilot fought and won a grim and savage battle with Louis Kreiger's dog Crib for the championship of America (Crib too was bred near Walsall). It is worth noting that in the 1880s Crib was a fairly common name for a British immigrant to call a fighting dog and many famous pit dogs of the time bore the name. In the same decade John Walls Crib, an all white dog, was a famous pit dog in and around Vancouver and it is said that Jack London saw this Crib fight and that it became the model for the bulldog that brought down White Fang in London's book of the same name – though London's description of the fight gives no indication that he had witnessed a battle involving a pit bred dog.

It would be ludicrous to state exactly when the bull terrier-types returned to Britain where they were referred to as American pit bull terriers but there is an account of a battle twixt an English London bred bull terrier called Bridget – that brought down an American pit dog called Conn in 1889 in Liverpool, England.

However, the name modern cynologists associate with importing the American pit bull terrier to Britain is Ed Reid who at one time published dog magazines from Pinfold Street in London but later moved to Boston, Lincs. Reid was the subject of much unfair publicity for some of the animals he bred from his imports were sold to men who were later convicted of using their dogs for pit fighting. It might be argued with the same conviction that a person who sells a pot for cooking onions to a man who insists on using the pot to boil live children is guilty of aiding and abetting the crime of murder. It should also be pointed out that some of the dogs featured in the unsavoury videos confiscated during a raid at one dog fight were English bred white bull terriers bought from the breeder of a particularly successful strain of bench-bred bull terrier.

Reid has written several books on the subject of bull terriers in general and American pit bull terriers in particular and has been instrumental in setting up weight pulling contests at which the American pit bull terrier excels and these activities have a great following in the American pit bull terrier fraternity.

As sporting dogs the very size of the American pit bull terrier (some dogs weigh over eighty pounds) place it at a disadvantage as a hunter in Britain. Most would find it impossible to get to a fox in most natural earths, though most pit bull magazines carry articles by Gwent based Anthony Johnson who has hunted fox, rat and feral cat with his team of American pit bull terriers.

The American pit bull terrier has, however, been used to good purpose by Australian feral pig hunters, though the excessive courage displayed by the breed often proves its downfall. Alan Parsons a part-time Queensland bounty hunter has this to say about the American pit bull terrier. 'Pure-bred pit bulls are seldom used. They are too game for their own good and dog haters so they can seldom be worked in conjunction with another dog. Really game pit bulls seldom last a full season without getting badly torn up. The best pig dogs are usually bull terrier-bred but have a dash – a quarter is enough – of Kelpie or collie. Pure-breds (pit bulls) seldom keep out of trouble – face a razor-back head on and suffer accordingly. I shan't use another pure-bred.'

The miniature bull terrier is a smaller version of the bull terrier produced by James Hinks and was once referred to as a Toy Bull terrier. In 1906 Sir Raymond Tyrriott Wilson is reputed to have owned a three pound bitch known as Pony Queen that was a perfect replica of the bull terriers of the time. Hinks did in fact keep a number of tiny bull terriers and exhibited bull terriers of ten pounds in weight at the International Show at the Agricultural Hall, London in 1863. Modern specimens should be under fourteen inches at the shoulder, twenty-four to twenty-five pounds in weight and be of the same conformation as the larger bull terrier specimens.

Few miniature bull terriers are worked though the type is small enough to work to rat and fairly agile to boot. It is however a fact that the majority of miniature bull terriers can only be born with the help of a Caesarian section. There is some evidence that Cheshire breeders used some miniature bull terrier bitches to badger in the 1960s and more evidence to suggest that terriers from Gwyllim Hardwick of Blaengarw were mated to these miniature bull terriers to produce badger digging and fox killing terriers. Some very tiny prick-eared terriers similar to very tiny miniature bull terriers (most had the typical bull terrier Roman nose) were shown without success in the under ten inch classes in Northants during the 1960s. It is interesting to note that the terriers owned by Mr Cowley during his dig at Loughborough in conjunction with Lucas's Sealyham terriers (see photograph in Lucas book *The Sealyham Terrier*) were a type of miniature bull terrier though this can only be ascertained if the photograph in Lucas book is subject to great magnification.

Pure-bred bull terriers are seldom of much use as working terriers in Britain. Their large size clearly places them at a disadvantage when working fox, though most were capable of getting to ground in the majority of established badger sets. The 1973 Badger Protection Act reinforced by the 1981 Wildlife and Countryside Act has effectively made badger digging an illegal pursuit however and thus the bull terrier can no longer be regarded as a working terrier that can find work in the British countryside.

Bull terrier blood has however been used to 'fire' many types of terrier to give the breeds both courage and strength of jaw. There are few breeds of southern terrier that do not have a history of bull terrier or bulldog blood bred into their bloodlines. Blome inadvertantly stressed the importance of the bulldog or degenerate mastiff in the creation of the working terrier and his notions have proved surprisingly correct.

Jack Reid apparently used a small Staffordshire terrier bull type (the breed had not achieved recognition at the time) to tidy up the coats and reduce the Bedlington terrier influence on his Norwich/Norfolk terrier stock and the cross also produced specimens with heavier jaws.

Sealyhams too owe much of their courage to the fact that John Tucker

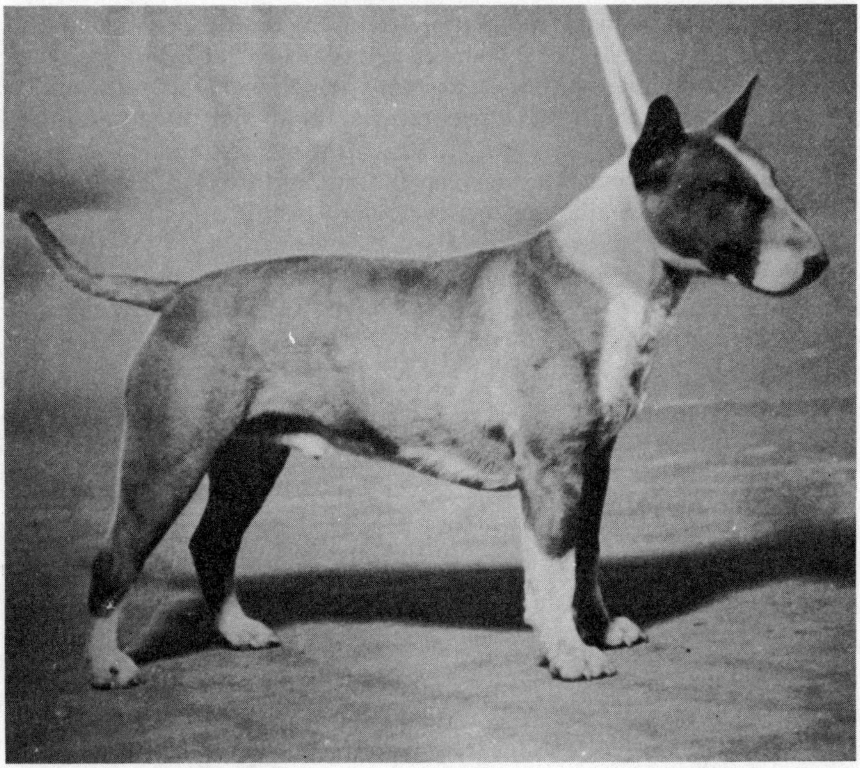

Miniature bull terrier

Edwardes used a type of small bull terrier called the Cheshire terrier to fire the bloodlines. As to these Cheshire terriers Lucas believed that as late as the 1900s this type of small pit bull was being bred by certain working terrier breeders. Rawden Lee tells of a Cheshire based kennel of terriers that were famous for their extreme courage. The kennel, owned by a Mr John Walker kept some seven couple of terriers which were game for anything from 'a pig to a postman' and Lucas states that these terriers did actually set upon a postman and mangled his legs so badly that the postman died as a result of the attack. Lucas was convinced that Walker bred the last of the true Cheshire terrier strains.

The black fell strains descended at least in part from the stud Black Davy and closely related dogs bred by Cyril Breay of Mallerstang and Kirkby Lonsdale and Frank Buck of Leyburn often manifest huge bull terrier-type heads. Breay and Buck both protested that they used no bull terrier blood in the creation of this strain and that large heads appeared simply because line breeding so close as to be inbreeding had 'fixed' the genes that produced huge bull terrier heads with strong masseter muscles. Bull terrier blood has however almost certainly been introduced into various black fell terrier strains in recent years. Why this hybridising and infusing of fell strains with bull terrier blood has taken place is questionable. Nuttall of Holmes Chapel, 1981, an authority on the type, stated that the bull terrier crosses would have done nothing to improve the courage of the type. He adds 'a dash of Patterdale (black fell terrier) could do wonders to perk up the Stafford if you ask me.' However there is little doubt that many modern strains of fell terrier have bull terrier in their ancestry.

Thus while it is true that bull terriers are seldom used as working terriers in Britain, the impact of bull terrier blood on many types of working terrier has been tremendous.

The Plummer Terrier

At one time this true breeding type of terrier was classed as a variety of Jack Russell terrier. Indeed many were shown with some success at Jack Russell terrier classes at hunt shows and some thirty-six were passed for the Jack Russell Terrier Club of Great Britain Advanced Register. However the type is so dissimilar to that of the Jack Russell terrier and the markings so distinctive that in 1976 Muriel Jones, then registration officer for the Jack Russell Terrier Club of Great Britain, stated 'The type is so dissimilar to that required by the standard of the Jack Russell Terrier Club of Great Britain that they can no longer be considered as Jack Russell terriers.'

However, long before the club meeting when Muriel Jones made her statement the type was breeding remarkably true to type and had become so distinctive as to be easily recognised by any working terrier enthusiast in Britain. At first the type was known as the Huddlesford terrier or the Huddlesford working terrier as for some twenty years the type or breed was kennelled at Huddlesford near Lichfield, but the breed type originated some five years prior to the pack coming to Huddlesford.

The ancestors of the type were rough-coated rather mute terriers that were bred in the valleys of South Wales but these dogs, while they were almost recklessly courageous, were lacking in voice and nose. Hence blood from Joan Begbie of Worth Maltravers, Wiltshire was added to the strain, yet a dichotomy between the breed and conventional Jack Russell types did not occur for a number of years. The curious markings one now associates with the breed had appeared some time before when a bitch called Class was born to a litter bred by mating a dog called Rupert to his aunt Jade, but Class had proven a difficult whelper and after her one and only litter she never came in season again.

The breed became fixed so to speak only when beagle blood was introduced into the lines. At that time the terriers from the pack had been used primarily as badger digging dogs and were worked with great regularity to fox by local hunts and badgers from Derby to Melton Mowbray in Leicestershire. Quite a few diggers accompanied the pack on their outings and one of these, a schoolteacher called Phillip Ainstey, owned a show-bred beagle bred from imported American stock and carrying the Rosset prefix. The dog was quite a chunky animal but measured only twelve or thirteen inches at the shoulder and had a

Huddlesford terriers

simply incredible nose and worked above ground and below with equal enthusiasm. Despite the fact that Ainstey was not a terrier enthusiast and was simply absorbed into the badger digging group – and the sport was both legal and considered respectable at this time – the beagle became quite a famous badger dog and showed more propensity to go to ground than to hunt hares. The dog once stayed for two days to a badger during a dig at Melton giving tongue all the while and not sustaining serious injury. Subsequently a terrier bitch was mated to the dog.

The first cross beagle terrier hybrids were quite hideous and sported huge pendulous ears though the cross did breed out the tiny prick ears which were common in the terriers bred at this time. Despite the appearance of these hound terrier crosses the hybrids were incredibly good below ground and had noses which put most pure-bred terriers to shame. Beagle blooded terriers were not uncommon at this time. Barry Dainty used a half-bred beagle terrier cross to produce many of the terriers that ran in his amazingly efficient bobbery pack of the early 1970s and it is said that Brockley's bitch Tussle had more than just a hint of beagle in her ancestry. Furthermore beagle blood seems to be so easily absorbed into terrier strains and within three generations there was little trace of the blood of Ainstey's beagle save for the blanket markings and fiery red-tan colour the dog had introduced to the breed type.

Inbreeding brought its inevitable problems and it took many years to breed out both the cleft pallets and the hydrocephally that were commonly carried by the early terriers of the type. At one point a blanket marked terrier from the Chiddingfold and Leconfield Foxhounds was introduced, but this cross also introduced a tendency for odd puppies to manifest patella weaknesses and small weak mousey heads. However this strain of terrier was both typey and had an excellent reputation for working below ground.

Weak heads were bred out by the introduction of the blood of a bull terrier called the Hackett White a dog bred down from an illustrious bull terrier – one of the most famous of fighting dogs and marked similarly to the type of terrier that was evolving at Huddlesford.

However, both the Chiddingfold and Leconfield terrier and the Hackett White contributed to the weak washy tan colour that began appearing in the strain in the mid-1970s and specimens manifesting this colour still appear in some litters. Furthermore many of the terriers of this time were very bad fighters and were notoriously difficult to kennel together. Dogs often fought bitches with great fury and kennel deaths were not unknown.

Two other dogs were introduced into the strain in an effort to correct these peculiarities. The first a very straight-fronted but ugly red fell terrier called Yaegar bred by Nigel Hinchcliffe from the dogs of Cyril Breay and Brian Nuttall did much to subdue the aggression of the type while maintaining the working qualities of the breed. Later a Russell type, Forsyth's Pip, was also mated to the line to correct shouldery stock and further additions of Nuttall bred fell introduced from time to time.

The type has levelled out as a twelve to thirteen inch neatly constructed terrier, fiery tan and white in colour with houndy markings. The breed has two pattern types – a blanket-marked collared type and a full caped tan and white variation, tan marked from head to tail with white legs front and belly.

For many years a pack of these terriers was hunted in and around Lichfield primarily at rat – some two or three nights a week – and rabbit though many dogs were placed at hunt service and at one time the pack boasted seventy dogs with working certificates. Nose, always a prime consideration, has been maintained and type and agility has been of great importance in the development of the type. Fast, hard biting agile dogs with neat fronts have evolved – dogs more akin to ballet dancers rather than heavy coarse street brawlers are the desired type.

The breed comes very true to type and the final accolade was afforded the breed by Kennel Club judge Ken Bowden in 1990 who wrote of the breed in *Our Dogs* (Bedlington Terrier Notes) 'At the show was a small pack of Plummer terriers. They are a most attractive terrier, rich tan and white . . . they have beagle as well as bull in them though they seem to owe something to the fox terrier in type. They are far more even than the Parson Jack Russells some of which look like a variety class.'

Although the breed was the creation of one man several working terrier enthusiasts now work and breed the type hunting fox, rabbit and rat with teams of these dogs, and it is now popular to run several of these dogs in a pack as the beagle blood ensures the pack will stay together. Three main breeders of the type, W. Mossman of Devon, J. Alker of Copple, Lancs and Curtis Price of Powys field spectacular packs of these terriers and periodically packs of these terriers unite to provide excellent sport for both their owners and the field who follow them.

There is still much room for improvement in type in this breed but careful selection and scientific breeding programmes are breeding out the defects that the breed has manifested over the years – and not until the various faults have been ironed out will breeders consider applying for Kennel Club recognition.

The Border Terrier

It would be difficult to find a more controversial breed of terrier than the Border terrier. Some working terrier owners will not tolerate them, declare the breed as non-workers with little or no instinct to hunt and less instinct to face a fox below ground. Other enthusiasts swear by them forsaking all other breeds of terrier and state that once a terrier enthusiast has had good Border terriers no other breed of terrier will satisfy. However far from being a recent opinion it is fair to say the breed has always had its advocates and adversaries, though in recent years the working terrier enthusiasts have certainly fallen out of love with the Border terrier.

As with all northern breeds of working terrier the origin of the Border terrier is obscure though there has been much speculation as to how the breed was first created and developed out of the heterogenous mish-mash of types that spawned not only the Border, but also the Dandie Dinmont, the Bedlington and possibly the Lakeland terrier. Several theories concerning the origin of this terrier can be considered however.

It is just possible that the Border terrier together with certain fell terrier types and the unregistered unrefined strains of Welsh terrier – the Ynysfor Otter-hound Kennels strain – are pure or fairly pure forms of the Old English rough-coated black-and-tan terrier though certain Border terriers bear a superficial resemblance to early Bedlington and Dandie Dinmont terriers that indicate that the common stock that spawned both types may have adulterated the strains of Old English rough-coated black-and-tan terrier to produce the Border terrier. Some Borders still manifest the remnants of the silky top-knot that characterised the Dandie and was considered by Captain Jack Howell of Sealyham fame to be a hall mark of courage in a terrier. It is however possible that certain strains of the Old English rough-coated black-and-tan terrier also manifested this silky topknot and as this peculiarity may have been considered as being an indication of the potential working ability of a terrier, the topknot was bred into the early strains of Border terrier. At the risk of being a devil's advocate it should also be stated that the silky topknot of the Border, the Bedlington and the Dandie Dinmont may well have come from certain strains of Old English rough-coated black-and-tan terrier.

It is also possible that the Border terrier may well share identical

Border terrier

ancestors with the Bedlington, the Dandie and the fell strains and that the different types arose by a combination of the isolation of certain localities and the subsequent limitation of the terrier gene pool in certain areas. Unintentional inbreeding would have produced homogenous types in certain areas and if a prolific and successful sire had been used on local bitches the dog would have stamped its type for many generations to come. This was the case in Derbyshire in the 1960s where most Russell type terriers were heavily marked simply because Bill Brockley, a successful terrier breeder, offered two heavily marked stud dogs Scamp and Driver at public stud. The presence of a particular type of prolific or popularly used male can change the shape of local terriers for several generations. The heavy unsightly bull terrier hindquarters thrown by Driver are still found in many Jack Russell-type terriers bred in and around Burton on Trent today. Certain types of terrier can be standardised and be breeding true to type within a few generations of the appearance of one potent sire.

James Dodd, one time landlord of the Coach and Horses Inn at Hexham, and a long time breeder of Border terriers, stated that he had definite proof that the Border terrier was the result of a cross between the Dandie Dinmont and the Bedlington terrier and offers as a rather shadowy and doubtful proof of his opinion that Dandie's, Bedlingtons and some Border terriers have liver coloured noses. This peculiarity however cannot be considered as indisputable evidence that the Border is simply the half way house twixt the Bedlington and the Dandie as many breeds display a liver coloured nose and claim no connection with the type of terrier bred around the Border counties. It is also worthy of note that Charles Cook in his masterly and much quoted book *The Dandie Dinmont Terrier: Its History and Characteristics* states that he believes the Dandie Dinmont terrier to be a direct descendant of old-fashioned types of Border terrier though Horner *Terriers of the World* questions as to whether Cook was referring to the conventional Border terrier or simply the motley terriers that were native to the Border counties.

It has also been argued that in common with all the Border terrier breeds the Border terrier may well have otter-hound ancestry or to be more exact some rough-coated hound that was used by otter hunters may have been crossed with some type of terrier to breed some of the ancestors of the Border, the Dandie and the Bedlington terrier. The Border terrier has a very superficial resemblance to the otter-hound – many Border terriers have thickly leathered ears which give the dogs a slightly houndy appearance. It is also argued that the water resistant coat of the Border terrier – most will clear water from their coats with a single shake – is also proof of the terrier's otter-hound ancestry and it is a fact that many Border terriers show a great readiness to work in water, but this may be due to the fact that Border terriers have worked for many years with otter-hound packs and there would have been a tendency to breed from dogs that showed a natural inclination to work in wet conditions. However it must also be stated that there are few breeds of terrier that cannot boast some sort of hound in their ancestry.

One of the families closely associated with the development of the Border terrier was the Robson family who had close associations with the Liddlesdale and Haydon Foxhounds, the Border Foxhounds and somewhat less close ties with the Northern Counties and Dumfriesshire Otter-hounds and the Robsons and the Dodds inter-married many times as both families had close connections with the various hound packs that hunted the Border counties.

There is a tradition that the Robsons never actually deliberately entered a terrier to fox and that terriers that were born at hunt kennels grew up 'in the yard' and ran with hounds from the nest onwards entering only when they were good and ready to face fox. Johnny Richardson one time huntsman for the Blencathra Foxhounds mentioned during an interview with him that this is probably the very best way of ensuring a high success rate with terriers of any breeds – particularly Border terriers which have a reputation for being notoriously slow to enter – though many will still enter like tigers and are afraid of nothing from the nest onward.

It can be argued that because these terriers were bred to follow the hounds a more leggy type of terrier seems to have been desirable and this may have facilitated the dichotemy between the low-slung Dandie

Dinmont-type terrier and the more leggy Border terrier type of dog. However there are other differences between the types that cannot be explained simply by the fact that the leggier Border terrier was required to run with hounds. Typey Border terriers have the most elastic bodies imaginable. Early judges of the breed frequently bent the fronts of the terriers in a U-shape against the stern and rears of the animals to test this elasticity. It can be argued that such a flexible physique enables a dog to weave its way through narrow crevices and seek out its fox in tree roots and rock piles. Jack Cobby, the south-west Wiltshire foxhound huntsman still judged Borders by bending them double to test this elasticity. Neither Dandie Dinmonts nor even the more slender Bedlington terriers seem to possess this almost rubbery elasticity.

This curious method of judging the type of Border terrier most suitable for working foxes pre-dates the recognition of this terrier by the Kennel Club however and even before the Kennel Club was formed in 1873 agricultural and county shows in the Border counties staged classes for Border terriers. Rawden Lee writing in 1894 states that the Border terrier was already breeding true to type before the turn of the century and that a Border terrier mated to a white-bodied terrier always produced brown or Border-coloured puppies (Rawden Lee seemingly knew little of the science of genetics and less about dominant and recessive factors in various breeds of dogs). Hence when the Kennel Club recognised the breed in 1920 the type was already fixed, true breeding and the type not disposed to the exaggeration that was to ruin and deform many other breeds of working terrier. Indeed the Border terrier was said to be one of the few breeds where champions could still be workers and workers champions – a somewhat glib aphorism that enthusiasts should always keep in mind when breeding terriers of any sort. A curious relic of the early days of the Border terrier is the fact that exhibitors consider a win at Bellingham, home of some strains of the breed, is as prestigious as a win at Crufts.

However, from its early days the Border terrier has had not only its advocates but those who found the breed somewhat less than first rate. Lucas interviewed a variety of terrier breeders who had at some time used Border terriers to fox, badger or otter and gathered many mixed opinions as to the worth of these terriers. In his book *Pedigree Dog Breeding* he quotes the Marchioness of Cambridge who owned a Border terrier bred by Andrew Drummond, a Northumberland shepherd, which 'can take any amount of punishment and give it too. At one time he was to ground four and a half hours until he was dug out . . . When the owner tries a white terrier that is not so keen as he should be about going into the earth the farmers in Wales shout ' "Let the little red dog go" and the red dog is in and at the fox or badger in a moment.'

Cartwright, the famous Gloucester terrier man, would not tolerate the breed however. He claimed they were slow to start, indifferent to work and inclined to be 'spade-shy' – tending to come off a fox or badger as the diggers broke through to the antagonists. Furness, who knew Cartwright intimately, states 'He had many great terriers in his kennels – some of which he bred and more he bought from Ireland, but there was seldom a Border or a coloured working terrier at his establishment.' It seems Cartwright had seen a coloured terrier worried by hounds in the early 1930s and this may have coloured his thinking.

However, Cartwright's dislike of the Border terrier was not shared by all. Prior to the 1960s John (Jack) Cobby, huntsman for the South West Wiltshire Foxhounds bred one of the most attractive strains of Jack Russell-type working terrier. The line descended from Nimrod Capell's Pincher – an unsightly terrier featured in Lucas' *Hunt and Working Terriers* later improved in type and possibly maintained working ability until Cobby bred Pickaxe considered by many to be the best looking working terrier of the early 1960s: a fiery red and white terrier similar in type to Ruth Haws' strain that won so well during this time. On the death of Pickaxe, Cobby did not continue the line but began to breed and work Border terriers. It is also noteworthy that during the early days of the Midland Working Terrier Club, Roma Moore attempted to interest her members in a challenge received from members of the various Border terrier clubs to the effect that one of the members of these Border terrier clubs was prepared to match a strain of Border terriers against any strain of Jack Russell terriers in Britain in a working test that would decide the merits of either type of terrier as a worker to ground or above ground. It was never actually made known who the champion of the Border terrier camp was to be, but it was common knowledge it was John (Jack) Cobby. It is also worthy of note that whoever the challengers were there were no takers!

At this time one of the Border terrier clubs which advocated 'champions can still be workers' instituted a scheme to record and publicise Border terriers that were awarded working certificates by Masters of Hounds and there were many excellent show specimens that boasted these working certificates. Jack Price's Oxcroft Rocket qualified for a working certificate from the Dumfriesshire Otterhound Pack, where Rocket's sire Millbank Tarka had actually served as a hunt terrier one should add, while Roger Clements Hanley Castle Russ worked with the Crome Foxhounds and obtained a Master of Foxhounds working certificate. Many other good typey Borders worked at hunt service throughout the county at that time and the working certificates awarded to suitable dogs were esteemed by club members. At one Midland working terrier show only three terriers appeared in the working certificate class – two were Border terriers. Many terrier enthusiasts questioned the value of a working certificate for the ranks of the working terrier enthusiasts boast a great many spiteful bitter people who pour scorn on the achievements of others and this silly and petty behaviour did much to reduce the credibility of dogs which had obtained working certificates with certain packs. Indeed in 1965 it was often stated that if the working terrier enthusiasts fought those who were as antipathetic to field sports with the same fervour as they fought each other field sports would be in no danger from those wishing to ban them! The working certificate scheme was a good one – and if it was abused from time to time (and it almost certainly was) it was still a worthwhile scheme.

A great advocate of the working Border terrier at this time was John Morgan who worked a a terrier man for the Whaddon Chase Foxhounds for a number of years: Morgan was perhaps better known for the very typey tricolour Jack Russell terriers he exhibited around the various working terrier shows, but he owned one extremely good terrier called Raisgill Pickle. At that time Morgan's great rival at the working terrier shows was Bill Brockley of Etwall, Derbyshire, but Bill was never stinting in his praise for Pickle; 'he didn't seem to know what pain was – he was the pluckiest terrier that drew breath and as good a worker as I have ever seen.' As it happened Pickle contributed little to influence the lines of further Border terriers, though he made a considerable impact on the lines of fell terrier bred around Dalston, Cumbria and this will be dealt with presently.

The same could not be said for Oxcroft Rocket, a very typey terrier bred by Jack Price who worked at Oxcroft colliery near Chesterfield and hence adopted the prefix Oxcroft. Rocket features in the pedigree of so many Kennel Club champions and working terrier show winners that it would be foolish to list examples, but Rocket's history should be of considerable interest to the working terrier enthusiast. During the 1960s it was by no means uncommon to find a classy unregistered Border terrier at hunt service and such a terrier was the Border terrier Tarka that served with the Dumfrieshire Otter-hounds. Tarka was bred from a rather unfashionable bitch mated to the great sire Champion Maxton Matchless – who bred not only high-class exhibition stock but a spate of excellent working terriers. Tarka had an excellent reputation as both a worker and a producer of workers for he had bred Willie Gray's dog Corrie an excellent terrier, a grand finder and a first-rate stayer to fox and badger. Tarka was not registered however but Jack Price who regularly journeyed north to hunt with the Dumfriesshire Otter-hound Pack somehow persuaded Tarka's owner Billy Scott to register the dog as Millbank Tarka and Price mated his bitch Daletyne Magic to the aging scarred and grizzled veteran otter-hound terrier.

Oxcroft Rocket a son of the union was an extremely typey dog which was narrow-fronted and strong headed. He never became a Kennel Club champion but he bred champions and most show winning lines have Rocket not too far back in their pedigrees. It is said that show judges were reluctant to 'put up' scarred dogs at this time but George Leatt gave Rocket his one and only challenge certificate.

At that time Price was a close associate of Terry Duggan, considered by many to be one of Britain's best terrier men who worked a strain of Jack Russell terrier bred from Eric Furness' Viper blood. Duggan took Rocket for training in order to polish the dog so that he might obtain an MOH certificate with the Dumfriesshire Otter-hounds with whom Duggan regularly hunted. Rocket was never a favourite dog of Duggans however. He was fearless, iron hard and a good finder but was never a careful dog below ground. Later Rocket bred an equally tough and hard bitch, Ch. Oxcroft Vixen, which not only won well at both hunt and working terrier and Kennel Club shows but was a great worker to fox and badger. The iron hard disposition of both dogs probably caused Price to utter his much quoted epigram 'If you've got a good'un in a Border, it isn't a good'un it's too hard.' It is well worth mentioning that Price is unique amongst working terrier enthusiasts for he has successfully bridged the gap twixt working terriers and showing them at Kennel Club Championship shows.

An interesting terrier that now appears in the pedigree of many working Border terriers today was an unfashionable terrier called Bugsy Malone owned by Jacqueline Fallon of Burton on Trent. Bugsy Malone was almost devoid of facial furnishings and would have had little chance of winning at a Kennel Club show though the dog was so typey that he often swept the board at working terrier shows. He was a furious little dog, prone to run deaf when he was on a scent, and Mrs Fallon frequently sought help to dig out the dog when it ran to ground while out at exercise. Bugsy was sent to hunt service at the Meynell Foxhounds at Sudbury where he served for a season before obtaining a hunt working certificate. Bugsy was a habitual hunter and somewhat difficult to control because of this fervour. His nose was literally incredible and he ran head down on scent in much the manner as would a beagle. He entered the pedigrees of many unfashionable strains of Border terrier and quite a number of strains of fell terrier claim descent from him. Despite his lack of facial furnishings he did much to maintain the working ability instinct the Border had once enjoyed at a time when the breed was already under fire from somewhat less than satisfied terrier trainers.

Something certainly happened to the Border terrier (or perhaps to the people who trained these dogs) in the early 1970s. There had always been tales that certain strains of Border terrier were somewhat less than satisfactory as working terriers. Lucas records some working terrier enthusists who stated that many strains made bad workers to ground. However by the early days of the 1980s the reputation of the Border terrier as a worker had plumetted. Few hunt kennels employed Border terriers and it became common practice to question the value or validity of a working certificate issued to a Border terrier. In 1980 Jacqueline Fallon again won Best-in-Show at a Northampton Hunt and Working Terrier Show with her working certificated Border terrier Bugsy Malone.

One of the competitors at the show questioned the award of the Best-in-Show shield and cup with 'You can't exactly call a Border a worker can you!' Yet sour grapes – ever on every menu at hunt and working terrier shows – aside, there was little love or respect for the Border terrier amongst working terrier buffs and one can offer three theories as to why this should be so.

a. There had been a decline in the overall working ability of the Border terrier.
b. There had been a decline in the overall ability of British terrier men.
c. Other, quicker entering, less sensitive breeds, had begun to 'shoulder out' the Border terrier in the kennels and hearts of working terrier buffs.

It is just possible that the appearance and use of a single typey prepotent Border terrier stud dog that neither manifested working ability nor bred it into his progeny could change or at least drastically alter the working qualities of an entire breed – particularly if that dog bred similar prepotent males to continue the line. It is worth noting that despite the fact that many Border terriers were shown at hunt and working terrier shows by the late 1960s a number of people that had not the slightest interest in working their terriers had started to exhibit and breed Border terriers. Thus stud males, always the most potent breeding force in any species of polygamous animals, that were never tested below ground would have been used to further lines of Border terriers and the effect on the working ability of the Border terrier would have been catastrophic. Breeds of dogs have certainly been changed beyond belief by the over-use of certain males that carried undesirable qualities. Yet at the risk of appearing a devil's advocate it should be pointed out that the pedigrees of strains that are known to still work to fox are almost identical to some of those of supposedly non-working strains or rather strains that produce an unacceptably low rate of good working terriers. A curious cult began appearing in the latter years of the 1970s: a cult that because of the tendency of certain top winning strains of Border terrier to produce a very high failure rate of working terriers, refrained from registering their Border terriers as if by the very act of registering a puppy with the Kennel Club the whelp lost some of its ability to work. This attitude indicates absolute lunacy – but the terrier world is peopled by many who give little thought to breeding plans or logic.

It is equally likely that a different type of person began to take an interest in working terriers in the mid-1970s. Cyril Breay speakng at Bramham Moor in the early 1960s commented on the less desirable people who were already taking an interest in working terriers and by the early 1970s thefts of working terriers were commonplace. Brian

Nuttall of Holmes Chapel – arguably the authority on the British working terrier, believes that the 1970s saw the birth of the cult of the instant expert – a person who buys a trained dog; becomes an expert within days of the purchase; is asked to judge shows as the result of this easily acquired, supposed expertise, but quits terriers and takes up other interests at the hint of a minor set-back in his meteoric rise to face. Borders are often quite slow to enter to fox and are totally unsuitable terriers for the person who requires instant success. Yet the early 1970s saw a spate of ephemeral *aficionados* swell the ranks of the working terrier enthusiasts. Border terriers are often sensitive dogs that do not thrive if bought and sold with the callous indifference of a speculator dabbling in stocks and shares – and many working terrier enthusiasts vie with lurcher owners as dog swoppers. People with these tendencies with pitifully low attention spans but with money burning in their pockets should stay well clear of the Border terrier for these terriers are terribly damaged by such treatment and misuse. Sadly at the time of writing more and more meddlers are becoming interested in working terriers, so the future of the Border terrier as a worker looks far from rosy.

It is also possible that other breeds have begun to shoulder out the Border terrier in the affections of workng terrier enthusiasts in Britain. In the early 1960s hunt and working terrier shows catered for the various types of terrier collectively known as Jack Russell terriers with classes for Border terriers and crossbreds. A fell or Lakeland terrier type in the show ring caused a raised eyebrow or so in the south of Britain. In the mid-1960s classes for Border, Lakeland or crossbred (at this time fell terriers were still regarded as crossbred by the working terrier fraternity in the Midlands and South, though the type was becoming relatively popualarin the north east). In the late 1960s the shows became inundated with black fell terrier types bred down from the type created or made popular by Breay and Buck though refined and standardised by Nuttall of Holmes Chapel. It is interesting to note that there was a corresponding decline in the number of Border terriers exhibited at working terrier shows after this time. What is likely is that the fell strains, both the Patterdale and the box-headed Lakeland blooded strains are usually earlier to mature and easier to start than are Border terriers which require a more careful entering programme to get the best from them. Furthermore, the fell strains suffer less (though even fell strains suffer) from the constant swopping, chopping, changing and selling that is now alas part and parcel of the world of the working terrier. Border terriers, even the most phlegmatic Border terriers, suffer terribly at the hands of 'grasshopper minded' people.

Whether or not the working Border terrier is still a breed that can be classed as a working terrier – 'where champions can still be workers' – is debatable. What is indisputable is the fact that Border terriers are still crossed with other breeds or types or working terrier to breed in qualities that are absent or in short supply in the breeds with which Border terriers are crossed.

In the 1930s, Sealyham-type terriers or Sealyham/Jack Russell-type terriers were popular in the South Welsh coalfields, but some of the almost legendary dogs bred at that time were hybrids between Sealyham and Border terriers bred by mating native Sealyham terriers with Major Pawson's Dipley strain Border terriers. Such crossbreds not only manifested the hybrid vigour expected when two very dissimilar types of terrier are mated together, but possessed an unusual degree of courage tempered with commonsense. By the 1950s many of these Sealyham-type terriers were becoming longer in the leg as a result of the Border terrier ancestry and had begun to display the whispy silky topknot they had inherited from the Dipley strain Border terriers. It is also worth mentioning that Dan Russell in his book *Working Terriers* (1948) makes mention of a similarly bred hybrid 'The best terrier I ever owned was one of these Border-Sealyhams. He weighed fifteen pounds and was immensely strong. For four seasons running he did two days a week with hounds during which time I dug eighty-three brace of fox with him and he bolted goodness knows how many, twenty badgers and three otters; in all that time he sustained no injury beyond an odd nip and never missed a day's hunting.' A fine record by any standards – though in his youth Dan Russell had an excellent reputation for being a good man with terriers.

It is said that Cyril Breay advised his accolytes that a cross with a Border terrier did much good for a strain of fell terrier. The fell strain later to be erroneously referred to as the Patterdale owed at least some of its qualities to the Border terrier. The litter that produced both Mick and Blitz were bred by mating the bitch Tiger to a red Bedale Hunt terrier which in turn was sired by a Border terrier though it should be pointed out that Breay never again introduced Border terrier blood into his strain.

John Parkes who continued Breay's strain of terrier has also brought in Border terrier blood in recent years however. Parkes strains bred down from Breay's Monty with a dash of classy red fell blood from Harry Hardasty's Turk has started to pepper his strain with Border terriers bred from Ray Walker's strain. Breay had in fact advised Parkes that it would benefit the fell strains if Parkes brought in the right Border terrier blood to improve and temper this type of fell terrier.

Richard Bland, huntsman of the Melbreck Foxhounds is also of the opinion that fell terriers need the occasional dash of Border terrier blood to give the resulting hybrids discretion and sense. Bland kennels terriers with hounds and hence gassy, aggressive terriers are not what he wants. His original line bred down in part at least from Johnny Richardson's Tarzan is now saturated with Border terrier blood bred by mating his bitches to the Border terriers owned by John Dickson of Otterburn – a district with strong Border terrier connections one should add. Terriers bred from the combination of Tarzan and doses of Border terrier blood are seldom typey but measure twelve inches or less at the shoulder and seem ideal for work in the Melbreck country.

Mention has already been made of Raisgill Pickle, a Border terrier that saw service with the Whaddon Chase Foxhounds when Jack Morgan was terrier man for the said pack. Pickle was used by Willy Gray of Dalston, Cumbria to mate to various local fell terriers to produce a fairly typey sort of fell terrier – heavier than the dogs favoured by Bland for Gray believes that a distinct type of fox – larger than the typical British fox – exists around Carlisle and that it requires a large pwoerful terrier to handle such a fox. Gray's Border/Lakeland terriers are in fact about sixteen pounds in weight with the strong otter head the Border terrier lends to any strain of fell terrier with which it is crossed.

At the time of writing one of the most successful red fell terrier breeders in Britain is Graham Ward of Consett, County Durham. Ward breeds a typey box-headed fell terrier strain bred in part at least from the dogs of Harry Hardasty. However Ward too has used Border terrier blood in the creation of this strain though the Border terrier he used to breed these red fells was a stray of pedigree unknown origin though extremely game and apparently an excellent finder below and above ground. The otter heads some of Wards early strain manifested as a result of the Border terrier blood have vanished in recent years and Wards' terriers now resemble very typey small Irish terriers.

Border terrier blood certainly influenced the strain of black fell terrier bred by Brian Nuttall of Holmes Chapel, though Nuttall must have used only tiny amounts of Border blood to create this strain. These black fells now breed amazingly true to type and only the hard crisp coat manifested by some of the terriers indicates the presence of Border terrier blood in this attractive fell strain.

There are still strains of Border terrier that are worked and will still give a good account of themselves both above and below ground, but it is also true that a great many Border terriers show little or no propensity to work.

The Terriers of Ireland

The Terriers of Ireland

Four breeds of terrier, or rather four breeds of terrier that are recognised by the Kennel Club, hail from Ireland: the Kerry Blue, the soft-coated Wheaten, the Irish terrier and the rather rare Glen of Imaal terrier, which in recent years seems to be making a comeback. Enthusiasts of each breed claim the other types of Irish terriers are descended from their own favoured breed, but the origin of these terriers is so obscure that it is difficult to state which type came first or exactly how the four types are related to each other. Horner suggests that all are descended from the Old English black-and-tan terrier and offers as proof that early Irish terriers could be traced to a black-and-tan bitch. However, all Irish Kennel Club registered breeds of terrier have one thing in common – since the abolition of badger digging they are all too large to be worked underground. Yet nowhere was there greater enthusiasm to ensure the native breeds would not lose their working ability than in Ireland.

Within fifteen years of the first dog show staged by W. R. Pape at Newcastle in 1859 the first classes for Irish terriers were staged at Dublin and by 1900 the Irish terrier was one of the most popular breeds of dog in Britain. The popularity of the breed caused some concern amongst the purists who believed that the various breeds of Irish terrier would be bred exclusively as pets and the working and guarding qualities of the breeds would suffer accordingly. Thus the Misneac Teastas trials were devised; questionable tests of the working ability of the dogs, tests which incidentally would only be tolerated in Ireland and would be abhorent to the rest of Great Britain even before the 1911 Protection of Animals Act had been passed.

The tests which skirted the 1835 Act (prevention of animal baiting) by a hair's width were divided into two parts – the Teastas Begg or small test which was designed to test the terriers ability to work or bolt rabbits and rats and the Teastas Mor a highly questionable test, which was designed to assess the terriers ability to work badger – the only subterranean quarry which the large size type of the Irish terriers were capable of working. The lax laws of Southern Ireland allowed these tests to be conducted without fear of criminal prosecution but both offended human decency and served no practical purpose – except to satiate the blood-lust of owners. Neither test constituted hunting in the accepted sense of the word and it was understandable that such tests fell out of favour with dog breeders and hunters alike though prior to 1966 it was impossible for any breed of Irish terrier to become a full champion in Ireland without it holding such a certificate.

If Glover *The Working Bedlington Terrier* is correct the Teastas Begg or small test consisted of allowing a captive wild rabbit loose in a field allowing it either law or better still an opportunity to escape and encouraging the terrier to hunt up the scent of the rabbit. Yet another aspect of the test consisted of releasing a captive rat into a stream and allowing the terrier to hunt up, catch and kill the rat. It is worth noting that there is absolutely nothing illegal about allowing a dog to pursue a released, once captive animal, providing the animal has a fair or reasonable chance of escaping and providing the animal has not been deliberately injured or incapacitated to prevent its escape.

The Teastas Mor or large test was indeed a different matter and if conducted in Great Britain would have justly merited prosecution. If one might once again refer to the description offered by Glover; an artificial set, some forty feet long and some two feet below the surface of the soil, was constructed and a captive badger released in the set or 'shore'. If the badger was reluctant to escape into the fastness of the 'shore' a small baying terrier was released to drive the badger into the end of the tunnel, but the terrier was prevented from following the badger by a trap-door operated by a man on the surface that allowed the badger through but barred the small baying dog's progress.

When the badger settled at the end of the artificial set an Irish breed of terrier: a Glen of Imaal, Kerry Blue, soft-coated Wheaten or Irish terrier was released at the mouth of the 'shore' and required to:

a. engage the badger in under a minute from the time of the dog's release;
b. draw the badger from the depths of the 'shore' to the surface in under six minutes;
c. remain totally mute during the entire process uttering not a sound in excitement or a cry of pain when the badger retaliated.

To assess the winner of these epics of futility a time-keeper and a series of judges who could detect as to whether or not the dog remained totally mute during the performance were appointed and the winning dog was the animal that performed best against the clock, engaging its badger quickly and drawing it from the 'shore' in the fastest possible time. Vociferous dogs were disqualified if they barked, whined or yelped with pain one should add. In passing it is worth noting that the sides of the 'shore' would need to be built of wood or earthenware to allow a dog to draw a badger some forty or so feet to the mouth of this artificial set for the task of drawing a badger from an earth-sided set into which the wretched beast could anchor itself with its claws would tax the capabilities and strength of a mastiff.

Even in a country such as Eire, seemingly relatively untouched by the ramifications of the 1835 Act that abolished baiting and the 1911 Protection of Animals Act, thinking people must have been repelled by the spectacle just described; a spectacle that offered no chance for the luckless badger to escape (though again according to Glover after each and every bait – and there is no other way to describe this degrading show – a fresh badger was provided and after an examination by a veterinary surgeon the badger that had been subjected to the ordeal described was released).

To confuse such a spectacle with hunting would be wrong and demeaning to the hunter and field sports in general; but it does explain why the general public seems confused about the difference between badger digging and badger baiting. Why the judges required the terriers to lie mute against a badger is also baffling though one supposes that a vociferous dog would find some difficulty in drawing a badger and baying while it did so.

In 1966 public opinion rather than legislation stopped these trials and brought an end to an ignoble spectacle that degraded man, caused unnecessary pain to dogs and terrified the badger. It should be pointed out that trials of this sort are still held in Ireland, though these performances are conducted clandestinely and tend to cater for those who wish to bait badgers with bull terrier breeds rather than the traditional Irish breeds of terrier. It should also be pointed out that such trials by their very example hasten the abolition of all field sports in Great Britain.

The Irish Terrier

Irish breeds of dog, particularly Irish hounds one should add, seem to invite weavers of verse and prose to pen eulogies in praise of them and the Irish terrier has certainly been the subject of much flowing praise. 'Tis wonder dogs they're breeding now' (*Mick an Irish Terrier*) certainly describes the mental qualities of the breed to a nicety. Robert Leighton *The Complete Book of the Dog* (1922) describes the breed in flowing prose 'a demon for sport: as capable on land as in water he will tackle anything with four legs and a furry skin. Rats are his mortal enemies'.

The origins of this breed are obscure though it seems reasonable that Horner may well be correct when he states the Irish terrier may well be a much altered form of the Old English rough-coated black-and-tan terrier. Indeed Waterhouse's great winning dog Killiney Boy was bred out of a black-and-tan bitch! Early terriers may well have been small enough to follow a fox to ground – Winch who believes that the modern Lakeland terrier owes much to its Irish terrier ancestors is inclined to believe that the modern eighteen inch giants are relatively recent innovations and Winch's theory is lent credibility by the fact that when the first classes for Irish terriers were staged at Dublin in 1874 two types of terrier were catered for – those above nine pounds in weight and those below that weight.

Early Irish terriers were not only variable in size, but also varied quite a lot in colour. Many terriers bred in County Cork were above thirty pounds in weight and wheaten in colour with softer more silky coats than one associates with present day Irish terriers. In 1887 classes were staged for silver- coloured Irish terriers, but some seven years later the type seems to have settled for Rawdon Lee *Modern Dogs* (1874) mentions that the Irish terrier was now a typey, fairly uniform breed of dog and was, according to opinion polls, the second most popular dog in Britain – the most popular was apparently the fox terrier. The breed was apparently half way between the Airedale and the Bedlington terrier in size.

It is of interest to note that terrier books written before the turn of the century mention that ancestors of the Irish terrier were Scottish terriers and this term needs to be explained before proceeding further. The Europeans in general have an annoying habit of grouping unrefined and heterogenous articles, verses or music in categories simply for the sake of convenience. Mozart calls his exotic sounding piece Rondo A La Turke (Turkish Rondo) simply because any strange or foreign musical pieces

Irish terrier. (Photo Monty)

were referred to as Turkish. Similarly any terrier that did not conform to the standard laid down for either the fox terrier or the many black-and-tan terriers was referred to as a 'Scottish' terrier even though the breed had no, or scarce, connections with Scotland.

Certainly the early Irish terriers were game and fiery. In their native land they were often fought against other terriers, pitted against badgers, the smaller terriers worked to otter, badger and fox and the breed had a renowned reputation as a ratter. Despite the breeds reputation for being quarrelsome, it also had a reputation for being extraordinarily game and a fiercely protective guard and several army regiments including the Durham Light Infantry adopted the breed as a regimental mascot, for by the start of World War I the breed had become a symbol of dauntless courage and seemingly had replaced the bulldog as the insignia of British honour, bravery and tenacity.

It is interesting to note that Jack London, one of the most successful dog book writers of all time, used an Irish terrier as one of his heroes. London knew little of dogs and matters canine and kept but two dogs in his life. He was however fiercely racist and utterly contemptuous of Africans and Asians alike. When towards the end of his short life he needed to earn a great deal of money, and earn it quickly, he forsook his political novels and sociological writings and reverted to writing novels about dogs. *Jerry of the Islands* however is a ludicrous tale of an Irish terrier which is the embodiment of not only white Anglo-Saxon supremacy but courage above and beyond the call of duty. The dog is able to distinguish between clean-cut honest Europeans and crafty dishonest Polynesians and Asiatics and protects its white masters from harm at the hands of the natives!

In passing, *Jerry of the Islands* was not a particularly successful book for London or Macmillan who published the book, at least not compared to *The Call of the Wild* or its brutal sequel *White Fang*, but the book *Michael: Brother of Jerry* that followed hot on the heels of *Jerry of the Islands* caused social changes never envisaged by London. Michael is a circus dog and London relates a shade too graphically perhaps the horrors that were perpetrated on performing animals to train them. *Michael: Brother of Jerry* was published posthumously, but the public indignation the book inspired prompted groups to form Jack London Clubs to protest and bring about legislation to protect circus animals for acts of wanton cruelty. In passing it should be mentioned that *Michael* was probably inspired by London's visit to watch a troupe of dancing geese that jigged up and down on a sheet of thin steel. London approached the troupe and found that the sheet was kept unbearably hot by a kerosene burner hidden beneath the stage!

By the turn of the twentieth century the Irish terrier had adopted the typical terrier shape, box-headed, straight-legged with a jaunty upright tail – a beau ideal of arrogance perhaps. Thus it was not surprising that the Irish terrier was used to refine or improve other less fashionable breeds of terrier. It seems likely that the original Airedale terriers were very houndy and ugly – indeed Colonel David Hancock *The Heritage of the Dog* states that he believes the Airedale terrier was simply a form of the rough wire-haired hound sometimes referred to as the Lancashire otter-hound. Irish terrier blood certainly played an important part in refining the Airedale terrier and giving it a more terrier-like appearance yet maintaining the courage and working ability for which the Airedale was once famous. Silhouettes of modern Irish and Airedale terriers are in fact very difficult to distinguish from each other.

Winch, an authority on the history of the northern English working terrier types is of the opinion that the dichotemy twixt the Lakeland-type fell terrier and the Border, the Dandie Dinmont and Bedlington terrier was as much due to Irish terriers brought to Cumbria by Irish immigrants after the potato famine, as to the Old English rough-coated black-and-tan terrier. Winch cites the incidence of Catholic-Irish residents at Cleator Moor – a fell terrier stronghold – as proof of his theory and adds that box-headed red fell terriers were common long before the formation of the Lakeland Terrier Association.

Irish terrier blood was certainly used to affect the transformation from fell terrier to Kennel Club registered Lakeland terrier. Mawson records that a small undersized Irish terrier was purchased from Gloucester and used on many fell terrier bitches and the progeny of these matings registered as Lakeland terriers. It is also worth mentioning that Ch. Oregill Copper Coin, a Lakeland terrier that influenced the evolution of the Lakeland terrier little but was used extensively on fell terrier bitches, was not favoured in Kennel Club circles as the dog resembled a black-and-tan Irish terrier.

As to whether the black-and-tan Scarteen terrier, a terrier used to bolt foxes and bred at the Scarteen Foxhound kennels in Ireland is a form of the Irish terrier or simply a fell-type terrier is questionable. The type may still exist in isolated pockets around the hunt kennels, but is seldom seen and rarely advertised. Terrier enthusiasts in the Scarteen hunt country claim these black-and-tan terriers – identical to unrefined fell terriers or Old English rough-coated black-and-tan terriers are the purest form of the native Irish terrier stock, but this would be a difficult claim to substantiate.

Whether or not a small Irish terrier influenced the development of the Norwich/Norfolk terrier is open to doubt though it is said that Jack Read used Irish terriers to correct the bad coat created by introducing Bedlington terrier blood into the breed. It may well be the case that any small box-headed terrier of pedigree unknown would be referred to as an Irish terrier by early breeders of Norwich/Norfolk terriers in the same way that a terrier that was neither fox terrier nor black-and-tan terrier was once called a Scottish terrier for convenience sake.

More recently Irish terrier blood has been used to create lurchers. A spate of Irish terrier greyhound hybrids were advertised in *Exchange and Mart* during the 1950s but the popularity of these hybrids diminished in the 1960s until an Irish terrier lurcher became a novelty. However in recent years Phillip King, an Irish terrier breeder, has advertised several Irish terrier lurchers, both first cross Irish terrier/greyhound hybrids and the second cross Irish terrier/greyhound/greyhound lurchers and has claimed that they are the most versatile of lurchers; gamer than collie-bred hybrids but equally as tractable and as at home on land as in water.

The typical Irish terrier is a hefty dog measuring eighteen inches at the shoulder and since the cessation of badger digging the breed has had little opportunity to work underground. As might be expected the Irish terrier is a mute dog, working silently and furiously, and this might well be an advantage if the dog is to be used as a base for lurcher breeding where a silent dog is deemed desirable for obvious reasons. The Irish terrier also boasts an exceptional nose and can still be an excellent worker to both rat and rabbit, however.

The Kerry Blue Terrier

It seems likely that the Kerry Blue terrier has such a unique appearance that it was almost inevitable that a host of theories as to the origin of the breed should have been invented or concocted.

Hubbard, an expert on the origin of antique and obscure breeds states in his *Dogs of Britain* (1948) that the ancestor of the Kerry Blue terrier was a sheep herding tyke known as the Gadhar – a breed used to guard as much as herd the flocks. How Hubbard comes to this conclusion is a mystery. References to the Gadhar are scant, and the connection between this type of dog and a terrier of any sort is to say the least tenuous.

Michael F. Norris, a contributor to Violet Handy's monograph on the Kerry Blue terrier advances an equally ludicrous notion. Norris believes that the Kerry and to a certain extent all Irish breeds of terrier are closely related to the Great Irish hound (a type which while it later became extinct was the ancestor of the Scottish deerhound and one of the ancestors of the Irish wolfhound.) Barlow argues, though scarcely scientifically, that peasants seeking to increase the hunting instinct of their terriers resorted to crossing their dogs with Irish hounds. It is always unwise for those interested in cynology or the aesthetic qualities of certain breeds to embark on a theory concerned with aspects of hunting. The working of the terrier is quite dissimilar to that of any sighthound and sighthound blood would contribute very little toward the development of a dog that is required to go to ground and seek out a fox or badger.

Michael F. Norris mentions that blue or blue/black terriers were not uncommon in Britain at one time – he cites the Blue Paul and the Bedlington terriers as examples of dogs that were so coloured, and relates a tale that many years ago a blue coloured terrier swam ashore at Tralee Bay when a ship foundered on the rocks. The terrier apparently proved so game that it was used on several local bitches and hence blue-coloured terriers became very common in and around this district. There is of course no reference to the name of the boat that came to grief in the bay and hence no indication of the origin of the terrier. A similar tale of how green-egg laying poultry came to Caithness exists and this tale too is likely to be pure hokum.

Ash *Practical Dog Book* (1930) speculates equally unwisely that the Kerry Blue terrier may well be a hybrid between the Bedlington terrier

Kerry Blue terrier

and the red Irish terrier, but offers no explanation as to why the cross was made or when the first blue terriers were bred. Ash's theory might be discounted as being pure guesswork though breeders of certain strains of fell terrier often produce slate grey puppies when pale wheaten-fawn fell terriers are mated to black fells.

Robert Leighton *The Complete Book of the Dog* (1922) finds it impossible not to suggest that a hound played a part in the creation of the Kerry Blue terrier and mentions the resemblance of the unclipped Kerry Blue terrier to that of an otter-hound. Likewise an unclipped, untidy soft-coated Wheaten terrier resembles a primitive otter-hound. It is also worth noting that in recent years there has been a revival of the theory that many breeds of terrier are simply tailored down hounds – a notion first suggested by Turbeville in 1576 who remarked that in the Low Countries hunters used a small rough-coated hound that showed an inclination to go to ground. Colonel D. Hancock in his interesting but extremely heretical book *The Heritage of the Dog* (1990) is of the opinion that many terriers are simply hounds bred on more traditional terrier-like lines.

It should however be mentioned that in 1886 a rabbit coursing meet staged at Cork was judged by Stonehenge (J. H. Walsh) whose masterly book *Dogs of the British Isles* had been published some six years earlier and had made Walsh something of a celebrity. Ash mentions that during this meet some blue-coloured Irish terriers acquitted themselves well at the sport. Ash is quick to mention that the 'Blue Devils' mentioned by a

Dublin paper in 1892 were Bedlington terriers not native blue terriers and this fact lends at least some substance to Ash's theory that the Kerry Blue terrier evolved as a cross between the Bedlington and the red Irish terrier. Dr Pierce also mentions that the Kerry Blue terrier was of a different temperament from the terriers of the rest of Ireland – a hotter more fiery terrier – and many attribute this more quarrelsome disposition to infusions of Bedlington terrier blood. In passing it is also worth noting that Bedlington lurcher hybrids are sometimes as blue/black as the most well-bred Kerry Blue terrier.

In 1922 a class for Kerry Blue terriers to be judged under Kennel Club rules had been staged and a fairly large terrier, some eighteen inches at the shoulder, was deemed to be ideal. It is worth noting that in the early days of the breed (indeed until as late as 1966) no Kerry Blue terrier could become a champion in Ireland until it had been tested for gameness, courage and working instinct in one of the two types of trial conducted under the Rules and Licence of the Irish Kennel Club. These epics of futility, the Teastas Begg or small test and the Teastas Mor or great test have been described earlier, but it should be mentioned that while the Kerry performed well at these trials it often proved too aggressive to be shown at Kennel Club events. It has been argued that the Kerry, in common with all Irish breeds of terrier one should add (and possibly in common with all breeds of terrier) has often been fought against other terriers and thus the temperament of the Kerry Blue terrier did not make the dog a suitable candidate for the show ring for the sight of other dogs often caused early Kerry Blue terriers to erupt into bouts of uncontrollable fury. This quality, while it endeared the Kerry to some, made other exhibitors extremely charry about breeding and showing Kerry Blue terriers and breeders of other dogs even more reluctant about allowing their exhibits near a benched Kerry Blue. It was a joke that Flynn placed the Kerry halfway between the Airedale and the Bedlington in size 'not a wise place to be unless one is prepared to see the fur fly' but during the 1920s the Kerry had a reputation for being far more aggressive than either breed.

Like all Irish terrier breeds the Kerry is too large for conventional terrier work though the early show dogs were also sold as sporting companions. As Caesar dogs, dogs required to fix and hold a badger at the end of a dig, the breed did find favour at one time, but the fractious disposition of the Kerry and its tendency to latch on to other terriers as enthusiastically as it latched on to a badger made many diggers reluctant to use such a Caesar dog.

The Kerry is still capable of being used as a ratter and a great rabbit hunting dog, and its sporting instincts are still strong – though in recent years dogs which show a tendency to be 'hot' or vicious with other dogs are becoming less common.

Since the 1970s Kerry Blue terrier blood has been used to tidy up strains of fell terrier and Lakeland-type fells with Kerry Blue heads, fronts and furnishings are becoming quite common on fell terrier exhibits shown at hunt and working terrier shows in recent years. The fact that the Kerry scales in at eighteen inches at the shoulder may cause readers to question why such a dog should be used to mate to working strains of fell terrier (and the Kerry's reputation for being totally mute below ground should cause even more concern) but Irish terriers (probably forms of the same stock that spawned the Kerry Blue terrier) have long been used to mate with Lakeland or fell terriers to improve both heads and fronts on working terriers. Few pure-bred Kerry Blue terriers are worked today, however.

The Soft-Coated Wheaten Terrier

It is said that Dr Gerard J. Pierse discontinued breeding Kerry Blue terriers because the breed had a reputation for being quarrelsome and aggressive and not typical of the working terriers of Ireland. So it was in 1934 Pierse took up the cause of another untidy type of terrier that had been bred on farms on the west of Ireland for 200 years – well at least according to Dr Gerard J. Pierse. Pierse stated that the type had been kept to keep down rats and rabbits but also to work badger – though like all Irish terrier enthusiasts certain breeders of these dogs insisted on matching their dogs in some of the badly organised dog fights that have been all too common in Ireland for hundreds of years. Every breed of Irish terrier has boasted specimens that have been pitted and Winch believes that Irish terrier blood featured in some of the types of bull terrier hybrids that were popular in the north east of England during the mid-1800s.

Early Wheaten terriers were a very variable bunch and appeared to be a type of terrier that could be regarded as an intermediate form of the Glen of Imaal terrier and the taller, leggier Irish and Kerry Blue terriers. In the early shows catering for this breed of terrier, short-legged terriers of the Glen of Imaal type mingled with taller, more typey specimens.

It is curious that Pierse considered the Kerry Blue terrier as a more furious and aggressive breed than this hotch-potch of terriers that was later to gel into a homogenous type that would become the soft-coated Wheaten terrier. Wheatens still have a terrific reputation for being utterly courageous animals that will still tackle not only badgers but other dogs with equal alacrity. In Ireland, where the J line of Staffordshire bull terrier (bred down from an incredibly courageous dog, Fearless Joe) is still worked to badger, Wheaten terriers, some admittedly from unregistered strains, are often ranked as being as game as some of the working Staffordshire bull terriers and tales of Wheatens capable of killing otters are legion. Yet it is fair to say that aggressive 'hot' Wheaten terriers are seldom seen at Kennel Club shows and furious dogs are considered untypical of the breed.

Wheaten terriers however have a reputation for being slow to develop physically – they attain their full coats only after they are two years of age and are often docile and reluctant to stand their ground against large vermin until they are second year. However it should be mentioned that

The Soft-Coated Wheaten Terrier

some of the legendary working terriers, Capell's Bluecap and the extremely game dog Pincher, were very slow to start and did not attain their legendary prowess to vermin until they were nearly four years of age and slow starting terriers are often the very best of workers when they decide they are ready to start.

It must be mentioned that an article which appeared in *The Working Terrier Year Book* describing the barbaric and illegal terrier trials, quite distinct from the trials conducted under the aegis of the Irish Kennel Club one should add, that are still conducted in Ireland, mentions that soft-coated Wheaten terriers often compete in these trials, tests that consist of encouraging a dog to rush up an artificial earth and drag out a captive badger that has no chance of escaping its captors. While it is sad that quasi-hunters find such thinly disguised baiting sessions necessary to justify keeping terriers, it has to be admitted that these terriers are still game enough to face powerful subterranean foes such as badgers. Sadly the existence of such trials acts as a powerful weapon to those who would see terrier-work made illegal.

In recent years (the first advertisement appeared in 1980) advertisements for lurchers bred by mating soft-coated Wheaten terriers to greyhounds have appeared in the sporting press and many of these lurchers bred by crossing Wheatens with greyhounds resemble small rather scruffy Norfolk-type lurchers or bearded collie lurchers. This type of lurcher has a reputation for great courage, but it is also fair to state that few of these hybrids seem to be trained to any standard and are never found competing in lurcher agility or obedience trials. More recently (1988) curious hybrids bred by mating Wheaten/bull terrier hybrids to greyhounds have made an appearance though it is fair to state that there are few reports of the ability of these lurcher composites.

The Glen of Imaal Terrier

While it can be said that the Irish terrier, the Kerry Blue and the soft-coated Wheaten terriers are simply colour and coat phases of the same type of dog – all are roughly of the same height and shape – it has to be admitted that the less popular Glen of Imaal terrier is 'different'.

Glen of Imaal terriers are lower on the leg, built like robust albeit untidy large Sealyham terriers and bear little resemblance to the other Irish breeds of terrier. The breed, once again in common with all Irish breeds of terrier was bred as a badger hunting dog and also a fighting dog in the remote districts of County Wicklow. Horner suggests that the breed was developed by Lowland and Hessian troops quartered in County Wicklow in the sixteenth and seventeenth centuries, but there is little to suggest that Horner could be correct though the Glen of Imaal certainly resembles some of the descriptions of the hounds kept in Flanders in the sixteenth century and recorded in Turbeville's *The Noble Art of Venerie and Hunting* (1575). However it is fanciful to suggest that Lowland troops automatically brought in these hounds to Wicklow and illogical to imagine that terriers did not exist in County Wicklow before the sixteenth and seventeenth centuries. What is more likely is that the breed is simply a form or some type of native Irish terrier that breeders and sportsmen in County Wicklow allowed or encouraged to develop along different lines until the breed was totally dissimilar to the other breeds of Irish terrier. The development of the Glen of Imaal and its relationship to the other Irish breeds might in fact be likened to the evolution of the Dandie Dinmont terrier and its close relatives the Border terrier and the Bedlington terrier.

Herbert Compton *The Twentieth Century Dog* (1904) believes that the metamorphosis of the Glen of Imaal terrier was in fact hastened by bulldog blood once again supposedly introduced by English troops quartered at the garrisons in County Wicklow, but this too is an illogical supposition, for a decade of selective breeding could easily alter a type of terrier until it no longer resembled the stock that originally spawned it, though it is interesting to note that early cynologists were reluctant to accept that a type of dog can metamorphose slowly to become a distinct breed without the addition of alien blood to facilitate the metamorphosis.

The dichotomy of type was noted but not approved of by Vero Shaw

Glen of Imaal terrier: Killarney Princess. (Photo Bord Failte)

who described a show staged in Dublin in 1876 where long low-slung dogs 'long, low and useful' were seen. Vero Shaw disapproved of these low-slung dogs which he considered as untypical of Irish terriers in general. Whether or not the dogs described by Vero Shaw were Glen of Imaals or (and this is more likely) the Irish terriers of the time were far from homogenous and that at one time low-slung dogs were common throughout Ireland and not just in County Wicklow, is open to question.

However, a few years later Herbert Compton writing in 1904 actually describes dogs bred in County Wicklow as long in the body, short on the leg and blue/black in colour though blue, wheaten or brindle Glen of Imaal terriers are more regularly seen today.

In a letter to the author of 1984 a retired schoolteacher, Arnold Collins once of County Wicklow, states 'You seem uncertain that the Glen of Imaal terrier is courageous and you state they are inclined to be nervous, but this is not the case. My father owned, but never bred, Glen of Imaal terriers for many years and the courage of these dogs was never in question. Disreputables from our village regularly fought the dogs against others of the breed and also against other breeds that were much bigger and these terriers were never wanting in courage. Badgers were also fought by these terriers and the badger is a most testing animal for a dog to face. I feel you may have underestimated the breed or else the Glen has changed greatly since the times when my father kept them. My father also mentioned a Jimmy Onions who kept a very good type of nearly black terrier that worked with some of the fox hound packs and were much smaller than the dogs bred locally.'

It is also worthy of note that Horner *Terriers of the World* mentions that during the days when the Irish Kennel Club allowed the Misneac Teastas tests to take place despite the fact that the Glen of Imaal terrier was smaller than the other Irish terrier breeds, the Glen of Imaal measures fourteen inches at the shoulder, the Glen won many of the Teastas Mor certificates and was seldom wantig in gameness. Horner adds that the hunting of the badger, considered to be abhorent in Britain, is still perfectly legal in Eire – for the time being one should add.

Horner's opinion is not shared by all. *The Working Terrier Year Book* records in a letter from an anonymous Irish terrier man that the Glen of Imaal was noticeable by its absence at the modern trials/cum baiting sessions – though this may possibly indicate that the owners and breeders of Glen of Imaal terriers are reluctant to allow their terriers to take part in such pointless, cruel and inhuman tests. Indeed the plight of a wretched captive badger released into an artificial earth that is blocked to prevent its escape and then baited by a succession of dogs should be repugnant to all genuine hunters.

At the time of writing the Glen of Imaal must be classed as a rare breed however and there are few serious and dedicated breeders of this curious and attractive breed of terrier. Liz Gay of Gamston, Nottinghamshire, keeps a small kennel of these terriers and curiously, for the breed was once known as a renowned grappler and frequently pitted against other dogs, Mrs Gay finds she is able to kennel three terriers together without desperate fights taking place (there is an old working terrier adage – kennel three, bury one – this is applicable to most breeds of working terrier). Mrs Gray is not a working terrier *aficionado* but tries to put out terriers to people who will work them and counts gamekeepers and fox diggers amongst her clients.

Glover *The Working Bedlington Terrier* mentions that one Jack Chisnell of Market Harborough has worked Glen of Imaal terriers to fox and seems quite happy with the working qualities of the breed though a fourteen inch dog weighing in at thirty-five pounds in weight must find in very difficult to get to its fox in most tight places and be desperately hard pressed to work foxes in tree roots. Glover states that a twenty-four pound terrier would appear to be the best weight for a working Glen of Imaal, but such an animal would seem woefully undersized to the purist Glen of Imaal breeder.

Glover puts forward an interesting theory that the Glen of Imaal terrier may well be used to recussitate the working ability of the Bedlington terrier for few people consider that the Bedlington – once a tiger of a dog – is a worthwhile prospect as a working terrier. Hence George Newcombe has endeavoured to recussitate the Bedlington terrier by dint of mating his bitches to fell/Lakeland terriers – though Newcombe's project is certainly viewed with suspicion by the majority of purist Bedlington terrier breeders.

Glover advocates using Glen of Imaal terrier blood to revive the flagging working instincts of the Bedlington terrier, but when held up to close scrutiny Glover's proposed breeding project has little to commend it. Glen of Imaal terriers are not related to Bedlington terriers though it has been suggested that the 'blue devils' shown at Dublin were Bedlington terriers and this blood may have entered into certain strains of Irish terrier – it must be added that Ash's hypothesis is pure speculation and has never been substantiated by fact. Newcombe used fell/Lakeland blood to revive the working qualities of his strain of Bedlington terrier and Lakelands/fells are closely related to Bedlington terriers and hence the outcross was easily assimilated by Newcombe's Bedlingtons.

What is more important however is the fact that neither the Glen of Imaal terrier nor the Bedlington terrier are worked by the majority of the people who keep or breed them and hence while it is mathematically sound to assume that the combination of two minuses may well produce a plus factor the premise is genetically unsound. Type-wise the Glen of Imaal terrier is very different from that of the Bedlington terrier though both breeds have coats which are not smooth (the Bedlington terrier has a linty coat, the Glen of Imaal has a jacket which is wirey with a soft undercoat). Frankly little seems to be gained by mating Glen of Imaal terriers to Bedlington terriers in an effort to revive the working qualities of the latter breed, except to produce a crossbred dog of a variable type that may or may not carry the copper toxicocis problems that are ruining the Bedlington terrier. A similar result could be obtained by testing the existing strains of Bedlington terrier for copper toxicocis and breeding from suitable selected males that did not carry copper toxicocis.

The Terriers of Scotland

The Terriers of Scotland

If a person researching matters canine and working terriers in particular was to seek out every gamekeeper, every hunt servant and every pest control officer in Scotland and request to view his terriers the researcher would encounter a rich variety of Jack Russell terriers, fell terriers of every type, particularly black fell terriers, and probably even a Border terrier or so. It would be highly unlikely that he would find a single hunter who fielded any of the Scottish breeds of terrier. However, this was not always the case.

Scotland boasts wide and varied scenery. In Border country the hare-hunting, rolling plains spill over from Northumberland. Scotland's central lowlands have always hosted an enthusiastic band of hunters while the Grampians and the Cairngorms must vie with the Ural mountains for the most spectacular scenery in Europe. North of Inverness lies the most sparsely populated country in Europe and there are areas of Sutherland that can be traversed only by the most determined walker.

In such a remote vastness game abounded. Wolves driven to extinction by the harrassment of English and Welsh hunters lingered for a further century or so in the remote glens of Scotland. The boar – 'and where he strikes his crooked tushes slay' – had become a park-bred animal in England long before Shakespeare had penned his *Venus and Adonis*. In Scotland it lived out its furious, truly wild existence for a further three centuries or so, sheltered by impenetrable thickets in thinly populated areas, skulking angrily amongst peat hags and heather. The wildcat, the catamount of Shakespeare once inhabited all of Britain. It still abounds in Scotland as does its curious relative, a black hybrid feline as baffling as the Chimaera, as elusive as a moonbeam. Otters, now rare in the brooks and rivers of England and Wales, are fairly common in Scotland – an otter crossing, a place where motorists are asked to drive with care lest they harm otters, exists in Orkney and other mustelids: stoats, weasels and even polecats and pine martens are commonly seen.

Foxes have always been regarded as vermin rather than sporting quarry north of Carlisle and are ruthlessly sought out and destroyed in the Highlands. Organised mounted and foot packs are relatively recent innovations in Scotland but tales of both wolves and marauding foxes being pursued by bobbery packs of sight and scent hounds date from pre-Celtic times.

Badgers, scarce in the Highlands, are plentiful in the Lowlands and to the west where the climate is mild enough for badgers to forage in the depths of mid-winter and to produce cubs as early as January. They were persecuted ruthlessly as their nocturnal, secretive ways inspired fear and enmity from a race where witchcraft and superstition had more credibility than in the rest of Britain.

Yet Scotland is a harsh land a country where freezing winters are often only punctuated by mild midge-filled summers and snows cling to the summits of mountains until late May. In the Highlands a wind, wicked as a harridan's tongue, begins to blow in September ceasing only as June brings a brief and all too transitory summer.

Rock piles, relics of a glacial age which wrought changes to a once gentle countryside scattered over thousands of acres, afford sanctuary to fox, badgers and smaller mustelids alike, while shallow earths excavated just above the water table undermine enormous areas of heather. Borrans deep enough to put Blaeberry Borran to shame scar many glen sides and offer refuges to foxes and badgers.

In such a country it was inevitable that terriers of a sort would evolve to cope with small and medium sized vermin – terriers, thick of coat to survive the icy winters, strong of jaw to kill rather than bolt foxes and robust in shape to survive the conflicts with fox and badger. Scottish terriers are in fact simply versions or variations of a type of terrier that was common from Cape Wrath to the Borders.

It is not surprising that this type of terrier was developed in Scotland. What is surprising is that this type of terrier is no longer worked in the land north of Carlisle.

The Cairn Terrier

It seems likely that the Cairn terrier or a type of terrier similar to the Cairn was the prototype of all the Scottish terrier breeds. The Cairn terrier is one of the smallest British terriers and measures around ten inches at the shoulder – an ideal size for a chunky, strongly made working terrier and has been changed little since it first appeared on the show bench in 1909 when the type was shown as a short-haired Skye terrier – and at the first dog show which catered for the breed, all the Cairn-type terriers shown had been bred on the Isle of Skye.

Skye in fact seems to have been a centre of terrier breeding in Scotland – and for fairly obvious reasons. The island warmed by the Gulf Stream hosts an incredible number of foxes and otters and a terrain that makes the hunting of these animals testing to dog and to man alike.

It seems likely that the Cairn-type terrier was bred by hunters from the Borders to Caithness and local variations of this type gave rise to the Skye, the West Highland white, the Aberdeen or Scottish terrier and possibly the ancestors of the Dandie Dinmont terrier – though many lay outrageous claims as to the ancestry of the Dandie!

That the Cairn was originally used to hunt down and destroy vermin is certain. Mr D. J. Thompson Gray, who wrote under the pseudonym of 'Whinstone' in his book *The Dogs of Scotland*, (1891) records:

> Previous to 1879 the type of terrier now recognised as the Scottish terrier was comparatively unknown. This is not surprising when we consider they were in the hands of sportsmen, fox hunters, gamekeepers and crofters living in the remote parts of the Highlands and islands of Scotland far removed from the influence of dog shows and having little communication with the world.

Robert Leighton recalls a macabre tale in his *The Complete Book of the Dog* (1922) when he was introduced to a stuffed Cairn terrier by Sir Paynton Piggott, but while today's dog keeping public would consider it anathema to have a beloved pet skinned and mounted our ancestors certainly did not. At Crufts Dog Show 1890, Class 220 catered for 'Stuffed dogs, or dogs made of wood, china etc.' Carson Ritchie *The British Dog* suggests that this passion for stuffed dogs had started in 1851 when at the Great Exhibition M. Ploucquet's exhibits of hounds and

Joan Hancock's noted working Cairn terrier

certain varieties of quarry the said hounds pursued attracted considerable attention and cases containing stuffed Scottish-type terriers silently baying at an equally silent 'brought to bay' Scottish wildcat were once popular exhibits in Victorian drawing rooms. It is interesting to note that Lucas complained that when one of his Sealyhams had died he sent the cadaver to an exhibitor who mounted the creature so badly that it no longer resembled a Sealyham terrier.

Baillie Flett too makes reference to Scottish terriers he had owned 'They were principally of a wheaten or sandy colour of the smartest possible contour. Several were not ' "hard-haired" but that was of minor importance when rodent killing was their special purpose.'

However rats were not the only quarry to which these small neatly made dogs were entered. Jimmy Overs whose father was kennelman to Mrs Graham Spense at the Egton Kennel of Lakeland terriers records that his father once worked an unregistered strain of Cairn terrier to fox and badger and that these terriers were equally as game as the fell terrier strains of today and surprisingly quick to enter to quarry. Overs spoke almot nostalgically about the decline of the Cairn terrier as a worker and lamented the fact that the breed had passed to the hands of the fancier rather than the hunter.

However, some fanciers still continued to prize the working qualities of their dogs. Mrs Mawson of Leeds who bred the winning Glenmacdhui strain foremost amongst which was the bitch Glenmacdhui Mohra seemingly prized the working qualities of her Cairns and obtained working certificates for her terriers during the 1960s. At one time during the early 1960s one of the doggy periodicals staged a working terrier forum and invited Mrs Mawson (Cairns) and John 'Jack' Cobby (Borders) to comment on the working of terriers to fox and badger and as to whether a single terrier was capable of killing a fox!

Jeff Burman of Louth, a working terrier enthusiast and one of the great 'diggers' of the 1960s, bought one of these terriers bred in part from Glenmacdhui bloodlines and worked the dog to fox and badger and stated 'there's nothing harder than a good Cairn.' Sadly Burman did not continue breeding this pure-bred type of Cairn but crossed his Cairn with a small black-and-tan working terrier possibly fell-bred and worked the half-bred progeny.

Frankly, there seems little reason why Cairn terriers are not worked today. The type is ideal, for the Cairn is a small ten inch terrier weighing in at fourteen pounds in prime condition though slightly less if the dog is exercised hard in readiness for work. The type has suffered little from the craze for breeding exaggerated features in dogs and the breed has strong powerful jaws which are more than capable of defending this neat and alert looking terrier. It is in fact quite sad that the majority of Cairn terrier breeders are antipathetic to allowing their dogs to exploit their natural tendency to work.

At the time of writing, there is a craze to revive the working qualities in almost inert breeds such as the modern Bedlington terrier and the methods advocated include mating these terriers to other breeds to revitalise them. Cairn terriers are tailor-made for any enthusiast wishing to exploit the working qualities of a breed that is still capable of performing well below and above ground.

The West Highland White Terrier

That the West Highland white terrier and the Cairn share a common origin is seldom disputed, in fact it might be said – though this statement may well offend the purest – that the West Highland white is merely a colour-phase of the Cairn terrier. Certainly during the early days of both the breeds white terriers born to Cairn terrier parents were often shown as West Highland white terriers and the slight dichotomy that exists between the two types today is the result of breeders deliberately attempting to produce distinct breeds.

There seems to be a marked antipathy to any white type of dog in the Highlands in particular and Scotland in general. At the time when dog fighters matched dogs throughout Britain white bulldogs and bull terriers were commonly seen in the south of Britain but white bulldogs were considered a novelty in Scotland. White Border collies born to black and white or to merle-coloured parents are usually regarded with suspicion by Scottish shepherds though this suspicion is often supposedly explained by the statement that white dogs confuse sheep and inspire no respect in the flocks (many continental herding breeds such as Maremmas are white however). Likewise hunters, vermin controllers and gamekeepers supposedly put down white puppies that appeared in litters of Cairn-type terriers.

It is said that Colonel E. D. Malcolm of Poltalloch kicked against public opinion however and kept back white terriers born to parents of dark-coloured Cairn-type terriers and these white or cream terriers bred true to type. Thus is was possible in a single generation to produce a gene pool for an entirely new type of white Cairn terrier.

Cw Cw

\ /

CC Cw Cw ww

CC Dark-coloured Cairn-type terrier

Cw Cairn coloured terriers carrying the genes that produce white Cairn-type stock

ww Pure breeding white Cairn-type terriers

It is however worth mentioning that the Poltalloch terriers were slightly

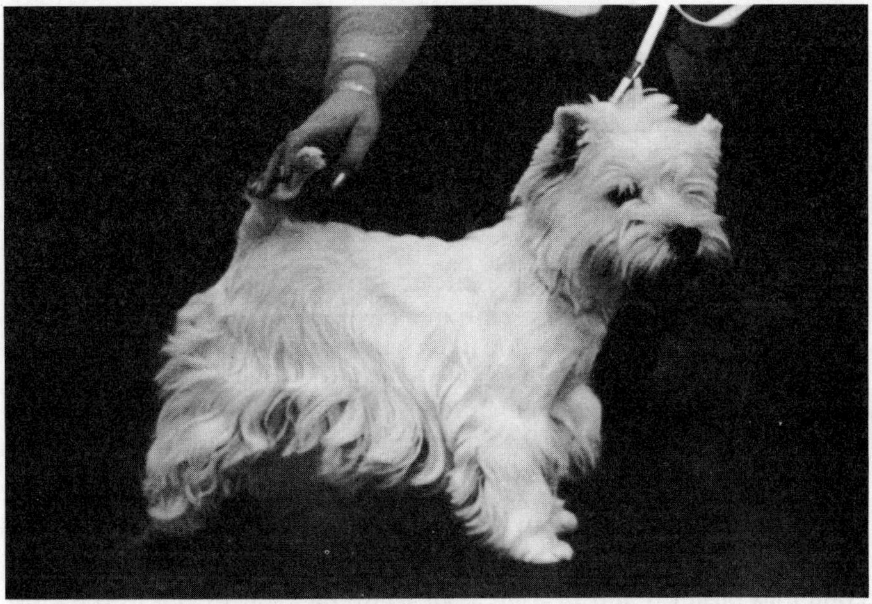

West Highland white terrier

larger than the traditional Cairns and weighed in at sixteen to twenty pounds (a Cairn terrier seldom exceeded a stone in weight).

Captain Mackie who visited Poltalloch to see these terriers says 'I have had the breed and hope to have it again. I know exactly what these dogs are fit for and may add that no water was ever too cold or no earth too deep for them.'

Colonel Malcolm quoted in Leighton's *New Book of the Dog* (1911) and wrote of the earths in which his terriers were required to seek out and destroy foxes. Malcolm talks of earths built in glacial morrains and composed of 'erratic' rocks some of which were three or four hundred tons in weight from which earths it was virtually impossible to extricate a terrier. He tells of one particular terrier drawn out of the very depths of a deep earth by a peculiar method.

> I remember a tale of one of my father's keepers terriers who got so lost the keepers went daily to the cairn (a cairn is a rock pile or borran earth one should add) hoping against hope. At last one day a pair of bright eyes were seen at the bottom of the hole. They did not disappear when the dog's name was called; a brilliant idea seized one of the keepers, the dog evidently could not get up, so a rabbit skin was folded into a small parcel around a stone and let down on a string. The dog at once seized the situation and the skin, held on and was drawn up and fainted on reaching the mouth of the hole. He was carried home, nursed and recovered.

However, Colonel Malcolm was not the only person to exploit the white 'sports' that appeared in litters of Scottish terriers – sports which if mated to Scottish-type terriers of their own colour bred absolutely true. Two other breeders of white terriers the bloodlines of which either became extinct or were absorbed into either the bloodlines of the West Highland white terrier or other Scottish breeds of terrier were Dr Flaxman whose strain of Aberdeen or Scottish terrier regularly produced the odd white puppy in its litters and these white terriers were known as Pittenweem terriers and the Roseneath terriers which according to Horner were originally bred by a gamekeeper called George Clarke. It is said that Colonel Malcolm did not like these terriers and hence refused to use them to breed his Poltalloch strain of terrier that eventually became known as the West Highland white.

Early enthusiasts of the breed, which was embraced by the Kennel Club in 1904, still exploited the considerable working ability of the West Highland white terrier. Mrs Lionel Portman writing in *The Field* (1910) states 'Badger digging is undoubtedly the supreme test of the working terrier. Rabbiting improves its nose and condition. Ratting combines business and pleasure. But to find a badger deep in the labyrinths of a large earth and to stick to him possibly for hours together, baying and sniffing at him so that he has no time to dig – a thing he can do faster than two men – is a task requiring perseverance, grit and stamina of the highest order. As we feel these qualities are worth at least as much encouragement as show points, we invariably enter all our terriers to badger soon after they have received their preliminary training.'

However a mere fifteen years later Mrs A. W. Bird writing in Lucas' *Pedigree Dog Breeding* states of the breed: 'They are wonderful ratters and although usually not strong enough in the jaw for badger digging I continually use my larger dogs with great success for this sport as well as badger digging.' Mrs Bird qualifies this statement with 'the average weight of a dog is twelve to fifteen pounds and the bitch a little less.'

However few breeders consider working their dogs today. This is a pity for the type is still unruined by exaggeration and is ideally shaped to work fox, rabbit and rat. The breed certainly offers an opening for a working terrier enthusiast who wishes to work a breed that is different from the run-of-the-mill terriers. One hears instances of the breed manifesting working qualities and many will run to ground on rabbit and fox if given a chance. Both the Cairn and the West Highland white are ideally suited as ratting terriers though in common with all Scottish breeds of terrier, West Highland whites are reluctant to pack or hold together well when hunting. This can be a problem if one wishes to hunt a small team of terriers to rat or particularly rabbit, for a team that splits while rabbit hunting where terriers can run to ground all too readily, is a great nuisance and a problem to control. At one time Lucas showed a great interest in this breed – he knew Mrs A. W. Bird and saw her team of Placemore West Highland white terriers badger digging, but the failure or reluctance of these dogs to hunt as a pack deterred further interest from Lucas.

The Skye Terrier

Whereas it can be said that both the Cairn and the West Highland white terrier have been altered little by the show breeders craze for exaggeration the same cannot be said for the Skye terrier.

Early Skye terriers would have been little different from Cairns. Indeed the common stock that spawned the Cairn and the West Highland white terrier also produced the Skye.

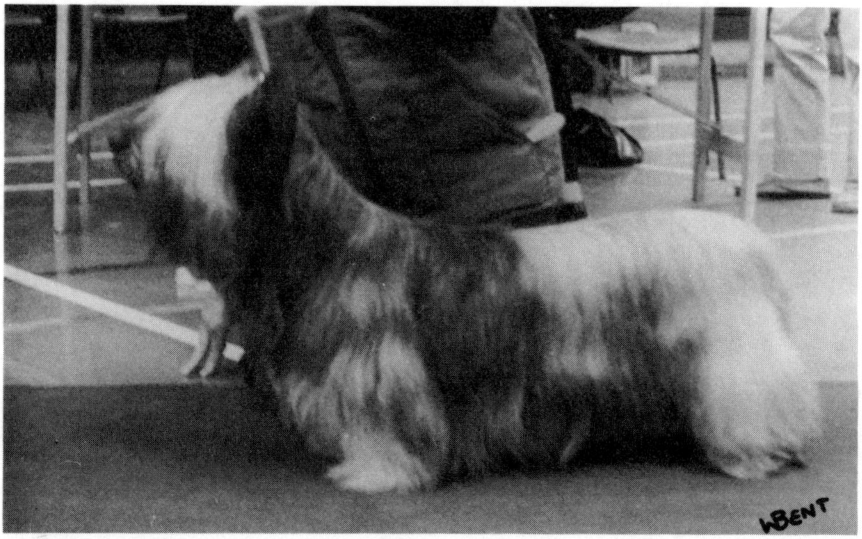

Skye terrier

Modern Skye terriers bear little resemblance to the Cairn however. A typical Skye terrier is forty-one-and-a-half inches long and ten inches tall and weighs in at twenty-five pounds. In addition to this the Skye has a long, silky coat perhaps the most unsuitable jacket ever to cover a working terrier for the coat balls up in mud, snow or clay.

At one time the breed had a bad reputation for being snappy and judges often examined Skye terrier exhibits with great care. Horner believes that this vice is gradually being bred out of the breed however, but the Skye terrier has little propensity as a working terrier breed.

The Scottish or Aberdeen Terrier

The characteristic Black-and-White whisky, box-headed Scottish or Aberdeen terrier is one of the most readily identified dogs and is regarded by many as the symbol of Scotland. In point of fact the breed is very closely related to the Skye, the Cairn and the West Highland white terrier and may well be remotely related to the Dandie Dinmont.

The Scottie too was once a renowned working terrier that was required to give a good account of itself at fox, badger, otter, wildcat and the various mustelids that still abound in the north east of Scotland and the terrier has retained the strong biting head of its working terrier ancestors.

To ascertain as to when a dichotomy in type between what are today called the Scottish terrier and the Cairn terrier occurred is difficult and in the early days of the breed-types terriers which resembled Skyes, West Highland white, Cairns and Scottish terriers were shown in the same classes – classes which catered for Scottish terriers as indeed each terrier shown could claim to be! However engravings dating from 1770 show terriers identical in type to the early Scottish terriers. It can probably be assumed that certain breed types arose in isolated districts and a process of none too judicious inbreeding fixed certain types of terrier.

As to when the Scottish terrier was last worked is yet another moot point. Many of these terriers will rat and rabbit as well as any terrier and would probably go to ground well if afforded an opportunity to do so.

Lucas writing in *Pedigree Dog Breeding* comments that the Scottish or Aberdeen terrier still possessed strong sporting instincts but once again remarks that the breed prefers to perform as individuals and is reluctant to pack 'a pack of fox terriers or Sealyham terriers may be worked as a pack and will all come to cry and horn, but half of a pack of Scotties would probably disappear in small parties before the day was over.' This is quite a serious problem if one intends to work a team in sheep country or wishes to hunt rat with a small pack of terriers.

Another peculiarity of the breed is its tendency to develop muscle cramps that are so unique as to merit the name Scottie cramp for no other breed other than Scottish terrier derivatives manifest this peculiarity – the Cesky terrier a derivative of the Scottie, the Sealyham and possibly the Dandie Dinmont terrier has been described in an earlier chapter (*The Sealyham*).

Terriers and their Quarry

The Principles of Entering a Terrier to Quarry

It is possible, just possible, to restrict a dog to kennels from puppyhood to adolescence, take it from the said kennels and enter it to fox on its first trip out. Indeed the number of terriers that are subjected to this method of training and entering must be legion. It is however equally fair to state that many, many working terriers in Britain are badly entered, loosely wed to their quarry, enjoy little reciprocity with their owners and are far from first class workers. More terriers are badly entered and totally ruined than are properly entered as the hordes of dogs that are passed to and from unlicenced dealers' kennels attests. If a terrier of any breed is properly entered and taken through the spectrum of quarry then it has a good chance of becoming a good worker to fox. True certain breeds which are still bred specifically to work fox will enter more readily or more easily but equally certainly a sensible caring terrier owner will make more of a success out of entering any type of terrier than will a person who ham-handedly prematurely enters a terrier to fox without judging the time and situation where the initial confrontation with fox should take place.

Sadly the world of the working terrier attracts the meddler, the instant expert, those with short lived interests in dogs, like a magnet. Such people ruin the dogs they acquire with alacrity and with even greater alacrity pass on their dispirited broken wards and straightaway acquire new animals to demoralise and ruin. Each year hosts of well-bred terriers are purchased, badly trained, prematurely entered and passed on to others who are even less meticulous, even less caring with their newly acquired dogs. Many of these dogs will know twenty or thirty uncaring, far from loving owners, until they find some person who will offer them a permanent home. Yet in the right hands, entered and trained properly and gradually the majority of terriers will make good and useful workers. Admittedly some terriers will not work or show little propensity to hunt, but the majority of failed terriers are simply the result of bad handling, careless training and premature entering. It should also be pointed out that it is far easier to train and enter a terrier, taking it through each step of its training programme, than to take up a damaged demoralised broken spirited dog and restart it to its rightful work. In the right hands most terriers will work all legal quarry, and while it has to be admitted some terriers will work better than others, this superiority is usually the result of training and entering as much as breeding and an innate disposition to work.

An excellent tale to illustrate this point is told by Marjorie Bunting in her book *The Norwich Terrier*. Another to bolt a fox which had gone to ground to escape from the hounds was Miss Eleanor Johnson's Champion Whinlatter Cain (a Norwich/Norfolk terrier). A terrier was needed and when Miss Johnson said 'here's one' pointing to Cain the hunt staff suggested he would not do at which point Miss Johnson put him in and soon showed he would do very well. The tale is not intended to show the superiority of the Norwich terrier or to illustrate that a bench bred dog will still work. What the tale does illustrate is that a terrier that is allowed time to develop, allowed opportunity to hunt the spectrum of available quarry from mice to foxes will usually enter well and perform the task for which it was originally bred. It is however equally true that a superbly bred working terrier in the wrong hands, prematurely entered by a far from discerning owner will perform extremely badly. Thus while it is true that almost any breed of terrier in the right hands can be trained to work all legal quarry after a fashion it is also true that the world of the working terrier seems to attract the sort of person who is singularly adept at making a sow's ear out of a perfectly good silk purse!

Further proof that the majority of terriers will, if given half a chance, work quite well is the fact that a great many very useful hunt terriers are donation terriers – terriers kept as pets and which have proved superfluous to the needs of the owner or have become spiteful or difficult to handle. The majority of these dogs are of pedigree unknown breeding of the sort which had they been offered the hunt staff as puppies would have probably been rejected. Their previous owners had shown no interest in working the terrier (it may have been less difficult to live with if the owners had worked the animal) and hence the terrier has 'self-entered' so to speak. It has hunted fieldmice at the bottom of the garden, chased rabbits on the waste ground on which it has exercised, been an absolute pest because it harrassed the cat next door and has been responsible for digging out rats and moles in the hedgerows near the house. Thus by the time its bored owner has decided to part with it the terrier has entered itself to small quarry and is ready for fox.

Tales of these dogs follow a pattern as predictable as a Wagnerian opera. The dogs grow to greatness in hunt service, and when other terriers fail to bolt foxes the rescued terrier goes in and drives out the fox, becoming famous throughout the country. When mated to numerous bitches (the majority of gift terriers coming to hunt service are males as bored male terriers are likely to cause their owners more trouble than are equally bored bitches) the dog breeds nothing of worth despite the reputation and breeding of the dam of the litters. In despair the hunter tries to seek out siblings of this now aging paragon but can find none, or those that are found are of little worth. Hence like the sword of Seigfried the blood line cannot be patched or repaired and passes into extinction for the vital alloy in the mixture is missing. The truth is that the terrier was probably not an innately good worker with genes that were capable of producing similar dogs in its progeny. The dog had experienced a slow gradual and natural process of self-entering and the greatness was the result of nurture rather than nature. There is scarcely a hunt servant in Britain that cannot tell a similar tale of an all-time great terrier that somehow failed to beget stock of equal worth.

Wally Wyld of the Grove and Rufford Foxhounds; possibly one of the most adept men at entering a hunt terrier in Britain today, tells a similar though not identical tale. Wyld's baptism to terrier work had been at the hands of a black fell terrier called Kipper bred in the purple by Cyril Breay in 1963 from Bingo and Tig and Kipper introduced Wally to the world of the working terrier and for a number of years he worked the Breay strain of fell. However when the terriers from Breay's line started to grow too big Wally fetched a free-to-a-good-home rough-coated terrier from a house in Sheffield for the terrier had, during a moment of boredom, gutted settees and sofas alike and had begun to bite strangers who visited the house. Wyld's tale does not have the predictable ending one might expect however for he continued the line from the house wrecking terrier and bred the present Grove and Rufford hunt terriers.

Barry Dainty one time kennelman for the Meynall Foxhounds and terrier man for the Warwickshire pack based at Kineton tells a similar story. A free-to-a-good-home terrier was offered Barry and the bitch turned out to resemble a Bambi model with a cherubic face and a far from impressive appearance. Penny the young bitch was, despite her innocent appearance, a cat worrier and a habitual hunter which if not restrained ran head down on a scent for miles. Whether or not she had seen a fox during her travels is questionable, but she caught and killed rabbits, rats and other vermin with great enthusiasm. She was an outstanding fox dog by the end of her first season at Kineton however and her death in a kennel fight was a great tragedy. Dainty continued her line by mating her to Taggart (bred by Brockley out of terriers from Eric Taylor's Mick and Jill line) and bred Pedlar another excellent hunt terrier and Penny also appears in the tail line of Greg Mousely's winning strain of Jack Russell terriers. Penny's virtue as a hunt terrier however was due as much to her gradual self-entering programme as to her breeding though she was bred from Seale Cottage/beagle blood as it so happens – a totally unsuitable type of terrier to be kept only as a pet.

If terriers are subjected to an interesting and exciting lifestyle, allowed to hunt small fry during the formative years of their life, never overmatched or prematurely entered they have an excellent chance of becoming good fox dogs and all-round hunters that will give the owner a long and useful life's work.

It is however true that many terriers survive premature entering, overmatching and yet go on to become useful terriers for working below and above ground. However it is also true that the majority of well-bred terriers that finish up mentally damaged, ruined and demoralised are also the result of this ill-conceived entering programme or the product of 'I can wait until he is really ready to try to fox' school of thought.

The majority of terriers of any breed will, if subjected to a careful entering programme, give a good account of themselves as hunting dogs though it is usually easier by far to enter a terrier that is specifically bred to work. It is interesting to note that during the 1960s Skinner the psychologist prepounded an interesting theory that if any course of study was broken up in to sufficiently small units anyone could undertake and succeed with the course particularly if the course was punctuated with rewards of the type that not only rewarded the efforts of the student, but encouraged him to continue with his course of study. Skinner's methods were often of a very lengthy nature, but they certainly worked and if a terrier is to be properly trained it must be subjected to the self-same gradual learning programme.

Training and Entering to Quarry

The oft repeated advice by Dandie Dinmont (Sir Walter Scott's *Guy Mannering*) to Captain Brown regarding the entering of young terriers still holds good 'first wi rottens then wi stots then wi tod then wi brocks – after which they fear nothing that ever came wi a hairy skin on it' still holds good now as then though the badger which became illegal to dig or harm under the 1973 and 1981 Wildlife and Countryside Acts should be best omitted from this list. Still start with rats, stoats or weasels and then enter the terrier to fox is an excellent piece of advice to the would-be trainer of the working terrier.

Considerable training can proceed entering the puppy to rat however. Within hours of a newly acquired puppy arriving at its new home it can be started to work the rag as they say in Black Country whippet racing parlance. Puppies and terriers and sighthounds in particular manifest an innate disposition to chase any object and this peculiarity should always be utilised. Encourage puppies to chase a rag from day one of their education programme and very soon a youngster will become wild with excitement when it looks as though the game is about to start. I make a point of skinning rabbits I catch and drying the skins so the pelts which are practically odourless can be rolled and folded to form dummies. These dummies attached to lengths of twine can be drawn before the puppies and the whelp encouraged to attack the dummy. At first some whelps may display a reluctance to attack the furry dummy and to shake or worry the pelt, but within minutes of seeing the object the majority of terriers will latch on to the rabbit skin and enjoy a game of 'cat and mouse' with the pelt. Other terrier puppies become instantly ecstatic at the appearance of a rabbit pelt and display almost a frenzy to attack it, but though reactions to the pelt may be different eventually almost every puppy will join in the worry. In 1988 I bred two terrier puppies from an elderly bitch Salem mated to an equally geriatric stud dog called Kotian. Pazzaz and Trembling were nearly identical but very different in temperament. Pazzaz attacked the pelt with gusto as soon as he saw it; Trembling would not go near it for nearly a week and stood tail between legs when I produced the pelt to start a game of cat and mouse. Pazzaz was so ecstatic that he once bit my hands when I took the pelt from him but Trembling was very slow to take an interest in the worry. Pazzaz's first summer saw him drawing adders from their holes as a thrush pulls out a worm and killing them with a single bite. Trembling seldom ventured on to the moor and stood shivering (hence his name) in the yard while his sibling hunted like an old hand. Later that summer Trembling experienced a metamorphosis and one day, with seemingly nothing to affect the change, he began running head down on every scent he encountered. Puppies mature at different rates and no animal should be written off before it is given a chance to mature. I have elaborated on this incident simply because a friend of mine who breeds a good quality small fell terrier enquired after a ten-week-old fell puppy he had given to a youth. 'I sold it', the youth replied with a bitterness and petulance that implied he had been cheated despite the fact he had been given the whelp – 'it weren't ragging and Chuggy's puppy was.' Such is the grasshopper mindedness that afflicts far too many modern terrier men I'm afraid.

It is not to everyone's taste, but I freely admit I stop my van to pick up road casualty cadavers and I will elaborate on this point carefully and quickly lest the reader suspects goulish behaviour.

Rabbits, foxes, stoats and weasels frequently become road casualties in Britain partly because once a cadaver of another animal is broken up by a vehicle, predators come to investigate the scent (and hence become road casualties themselves) and partly because rabbits seem to decide that the best time to cross a busy road is when the road is brightly lit by an oncoming vehicle. If they are not too damaged I collect cadavers to encourage my puppies to worry or rag them. Rabbits are also collected to feed to my ferrets I should add. Puppies may well act strangely when they first encounter a cadaver the owner is endeavouring to get them to 'rag'. Some take to the activity instantly; others are positively fearful of the carcass and hide rather than endure the sight of the cadaver. This phase too will pass. Warlock, one of the best terriers, and certainly one of the best stud dogs, I have ever owned, refused to go near a carcass until he was nearly four months of age though his litter-mates attacked any cadaver madly and refused to release their grips on the carcass. Still a cadaver used to teach a litter of puppies and hung out of reach to encourage whelps to jump at it hurts not at all and offends no one.

On the subject of causing offence, or rather not causing offence, a tale is now on the cards. At one time Moses Smith, a gypsy friend, and I were so down on our luck so to speak that we picked up road casualty rabbits and ate them. We had but to see a rabbit, white belly up, on the road for the van to screech to a halt and one of us leap out and pick up the cadaver. On one occasion we chanced on a cat that had fallen prey to a passing car and I picked up the carcass to feed to my ferrets. As I was returning to the van with the cat an elderly lady caused what I took to be her husband to stop the car and beckoned to me. With some trepidation I walked to her car, cat in hand, and awaited the tirade from the lady: none came. With a voice syrupy sweet she uttered 'It's so nice to find people who are kind to cats – even on their deaths' (I believe she meant the cat) and offered me a pound. As I've mentioned Moses and I were down on our luck so rather sheepishly I took the money and ran.

In South Wales it is a popularly held opinion that allowing a dog to rag a cadaver is a certain way of encouraging a terrier to false mark (or bay like thunder when nothing is present in the hole). The logic behind this train of thought is interesting and can possibly be explained by the belief that a dog confuses the scent of a carcass with the scent of an animal that has departed the earth so to speak – both are in a sense 'long gone'. Whatever the logic behind such a premise the reader should ignore it. Funnily enough the very first Sealyham terrier I ever saw was in 1947 and the dog had been passed from hunter to hunter because it had apparently been caused to false mark by allowing it to worry cadavers of foxes. It was more likely that the dog had been ruined by premature entering or perhaps by encouraging it to bay whether or not the earth was inhabited. If I remember correctly the bitch was mated to a Court Y Folan strain Border terrier and bred an incredibly game and vocal litter that did extremely well as badger dogs.

On the subject of badgers and road casualties it is a wise move to pass by a road casualty badger cadaver and leave the creature strictly alone. Such is the public's antipathy to badger hunting – quite distinct from badger baiting one should add – that the presence of a dead badger in one's car often literally begs prosecution. In 1985 I was asked to appear as expert witness in a trial when the prosecution had alleged the accused had caught and killed a badger. In point of fact the man was interested in taxidermy and had found the badger on the roadside and had taken it home to stuff and mount. A neighbour had seen him take the cadaver from his car and had reported him. As it happened the action was dropped as the man had never owned a dog but had he kept terriers it might have been a less pleasant ending to the tale. It is best never to invite trouble and it is an offence under Section 1(2) of the 1973 Badger Act to own or possess even a portion of a dead badger unless it can be proved (and this may be difficult) that the badger has been killed in circumstances which were not in contravention of the Act – namely following a road accident. As it happened numerous motorists had seen the cadaver before it was picked up by the taxidermist. A terrier man found with a road casualty carcass in his possession will find it difficult to convince a court that he had found the cadaver. Badgers alive or dead are best left strictly alone by the terrier man and this subject will be dealt with at a later date.

Once the terrier is innoculated against leptospirosis, distemper and hepatitis it is well to begin the process of training prior to entering. A terrier puppy should come instantly to hand long before it is entered. If the trainer calls the puppy's name and drops to a crouch to bring his face nearly level with that of the puppy most puppies will come to hand. It is so easy to teach dogs to come to hand quickly that it is amazing that so many terriers are so badly trained, but a working terrier that escapes its couple at a dog show invariably causes embarrassment because of its recalcitrance and the fact it refuses to come to hand. Yet terrier men with such badly trained animals are often found pouring scorn and ridicule on competitors who are displaying the aptitudes of their terriers in the obedience ring. Terriers must be taught to come on command long before they are old enough to enter to rat.

Regarding Skinner's theory that any parcel of learning should be split into many smaller parcels so the the learner may assimilate the skills he wishes to learn more efficiently, Curtis Price, who fields a pack of working terriers in Powys, advises his clients to start their terriers at mice rather than rats and his opinion seems to be echoed by his fellow terrier enthusiast Jed Alker of Copple who also fields a small pack of terriers. Price argues that if a puppy is started at quarry that will cause it little hurt – and rats cause terrific hurt as anyone who has experienced a rat bite can attest – then the puppy can be started so much younger and assimilated into the pack structure at a much earlier age. Price who once lived in the Blackpool area deliberately seeks out mills where mice abound and starts his puppies on mice bolted from piles of rubbish. Such a practice teaches a puppy to hunt at a very early age – Price and Alker start their whelps when they are twelve weeks of age and the puppies become very adept at hunting long before they are six months old. Price counters the scoffers who pour ridicule on his preliminary entering programme by the fact that the majority of his adult terriers see hunt service with local foxhound packs and his failure rate with his terriers is almost zero. It should also be added that it is lunacy to hunt uninnoculated puppies to mice. Mice are carriers of the deadly leptospirosis jaundice against which puppies can be successfully innoculated.

Rats are a far more testing quarry for a young terrier than most terrier men can appreciate. A rat's jaws exert a terrific pressure and the teeth are razor sharp. Puppies which experience the agony of a rat bite to the tongue during their first outings are invariably shy of tackling rats for months afterwards and the quantity of blood that escapes from a bite to the tongue is copious enough to alarm most terrier owners. Terrier books advise taking puppies ratting with older terriers so that they may see how to despatch these rodents, but this is often quite a dangerous practice. When two dogs simultaneously grab at a rat the rat can easily be killed by the breaking of the neck (the quick shake that quickly kills rats simply dislocates the rat's neck and causes instantaneous death). A rat so beset with two terriers neither of which can kill the rodent by shaking it often creates mayhem with its teeth before it expires. I have been bitten by many creatures ranging from pigs to mice but the most painful bite I have ever experienced was in 1978 when I had caught a rat that was endeavouring to escape. As it did so Battle – a Vampire daughter – seized the rat which promptly rounded on my hand and bit it savagely. With its teeth latched into my fingers, bulging eyes aglaze the rat seemed prepared to literally sit out the storm with Battle furiously trying to shake the creature which, because it had secured a hold on my hand, could not be shaken to death. The pain was excruciating and what was obviously a mere second or so before the rat expired seemed like an agonising eternity. I have seen terriers terribly disconcerted when rats latch to their lips and many extremely bold puppies overmatched by a large rat that stood its ground against them. It is in fact no uncommon sight to see young terriers ignore larger aggressive rats in order that the puppy can secure catches of smaller less hard biting grey young rats.

It must seem strange to anyone who has been plagued with rats and observed the ravages caused by these creatures that rats and mice are afforded some protection by law. Prior to 1911 it was a popular sport – if sport is the correct word – to tip piles of rats into an enclosure and set a terrier to kill the luckless beasts that piled on top of each other in the mistaken belief that they could escape the attentions of the terrier. However the 1911 Protection of Animals Act made the activity illegal for while it is not illegal to allow a dog to kill what must be described as bagged quarry, the captive beasts must be afforded some chance of escaping. Frankly I have yet to understand the pleasure anyone seems to get killing any bagged quarry that has no chance of escaping. The thrill of the hunt should be excitement enough: the kill is always an anticlimax to the genuine hunter. I have probably caught more rats than any man alive – I hunted a terrier pack four nights a week for twenty-three years and have ratted since I was eight – but I can honestly say I have never baited a captive animal of any species.

Puppies should be allowed to enter to rat when they are ready for the task and should never be jack-knifed into entering by allowing them to face a rat that has no way of escaping for the practice is not only illegal but counter-productive to the development of the terrier. It might be argued that catching a live rat in a cage trap and releasing it before the terrier might not be a violation of the 1911 Protection of Animals Act for the rat has a chance – albeit a slight chance – of escaping. Such a practice is however a rather pointless one for not only does the act engender great terror for the rat immediately prior to its release, but the prey presented to the terrier is in an unnatural situation and hence does little to help the terrier develop its hunting instincts. What is more important is the fact that the sight of a terrifed captive rat being released in front of a terrier gives the actual sport of terrier work a bad image – and at this time in the history of field sports a good sporting image is essential. No one actually likes rats – though I have met a few bizarre exceptions who did – but the spectacle of a terrified animal cast before a dog does not endear the terrier man to the general public. In an age where even the supposedly enlightened media confuses badger digging with badger baiting it is wise to avoid any practice which the general public might consider as cruel.

So just how does one enter a terrier to rat – and the answer must clearly be by taking the dog to a place where rats are known to congregate and allowing the terrier to take its chance catching one. Such a method of entering a terrier must seem long and tedious to some, but the enjoyment a hunter experiences should not be in the killing of a creature, but in the way dogs develop and improve their technique of hunting. I confess that many many times I have allowed rats to escape – sometimes to the chagrin of the owner of rat infested establishments – and I admit I do not enjoy the actual act of killing rats though I find dog work little short of fascinating.

Rats are naturally nocturnal and visit feeding grounds from late evening to dawn. When rat infestations are high or when young rats are plentiful it is not uncommon to see rats playing and feeding during daylight hours, but rats are furtive creatures and race back and forth to their burrows when the slightest danger presents itself. When I kept only a few terriers, long before I began to hunt a pack of fifteen couple, I would visit a rat infested area to watch the rodents at play before I took a terrier to such a place. If one sits and watches the feeding and playing rats the action teaches the hunter much of the way he has to plan his future hunt with the young terrier in tow. Rats invariably run for a particular hole when panicked and avoid burrow entrances near to that particular lair. My own method of starting a puppy was to try to get between the rat and its chosen lair and block the entrance to the burrow with my feet. The action often resulted in the rat running up my clothes and more than once with the rat running inside my trouser legs to escape the terrier, but I learned to tuck my trousers into my socks before ratting began and to tolerate a rodent racing up my trousers and jacket.

I have few qualities that commend me as a person, but I have great patience where dogs and hunting are concerned. Many times I have had to visit a rat infested spot twenty or more times before my terrier showed enthusiasm for the hunt and many times more before my terrier puppy actually caught a rat. In fact I can think of only one occasion when my terriers took to ratting on their first trip. My best bitch, Beltane, was mated to her brother Vampire and despite the fact that both parents were typey elegant dogs the offspring, I called them Phobos and Deimos, were decidedly ugly. Handsome is as handsome does however and on their first day's ratting they caught and killed twenty rats. Their mother Beltane was less precocious though she became a truly excellent rat killer. My diary indicates that she caught a rat only after some twenty trips out with the ratting team, but after that time her nose became so incredible and her agility such that no rat hunt was complete without her.

Ratting a puppy in the company of older dogs is rather a mixed blessing. True the youngster sees rats killed and begins to appreciate his purpose in life. Likewise the puppy soon becomes excited at the prospect of ratting alongside an older dog and often becomes hysterical with excitement as soon it witnesses an older dog killing rats. However puppies are so overmatched by the performances of an older dog that they often hunt badly or refuse to hunt at all when they realise that an older dog will always beat them to a kill. When this is seen to happen it is wise to leave the older dog at home for a night or two so that the slower developer can experience some success. When two puppies from the same litter are acquired by the same owner it is often the case that one only comes into its own after the other has died. Sometimes apparently slower whelps are passed on by disgruntled owners and in the hands of new owners (away from conflict with more precocious little mates) many slow starters begin to realise their potential. Bill Mossman a Devonshire terrier man tells the tale of two young terriers he purchased and one seemed so backward that he questioned as to whether she was capable of working well. At four years of age she was so far behind her kennel mate that Bill wondered if he had made a bad purchase when he bought the bitch. On the death of the older bitch the younger animal improved beyond recognition and she became the mother of Mossman's highly successful terrier team.

Yet another problem concerning starting a puppy alongside an older experienced ratter is that the older dog will usually seize the rat a split second before the puppy who also grabs at the rodent. When two ratting dogs seize the same rat neither can kill the rat by shaking it and the rat creates havoc with one or both of the terriers before it expires. An older terrier one that has already experienced considerable success at ratting will weather the biting regardless of the pain it experiences. A younger terrier will not usually be as resilient and may become extremely charry about tackling a rat for months after the incident. Such was the case with Blaze a bitch I once owned. Blaze was sired by Warlock an excellent sire with a track record for producing game and gutsy terriers and Blaze showed terrific early promise. At five months of age she was mad keen to rat, but on her first trip she ran in on Beltane her aunt who had seized a particularly large old doe rat and Blaze prevented Beltane dispatching the rat quickly. In seconds Blaze and Beltanes' faces were awash with blood and the younger bitch leaped back thereby allowing Beltane a chance to kill her rat neatly. I noticed that for the rest of the evening the puppy stayed well clear of the scrimmages that go hand in hand with most catches and was shy of catching rats that raced past her. She continued to behave in this manner for two weeks, so she was relegated to the rank of first reserve and left at home for a month or so. After having forgotten the incident she returned to the fray and became a seasoned ratter for the rest of her life.

It is always wise to seek out good ratting spots and work them regularly so that the owners of such places can see that your visits are having some effect on a rat infested area. Poisoning is a much more effective method of reducing rats than is hunting them with dogs, so owners of rat infested properties need to see rapid results lest they use poison in preference to allowing a person to rat with terriers. For this reason I always visited the place I intended to rat several times making some excuse for leaving my terriers behind and only when I was well aquainted with the layout of the property and the rat runs did I allow my terriers to accompany me on my trips. I was thus able to block exits and conduct the hunt in an efficent manner that convinced the owner of the property that my terrier pack was effective. In my early days I frequently fielded some very efficient ratting terriers to little avail and lost many good ratting places before I learned that reconnaisance was absolutely essential before I conducted a rat hunt. Rats know the area where they live and feed well: in fact their very lives depend on whether or not they are able to return to their warrens quickly and efficiently when danger threatens. Dogs often take considerable time to learn the layout of an area (and thereby intercept the flight of rats to their lairs) and often look terribly inefficient while aquainting themselves with the plot they are required to hunt. When I lived in Rotherham I owned a superb ratting terrier called San – he had a good if not superb nose, was a lightning quick catch dog and had that almost innate quality known as ratting sense (he could predict when and how rats would bolt). I hunted him every weekend and twice during the week and I was justly proud of him. During San's prime I was once asked to hunt a pig farm near Rotherham and unwisely I allowed him to hunt the spot without prior reconnaisance of the area. San tried his hardest and so did I, but we made a pitiful show of ratting the farm in front of the owner and his far from complimentary sons. We were never given a second chance to rat the farm – the owner simply laid down poison after he dismissed our ratting team as useless. Had I been allowed time to reconnoitre the farm prior to hunting it, it would have been a different matter.

On the subject of a ratting team – ratting terriers and human assistants – it is wise to assemble such a group with care. It took me five years to select a suitable team of human assistants to aid my terrier team and there were many unfortunate accidents during the selection process. Rats inspire such a fear amongst people that they often act erratically and kick and flail at the rats that approach them. Terriers are small tough dogs but easily damaged by such frantic actions and more than once have I seen dogs knocked unconscious by a hitherto apparently sane and sensible person lashing out madly with a stick. I forbade sticks after a while, and lunatics who turned up with guns were never invited again – guns and ratting terriers constitute a recipe for disaster and I have never allowed gunmen near my ratting team. No one, not even a person with the skills of a Daniel Boone, is able to shoot at rats that are flushed by dogs without endangering the lives of terriers.

It is also good policy to discourage bizarrely dressed people to ones' hunts. Many are admittedly harmless but farmers and landowners are conservative in their habits and view the appearance of curiously clad people with some reservations. Ratting places, excellent spots where a terrier team can be hunted for a lifetime are hard to come by and all efforts should be made to ensure that one's team is always welcome at such places. I vetted every person in my team with great care – I made some mistakes admittedly but my careful selection programme meant that I kept my ratting places for many years – though I freely admit I offended many people.

Ratting is such an exciting sport that it can be considered not only as a way of starting terriers to hunt larger quarry but as an end in itself. During the years I ran the Huddlesford Rat Pack I had great pleasure and would not have changed a single night's hunting. Our hauls were sometimes enormous and at other times small, but because the team of terriers were well trained and the 'field' equally well trained the sport and social life was terrific.

Our principal 'meet' was on a Thursday night and the field arrived shortly before sundown. We allowed an hour for the rats to come out to feed and crated our terrier pack – at one time we fielded thirty adult terriers. We hunted poultry farms on Thursday, deep litter pens where thousands of Cobbs ate themselves to a state of fleshy helplessness before slaughter or thousand upon thousand of Thombers hybrids lived out their days cramped in two by two cages converting four ounces of meal per day into pale brown eggs before growing prematurely old and fit only for the boiler market. The stench in these poultry houses was often ghastly, the excrescence exuded ammonia strong enough to deter a hyena, and the heat made ones eyebrow's crawl. Feeding in, and nesting under, these poultry houses were hundreds and hundreds of rats which emerged to feed as soon as the sun set and dined and cavorted until dawn. Hardly the most pleasant of places perhaps but each hunt night terriers and human beings alike experienced an 'adrenalin high' at the prospect of hunting such places.

Our plan of action was simple and highly organised. The terriers had been completely stock broken before we allowed them to hunt poultry pens and all congregated at the doors of the battery houses we intended to hunt. The doors were opened, the field and terriers flashed inside the sheds with the field taking up prearranged positions and the terriers hunting in the dung and mess under the battery cages. At a signal members of the field began to prod the mounds under the cages to encourage the rats to run to the floor while others of the 'field' blocked holes to prevent the rats escaping from the building. The whole process was enacted quickly, quietly and efficiently with not so much as a hint of pandemonium. Each member of the field knew his or her task (a third of the field were usually women) and each dog knew exactly what to do. The hunts were spectacular and successful because the meets were highly organised. Over the years the quality of the meets and the sport engendered by the pack attracted numerous celebrities: boxers, film and stage actors and actresses and numerous television producers and stars and we kept the ratting places and the spectators simply because the event was highly organised and the dogs completely trained and stock broken. Not one of the team was allowed to use a stick to intercept the rats though sticks were used to push out rats from the mounds of dung in which they were hiding. A dozen international newspapers reported the hunts and it became an extremely prestigious honour to be invited as a spectator on a Thursday night.

Rats are curious creatures and have the most peculiar effect on people who come in contact with them. The sight of a single rat causes the spectator to exclaim that the place is 'overrun with rats' and quite an ordinary sized rat will be considered 'the size of a cat' by an untrained observer. The fact is that few rats are larger than twelve ounces in weight and a rat weighing a pound would be a very large animal indeed. Giant rats are rare: I have seen few that exceeded a pound in weight and fewer still that were the size of a large kitten let alone the size of a cat. Our largest rat – and we caught many thousand rats – weighed in at two pounds four ounces, less than a third the size of the average cat, but surely the British record for a brown rat.

These Huddlesford Rat Pack meets were both spectacular and highly organised and celebrities such as Tora Koruwa and Teddy Moritz journeyed from Japan and America respectively to watch a single night's hunting. However, it is possible to experience equally exciting sessions of hunting in less spectacular surroundings though admittedly with smaller bags. Any waterway even a small brook that passes near an urban connurbation will have a fairly healthy rat population. Rats are none too choosy about the food they eat and a single family of rats will seemingly exist on the poorest quality diet. The proximity of a barley mill to a stream or brook, or better still an abbatoir, is almost a guarantee of the presence of rats. Indeed I find it hard not to relate the tale of a horse slaughterhouse at Monfaucon where the soil surrounding the abbatoir was so undermined by the burrowing of rats that no one could approach the building without falling into the myriad tunnels dug by these rodents.

Few brooks will sustain such a rat population though my earliest ratting forays were carried out along a black brook that fed the coal washers ad carried such a quantity of fine coal dust silt that the banks of the stream could be ignited with a blowtorch. Piles of twigs and rubbish formed islands in the stream in summer and once these twigs had time to subside they hosted a fairly large rat population. I learned much of my rat work from hunting these islands of garbage, my terrier sniffing out the presence of rats in the rubbish while I poked and pried until the rats panicked into bolting in the stream. These early ratting trips taught me much of the ways of terriers and to appreciate the value of a good nose in a hunting dog. A good nose is seldom rated by modern terrier men, many of whom seem content to simply take terriers on couples and release them into the mouths of inhabited fox earths. This type of hunting does little to exploit the full potential of working terriers and certainly limits the sport one can obtain from terriers. For some curious reason many terrier men are derisive about a man who uses his terrier team to hunt rat – though I have a sneaking suspicion that many terrier men who scoff at rat hunting are secretly terrified of rats. Nothing teaches the terrier man the merits of a good nose in a terrier as much as ratting and nothing more than a rat hunt on a river bank or amongst garbage.

The best 'nose' for rat work I have ever seen was my own terrier Beltane. By the time she was born the beagle, bull terrier, fell and Jack Russell blood I had introduced into the strain had jelled until the type had become level and in my own opinion extemely attractive. The family or type had however retained much of the nose it had inherited from its beagle ancestors, and in Beltane this incredible nose could be seen to good advantage. If she sniffed at a rat warren more than once the place was inhabited and she could determine the difference between a hole into which a rat had just run and escaped from another exit and a lair that still held a rat. It is illogical to suggest that any animal is infallible in any way – and courting disaster to state so, one should add, but throughout Beltane's fifteen years on this earth I never found her to make a single mistake when marking rats. Her ultimate triumph occurred in 1984 when we filmed the first half of a television documentary called *A Lone Furrow* ('a man who would be his own man must indeed follow a lone furrow'). Steve Jones had invented a gas gun – a motorcycle engine that belched forth fumes, carbon monoxide and smoke to remove rats from a piggery and the machine had caused the collapse of some of my dogs that stood reeling and swaying around the holes from which these rats were exploding. Beltane too stood swaying and tottering but marked the presence of every rat in the wall. Ironically, her children had only moderate noses and her grandchildren even less than moderate senses of smell but her great-grandchildren have somehow inherited their ancestors incredible olfactory senses.

Two of her great-grandchildren, Paul Florkovski's dog Sid and Richard Morley's dog Toby both marked burrows and rat lairs from the nest and by the age of five months were marking holes like seasoned veterans – but the subject of teaching or encouraging a dog to mark holes will be dealt with at a later stage in the book.

The process of ratting along a brookside requires a dog that is willing and eager to take to the water and when dogs are excited by the chase they seldom refuse to take to water when a rat plops out of its lair into a stream. Ratting along a brook bank is indeed an excellent way of encouraging water-shy dogs to swim. Only once have I owned a terrier that did not take to water readily and willingly. In 1964 I bred a bitch called Ping (it is perhaps a mistake to allow four year old children to name terriers) that was a nailer to rat, rabbit or fox but was decidedly water shy during her first season. When rats plopped into the brook she ran up and down the bank barking while other dogs swan after their rats and killed them. Ping was decidedly water shy, but to throw her into the stream to encourage her to swim would have been a terrible mistake that would have rendered her water shy for ever. I broke her of her water shyness by walking into the brook until the water lapped around the top of my Wellington boots and after a spell of barking and whining piteously Ping decided to join me. For some reason best known to her she became a passionate hunter of rats along river banks after that time and preferred to stand chest deep in water to await the rats that exploded from their lairs when I put a ferret into the bank.

I have always kept a diary since I was old enough to write and an entry in 1946 must surely have been an indication of the life I was to lead. The entry reads 'Dogs can't kill rats when they are swimming' – a somewhat ungrammatical attempt at explaining that when dogs are treading water they are unable to shake a rat to death. My father, never an understanding sort of parent, read my private diary and commented angrily 'Do you think you'll be able to earn your living writing about rats!' Yet even at the age of nine I was aware that dogs had trouble not only in catching but in killing rats in deep brooks. Unless a dog's feet are on terra firma it will seldom even attempt to shake a rat and will often carry the rat in its mouth enduring terrific lacerations before it can find solid ground beneath its feet and kill the rat. Jack Ivester Lloyd writing in one of the early Midland Working Terrier Club booklets records that he observed his West Highland white terrier carry rats back to the bank before dispatching them, but the truth is very few rats are killed in deep water which is maybe why ratters living along the banks of the river Aire in Yorkshire tended to prefer a leggy terrier-cum-hound that eventually became known as the Airedale terrier. Leggy terriers usually make the best ratting terriers for working in water if not on land though I would prefer a ratting dog that was agile rather than simply leggy but clumsy. Some of the best terriers for ratting in deep water were Border terriers bred down from Ch. Deerstone Destiny and owned by Tony Bell of Swinton, Yorkshire. These dogs swam like otters and were happier in rather than out of water. When Bell swam the river – and I have seen him do so in mid-winter – his Borders followed him like dab chicks following a moorhen. In deep water his terriers put my own dogs to shame.

On the subject of a dog being unable to kill a rat while the dog is treading water a tale concerning the river adjoining the Swinton maggot factory comes readily to mind. Ping had recently mastered the art of swimming after rats and become addicted to the activity. One rat bolted into the river near the factory and failing to find a sanctuary on the home bank, struck out for the far side of the river with Ping swimming after it. She caught her rat lifting it high out of the water but because she was still treading water failed to kill the creature. As she was swimming to the home bank I saw her flinch a dozen or so times and her face was awash with blood as she proceeded to kill the rat on the near side bank. A gash extending from her eye to her nose caused a flap of skin and muscle to part company with the rest of the face and the rip needed professional stitching to close it. Poor old Ping – she still bore the scars of the encounter when I identified her body a month later. Thieves had stolen her from my kennels and she escaped from their car only to be struck by a passing van. It was my first encounter with terrier thieves – sadly it was not my last. Good working terriers attract thieves like honey attracts flies these days.

In passing I should add that Ping was the prototype of the Plummer terrier. She was chestnut red and white in colour, straight fronted, very game and measured twelve inches at the shoulder. She was the first blanket-marked terrier I ever produced and frankly one of the best looking. Had she lived to produce a litter she would have shortened my breeding programme by twenty years or so. Thieves literally dogged the creation of a distinct type of terrier.

Terrier men who insist they only hunt fox – does such a claim add to a man's masculinity I wonder – are unaware of the amount of training and practice a good ratting dog requires particularly if the dog is required to dig out rats from their lairs. At one time I hunted a really great ratting spot ajacent to a maggot factory in Mexborough, a place where rats could always be found at one time but for some reason – a rodent killing epidemic perhaps – one year the rats disappeared and never returned in the same number ever again. The land around the meat piles – for maggots are fed on cadavers of creatures long dead – was honeycombed with rat warrens and each day as soon as school closed I put a spade in my vehicle and went to dig out the rats at the Mexborough maggot factory. San, who never could lay claim to having a great nose, became amazingly adept at winkling out and killing rats in these places. His technique was to dig frantically, keeping a weather eye open for rats which were panicked into flight by his digging action while I slotted the rat warrens gently with a spade to facilitate his digging. We learned to work in accord with one another and as we did so our haul of rats increased accordingly. On Boxing Day 1964, while others with more social graces followed the local fox hounds, I dug one hundred and six rats with him before lunchtime and a further eighty-six after I had rinsed my hands in a stagnant brook and eaten my sandwiches. It is amazing that during my entire spell in Rotherham I was never ill except for one spell when comedian Tony Capstick and I drank a spirit distilled from decayed beetroot by a local lunatic.

However, to regularly obtain large hauls of rats during daylight hours it is necessary to find some way of causing the rats to leave their lairs and the best pieces of equipment to move rats from deep lairs are ferrets.

Ferrets

Apart from one brief spell when in 1972 a mild distemper outbreak wiped out all my puppies and kits alike, I have seldom not been associated with ferrets. Indeed I have always thought that my only claim to fame is the fact that I once was recognised by hunting enthusiast and anti-hunters alike by the fact that my interview twith Richard Whitely to promote my book *Modern Ferreting* was voted the worst piece of television coverage by the viewers of Denis Norden's *It Will Be All Right on the Night*. For the few who did not watch this horrendous howler I had best explain. In order to publicise my book I had agreed to an interview with Richard Whitely of *Calendar* and *Countdown* fame and brought along a box of ferrets as visual aids, so to speak. My own ferrets are or rather were dark polecat coloured specimens but to create more interest I had borrowed a pair of white ferrets from a friend known as Paddy Danks who died early in 1988 I should add. Ferrets need to be handled from the nest onwards if they are not to become a bit nippy and to cut a very long story short Paddy seldom handled his kits. They were 'sharp' when I fetched them out of the cage at 'Chez Danks' but if one intends to perform in front of a camera with ferrets they can be gentled – for a time at least – by allowing the kits to glut themselves with milk, and ferrets are inordinately fond of milk one should add.

Thus just prior to the interview I allowed all the ferrets, my own and Danks' 'biters' to fill up on milk and thus the ferrets suitably doped or calmed were easily handled – for a time at least. My interview took longer than expected and I waited for Roger de Courcy to finish his ventriloquist act with Nookie his incredibly rude Teddy Bear. An hour later I performed in front of the camera with my own extremely docile ferrets while Richard Whitely stroked and petted the Dank's biters – that no longer replete with milk had become a little playful and that proved to be a slight understatement. The upshot of the matter was that while Whitely stroked the white jill ferret with his hands the jill examined Whitely's fingers with her teeth and my interview degenerated into chaos. This I believe is my one and only claim to fame – a poor sort of boast for a man who has lived some fifty years on this planet. Still that's show business one supposes.

Properly handled, properly fed ferrets seldom bite. Indeed at Abbott Brothers, Britain's biggest ferret breeders relatively unhandled stock is gentled by overfeeding for fat ferrets are seldom fierce ferrets. Kits straight from the nest may attempt to bite ones fingers but I believe this is more in play than a manifestation of anger. I simply do not expect my adult ferrets to bite in any circumstances and when I crate them before light for a day's hunting I simply reach into the nest boxes and take out the ferrets I want. I gaze in wonder at the gloved hands of some ferret keepers, for frankly I cannot imagine how people allow ferrets to get so out of hand.

I have known only two biters I have literally given up on and those were bred by a man in Tamworth who clearly had not even tried to gentle the kits. I was 'low' on ferrets at the time and hence I paid lurcher enthusiast Terry Ahern £2.50 a kit to get me replacements. Terry promptly produced two kits that bit me as soon as they left the box. My fingers poured blood from the bites, but I soldiered on and allowed the kits to drink themselves full from a bowl of milk. When I deemed them to be full gorged I handled them again and received a savage biting for my troubles. When I allowed them to run around the floor they sought out my ankles and in seconds blood began to seep through my socks. If I am nothing else I am tenacious and stubbornly persistent, so for the next few days I continued to try to handle the kits and gentle them. If I offered them milk from the palm of my hand they sniffed the milk and promptly savaged the palm of my hand. Many kits nip in play or to encourage their owners to play with them. These kits however were loathe to play and displayed an almost reptilian indifference to overtures of friendship from me. After a fortnight they were given away to Jack Legge who used a glove to handle the kits. They were totally unsuitable to use as ratting ferrets which need to be easily handled, but it should be stated that kits of this sort are extremely rare, and I have yet to see their like during my many years of rat hunting. Most ferrets are, despite their reputation, extremely friendly creatures and it should be stated that one has more chance of being bitten by a kitten than by the average ferret kit.

Basically ferrets come in two colour phases – the dark fitch or polecat coloured ferrets commonly referred to as polecats, though the polecat is the wild ancestor of the domesticated ferret, and the white albino ferret. In addition tp the polecat ferret, the sandy ferret also occurs and these can range from pale polecat coloured specimens to very light sandy ferrets. Colour is unimportant however for each colour phase boasts good and bad specimens. Most ratters favour white ferrets for it is argued that in the rough and tumble of a rat hunt a brown ferret might be mistaken for a rat. This just is not true, for a terrier that will kill a brown ferret will be equally unfriendly to a white one. It is good policy to let ratting terriers see ferrets every day so that they may become truly familiar with their allies.

However, while it can be argued that the colour of a ratting ferret is unimportant, the sex of the said ferret is (and not merely to another ferret one should add). Hobs (males) which are nearly twice as big as jills are seldom small enough to venture into a rat hole to flush a rat and hence only the smaller jills are used for ratting. Hobs are not without courage enough to face a rat – far from it for in places where a hob can crawl few rats will stand their ground against them and many will kill rats in seconds if the rat refuses to bolt. Few hobs are small enough to negotiate small tunnels however and hence jills particularly large powerful jills are ideal for ratting.

Shortly after World War I advertisements for greyhound ferrets started appearing in the pages of the sporting press. Greyhound ferrets were long lean ferrets but very heavy and powerfully muscled creatures bred specifically to work rats. These greyhound ferrets most of which were white but sandy and polecat 'greyhounds' certainly existed were highly priced and reputedly more aggressive with rats than conventional ferrets. Furthermore they had a reputation for being fleet of foot and extraordinarily agile creatures so that they were of little use as rabbiting ferrets as they were reluctant to allow a rabbit to bolt. During the myxamatosis era from 1953 onwards, it was difficult to sell ferrets for rabbits teetered on the brink of extinction so the majority of ferrets were sold as 'greyhounds'. The term now bastardised fell into disuse and though advertisements for greyhound ferrets were seen as late as 1963 seldom does one hear of greyhound ferrets today, though from time to time long heavy fast moving greyhound types appear in litters of quite ordinary rabbiting ferrets.

A ratting ferret's life is relatively short, particularly if a ferret is ratted regularly or more to the point ratted during the summer months. Ferrets often bluff rats into bolting and large heavy rats will often flee before tiny ferrets that would come off extremely badly in a tangle with a rat should the rat choose to stand its ground and fight. Buck rats rarely retaliate against a ferret even when the ferret sets to to eat the rat alive – a hideous practise that mustelids commonly perform in the wild Does are often another matter. When a doe has tiny pink young she will (when she is mature) stand her ground against stoat, weasel or ferret, though as soon as the young are capable of bolting she will escape alongside them. Does that have just drawn bedding to make a nest are particularly aggressive with a ferret and will drive them out of the hole and sometimes pursue them on the surface of the soil. Once when ferreting in Harlaston near Mexborough I watched a ferret 'tail in a gale' back out of a rat warren as if the devil pursued it. A large doe rat bloated with young followed her out, startling my dogs which were astonished to witness the spectacle and then she escaped back into the hole from whence she had come. To try to bolt such a rat a second time is lunacy and extremely destructive to ferrets. Furthermore a doe such as this will bite and molest even the bravest ferret so savagely that ferrets will be reluctant to face a rat ever again.

If jills are not rested during the summer months they are seldom prepared to face a rat after the first season and will often refuse to enter a rat warren after they have received a mauling from a doe with young or a female rat that has drawn a nest. Jills worked only during the winter months when rats do not usually breed will often continue to rat for several years, but once they have experienced a particularly bad mauling they are usually shy of facing a rat again. Ivor Hawkins a Yorkshire rat catcher once told me that he kept several dozen jills – mostly panda faced polecat ferrets were his preference, but as soon as they were mauled by rats he put them in a separate cage and sold them to rabbit hunters, for they were no longer of use to him.

Sometimes however a particularly tenacious ferret is born and these are worth their weight in gold. I bought such a paragon from Doncaster market in the mid-1960s and the purchase was the best 75p I have ever spent. She survived tangle after tangle with rats and killed many hundred and bolted ten times that number. She was so tame that even tail in a gale – a ferret warning sign one should add – hot from a battle with a rat she would allow me to pick her up and handle her.

Before proceeding further it should be mentioned that many keen ferret keepers refuse to 'rat' their wards because of the hurt a rat may cause the ferrets. Indeed many modern ferreting books hint it is almost immoral to hunt rat with a ferret. There is of course more than a hint of truth in this belief and I confess I have seen many ferrets bitten by rats. If it is any consolation to these ferret keepers it should be pointed out that a rat rarely kills a ferret and once the ferret senses it is over-matched by a rat it makes a discreet exit from the scene of the battle. Henceforth it refuses to engage the said rat again. Still it must be pointed out that rats can and do bite ferrets.

When I lived in Rotherham I believe I was regarded as the local crank who kept dogs and ferrets and numerous stray animals and birds were brought to my house. If I had been a rabbit hunter I would have never wanted for ferrets for every stray ferret found wandering in Rotherham was taken to my house. Stray ferrets usually work rabbit extremely well, particularly if they are found wandering in a district which has a healthy population of rabbits. Many strays have also encountered rats in their wanderings and have usually had such a bad time with these rodents that they are reluctant to go to ground in inhabited lairs. During my stay in Rotherham I was given some thirty stray ferrets by well wishers who believed I ran an animal sanctuary, but not one ferret proved to be a good ratter.

I made a rule of never working a kitten ferret to rat before its first Christmas and even then I endeavoured to give a kitten some experience at hunting rabbits in the months leading up to Christmas. So many kittens are ruined by over-matching to rat too soon and once a kitten is over-matched it will never work rat again. A half season working rabbit usually works wonders and shortly after Christmas a kitten is usually mature enough to face most rats. It is also policy to stop working rats with ferrets as soon as young rats start to appear, not because rats should be afforded a respite in order to breed, but simply because doe rats are extremely ferocious with ferrets during the rat breeding season. A ferret so managed will usually give a season and a half of work before it decides to quit cold, after which it is of no use as a ratting ferret.

During a ferreting session it is not uncommon for a jill ferret to follow hot on the heels of the bolting rat, or even to be latched to the rat which drags the ferret from the hole as the rodent tries to escape. The whole process, ferret inserted into hole – ferret locates rat, rat bolts, ferret follows – can take place in a split second or so and hence dogs must be completely familiar with ferrets and must understand that they are never under any circumstances allowed to bite ferrets. So a complex process of familiarising ferrets with dogs and vice versa must take place and should this training process not be properly conducted the ratter's turnover of ferrets will be truly staggering.

A chapter heading in that enormous tome *Famous Last Words* must surely read 'I'm sure he'll be all right with ferrets' – a statement that is usually a prelude to an incident that is both unpleasant and also costly. Terriers are not automatically 'all right with ferrets' nor are they born 'ferret broken'. Terriers are natural killers which if not trained, will kill a ferret as eagerly as they would kill a rat. It is also worth remembering that the majority of working terriers are extremely badly trained and are seldom broken to ferret. Yet when I regularly ferreted rat for my terrier team I often had visitors turn up, half mad terriers on slips or couples to ask to try their dogs. Each and every one assured me that they were sure their terriers were 'all right with ferrets' despite the fact that the lunges of the crazy beasts towards my ferrets convinced me otherwise. A sub-heading of the chapter 'I'm sure he'll be all right with ferrets' usually reads 'I'll keep him on the lead while we hunt' which usually means 'He'll take a little longer to kill your ferret, but he'll get there, never fear'. At one time I ferreted rats every weekend and groaned aloud when I saw a man, terrier on leash, walking towards me. When I saw such a sight I boxed my ferrets and walked away. It just was not worth the trouble arguing with someone who was bound to assure me he had – (a) control of his dog (b) a terrier that was fine with ferrets or (c) a lead on which he would keep the terrier during the hunt. Unless my visitor too carried a box of ferrets and was prepared to use them in preference to my own jills I simply packed up and went home. Yet a terrier that is unbroken to ferret is denied ninety per cent of its sporting potential.

Puppies are so easily broken to ferrets though adult terriers, particularly adult terriers that have killed rats, can be perfectly hellish to break to ferrets. I encourage all my puppies to become well and truly acquainted with ferrets, smack the puppies if they become boisterous with the ferrets and allow the ferrets to nip a puppy if the terrier becomes obstreperous. Once and only once has my system of ferret breaking come unstuck and I believe this incident could have been avoided had I been more vigilant.

In 1989 I owned a white hob – a gift hob I had reluctantly taken on when a local farmer had found it wandering on his land. The hob was tame, friendly and not a particularly good worker to rabbit. Hence I decided he was absolutely ideal to use to break puppies to ferret. I placed him on my kitchen floor and allowed Trembling a grandson of Vampire to sniff at the ferret. Trembling, never a brave dog, wagged his tail at the sight of the ferret and all looked well. Suddenly the telephone rang and I hastened to answer it leaving Trembling sniffing the ferret. The call turned out to be a rather strange sounding woman asking where she could get a Tibetan terrier without actually leaving Caithness – I am listed in Yellow Pages under Kennels. Politely I explained I could not help the lady and as I did I heard a gurgling sound from the kitchen. I terminated the call a little less than politely and raced into the kitchen only to find the ferret was trying to bite Trembling through the base of his skull. Clearly the ferret was not broken to terriers. Trembling recovered, but the incident left him with an implacable hatred of ferrets that will be hard to erradicate. We all make mistakes – and I have made a great many mistakes in my time.

I always allow great familiarity twixt terriers and ferrets once I am certain one species will not harm the other and encourage the puppy and ferrets to cavort and play together. It is absolutely essential that a terrier should regard the ferret as an ally and be able to recognise the difference between a rat and a ferret instantly. Terriers with phenomenal reflexes – I have owned only one such terrier in my life I should add and I have seen but two of these wonderful dogs – often make a dart at a ferret as it appears in the mouth of an earth but recoil as quickly as they move once they realise the creature is a ferret not a rat.

At this point it is perhaps expedient to discuss the subject of teaching a dog to mark inhabited rat warrens and lairs. Considerable time can be saved if a dog can be taught to mark a warren that is inhabited and communicate its message to the owner. A dog that will seek out, find and communicate to its owner that a rat or rats are living in a certain hole is an absolute treasure to own and it is relatively easy to teach such a dog. If I might digress a little to illustrate a point: many years ago archaeologists were baffled by the presence of picture writing on the tombs of long dead Egyptian Kings, yet no one could translate this curious script into something meaningful. Then one day during the Napoleonic Wars a French soldier unearthed a tablet of stone (the Rosetta Stone) on one portion of which was a message written in heiroglyphics while the other bore the translation in Ancient Greek.

Scholars were able to translate Ancient Greek and hence were now able to translate heiroglyphics.

It is my belief that dogs try to communicate with their handlers – and not just my belief for Conrad Lorenz expresses this view in his book *King Solomon's Ring*. The problem is that dogs are unable to speak in a human tongue and hence have to communicate their rather limited messages by a series of gestures or facial expressions. What is needed is a Rosetta Stone to interpret what the dog is trying to tell the handler.

Different dogs use different techniques to communicate their messages to their handlers and it is the duty of the handler to learn the language the dog is trying to speak – and some dogs do try so hard to speak. In order to learn the way a dog is trying to indicate that a rat lair is occupied and not recently vacated but with a strong scent of rat still lingering around the lair, dogs may point one paw raised, whine at the mouth of the earth or scratch at the hole, but can the handler learn exactly what these gestures mean? If a hunter observes a rat running down a lair and not appearing from another hole he can assume the lair is occupied. Hence the behaviour of the dog, the gestures, the facial expressions the dog manifests when examining the hole, indicate the hole is occupied. The handler knows the lair is occupied – he has just observed the rat disappearing into the confines of the lair – hence the lair that is known to be inhabited takes on the nature of a Rosetta Stone.

Marking improves ten-fold if the mark is honoured by ferreting the hole the dog has marked immediately. This action reinforces the action of marking for the action of inserting a ferret in the hole the dog has marked to produce a rat for the dog to pursue and possibly catch, gives the dog pleasure and hence the animal becomes wed to the process of marking an earth. If I see a terrier mark a rat I endeavour to bolt it for the dog (even if I do not have a ferret with me) by poking and prodding the soil surrounding the lairs or digging out the rat for the dog to pursue, particularly if the terrier is a puppy, for nothing improves a dog's propensity to mark inhabited holes as much as 'honouring' the action of marking.

Terriers should be under control while a ferret works a rat below ground and should not scamper from lair to lair scratching at the holes and hence actively preventing or delaying the rat from bolting. Most successful ferreters – and the majority of terrier men seldom have enough control of their dogs to justify the title 'successful ferreter' sit their dogs next to the lair to await the bolting of the rat. 'Sitting a dog' while a ferret works below ground to bolt the rat is a counter-productive action. Rats flash from their lairs and in the space of a micro-second seem to find sanctuary in another hole or place of refuge from which they usually refuse to bolt if ferreted a second time. Hence if the dog is to catch the rat in the split second available the dog needs to be standing near the hole for a sitting dog needs to perform two distinct movements to be able to errupt into flight after the fleeing rat. In the time a terrier takes to galvanise into action from the sit position the rat will usually make good its escape. Hence it is policy to have the dog standing near the hole rather than sitting some feet from the lair. This method of fixing a dog is easily taught and if the handler simply places a hand on the shoulder of the terrier to restrict it from wandering or sniffling at holes in a few sessions of training the terrier will learn to freeze when a ferret is inserted in a rat warren. I have never restricted terriers or lurchers when I ferret rat or rabbits and I allow them to pussy-foot gingerly between the warrens. Terriers which adopt this technique of ratting over ferrets are usually extremely successful at nailing rats just as they leave the holes. My rough-coated terrier San developed this skill to the level of an art form. He would walk as gently as if he was walking on eggs to the hole where he judged the ferret was engaging a rat and freeze, not moving a muscle, not blinking an eye, immobile as a stone as a rat crept out of a hole, and then San would snatch at the rat only when the tip of its tail left the hole and it had no means of escape. Curiously not one of his children manifested this peculiarity but many of his grand-children inherited this curious and highly efficient hunting technique. This was an instinctive method of hunting, an innate disposition that I have observed caged dingoes exploit in earth floored cages under which rats had burrowed. Later in the family Omega inherited this propensity to a degree that put the ancient dog to shame for she would freeze for an hour or more while a rat slowly made up its mind to bolt rather than face a ferret that was working the warren behind it. I believe this instinctive behaviour reached its highest state of development in Omega, for not one of her many great grandchildren has shown a tendency to work rat with such intense concentration. She was perhaps my ultimate ratting terrier in some ways: bright, lightening quick with an attention span to put a Buddhist monk to shame and in all probability she represents the three minute mile in the development of my terriers – a goal I shall never achieve again!

Successful ratting requires careful organisation if it is to be effective. As soon as a dog marks an inhabited rat warren and long before a ferret is put to ground to bolt the rats the handler should be viewing the area round the warren to ascertain where the rat will bolt. Holes adjacent to the inhabited lair should be blocked or if the holes have been dug in an earth bank stamped in or filled in with a spade. Rats are quick rather than fast and are capable of flashing from one hole to the next, but are rarely capable of affording a terrier a lengthy chase. From the time the rat bolts until it takes refuge in another hole is often less than a second. Hence holes near the inhabited lair should be blocked before ferreting a rat warren takes place. Likewise equipment, rubbish, waste or any other material under which rats may take cover should be removed or shifted so that the landscape over which the rats may bolt will be unfamiliar to the rodent. Rats can flash to and fro over a familiar landscape at a pace considerably in excess of that of a dog. If the hunter intends to be successful at the art of catching rats – and the technique of catching rats is indeed an art – great care has to be taken before the hunt begins. Punctilious attention to detail, anticipation of the possible flight paths of rats, and an understanding of the ways of rats will turn possible bedlam into a successful hunt.

Ratting is an ideal way of preparing a terrier for other work, but many terrier men are not enthusiastic about allowing terriers to hunt rat. Brian Nuttall arguably one of the most scientific breeders of working terriers in the world, avoids rat hunting his terriers. Nuttall acts as terrier man for a mink pack and as mink often take refuge in rat holes during a hunt Nuttall has found that terriers that are ratted regularly often mark and bay at rats as readily as they do mink. Hence Nuttall is reluctant to use his terriers to rat and obviously because mink, like ferrets, are mustelids Nuttall's terriers are not worked in conjunction with ferrets.

Yet ratting can be regarded as a sport in itself let alone a preparation for hunting larger more testing quarry. The Duke of Beaufort, never noted for his epigrams, once stated that ratting came a close second only to fox hunting as a pastime and I can do nothing but agree with this gentleman's sentiments.

Rabbit Hunting with Terriers

Rabbit hunting or rather the hunting of rabbits with terriers is often frowned on by working terrier purists simply because foxes often live in enlarged rabbit warrens and hence fox catching terriers should be absolutely steady to rabbit. Dogs which are regularly used for rabbit hunting, or started on rabbits will invariably mark or bay at rabbits as freely as they will at fox. Hunt terriers that bay at rabbits during a day's work with the hounds are a great nuisance. In fact 'rabbiter' is often used as a derogatory term for a reject hunt terrier, for it is upsetting for a hunt servant to remove twenty tons of earth only to find that the terrier is baying at a terrified rabbit that is wedged into the blind end of a stop.

Yet few terriers are absolutely steady to rabbit. Rabbits seem to excite terriers as much if not more than rats possibly because rabbits are heavily scented but also because rabbits opt for flight when disturbed and the sight of a fleeing animal excites any dog. Puppies start quite easily at rabbits – many terrier men, living in rat free areas, if any areas are completely rat free, often start terriers hunting by allowing them to pursue and catch rabbits. This practice is however condemned by many professional terrier men as it makes terriers 'unsteady' below ground.

However, not everyone shares the view that working hunt terriers to rabbit makes a terrier unsteady to fox. Cyril Breay of Mallerstang and Kirkby Lonsdale described by Wally Wyld and Brian Nuttall as a master at entering a terrier, allowed his puppies to hunt rabbit whenever they were able to do so. Terry Breay, son of Cyril, recalls how as a child he hunted rabbits with Gem a black terrier that is considered by many to be the foundation bitch of the strain of black fell terrier erroneously referred to as the Patterdale. Yet Gem saw considerable work with the Lunesdale Foxhounds and may well have been the terrier that first caused Maurice Bell to ask exactly what breed the terrier was. However at the risk of appearing a devil's advocate it can also be argued that Breay worked the high limestone fells with the Lunesdale Foxhounds and many of the earths found in these fells are created by the effects of the erosion by carbon dioxide charged rain and are relatively rabbit free. It is also worth noting that associates of Breay often remarked on his highly unorthodox ways of entering terriers. Akerigg in 1980 remarked 'It was Mr. Breay's way to break all the rules and still to produce the very best entered terriers one could hope for!'

It is, however, ludicrous to imagine that any terrier is capable of running down a rabbit that has attained top speed though few terriers can resist chasing them. Even Bedlington terriers – more diminutive lurchers than true terriers perhaps – are hard pressed to come to terms with a free running rabbit. However it is equally true to state that many many rabbits are caught by terriers and some terriers have achieved incredible bags of rabbits during a season's hunting. In the 1960s I ran a very uneven pack of terriers at rabbits over rubbish dumps and rough wasteland in Rotherham and secured over thirty rabbits a season while merely exercising the dogs during the evenings and allowing them to chase rabbits that were feeding near their burrows. In 1966 my pack caught sixty-seven rabbits most of which were run to ground in rock piles and drawn by the terriers from the depths of their rock warrens.

It is in fact quite amazing how rabbits adapt to an urban lifestyle. The rock piles I hunted were simply blocks of stone that had been dumped near the motorway that was being built along the bottom of Meadow Bank Road, Rotherham, yet within weeks of the gangs dumping their blocks the piles sported a healthy colony of rabbits. The rabbits appeared as if from nowhere – and while rabbits certainly bred on the railway lines near the motorway the piles of block and rubble tipped in readiness for motorway construction obviously stimulated an upsurge in the rabbit population near Holmes.

It was the custom of the Highways Department of Lichfield Council to tip piles of twigs collected from overhanging trees in certain spots along the county lanes near Lichfield. Mounds of twigs would be tipped in late January and by April these mounds would have consolidated to form dense clumps of branches and earth. By June most of these mounds were honeycombed with rabbits particularly if the mounds were large enough to afford the crowns of these piles good drainage. Rabbits were originally natives of the warmer climes of the Mediterranean lands and hence do not take kindly to nesting in damp and cold earths. It is interesting to note that rabbits that are forced to burrow and breed in damp areas are seldom as large as rabbits that live on the scant herbage of well drained sand dunes.

Strange and curious objects are often utilised as breeding earths by the rabbit. Kits are often produced on rubbish tips – again it should be noted that the clutter affords the rubbish mounds good drainage and does often nest alongside rats amongst drums, barrels and 'seen better days' buckets and pails. In places like this a terrier can be a far more successful rabbit hunter than the fastest lurcher. Swinton Mexborough rubbish tip once housed an incredibly large rabbit population which nested amongst the most frightful rubbish and produced strong healthy coccidiosis free rabbits, though rabbits taken in nearby Harlington which fed on the more lush grasses in that area often manifested livers which were riddled with coccidiosis. Rabbits will in fact live, and even do best, on the roughest and porrest of viands if they can breed in well-drained burrows. Sufficient to say that during my stay in Yorkshire I caught dozens of rabbits on these rubbish tips though it is fair to mention it is virtually impossible for a rabbit hunter to obtain permission to hunt these rubbish tips these days. Refuse dumps are decidedly dangerous places and the possibility of a hunter seeking compensation for the damage done to him while hunting a rubbish tip usually deters owners of such places granting anyone permission to hunt refuse dumps.

It is frequently stated that certain breeds of terrier have long since lost their sporting propensity and to a certain extent this may be the truth. However few terriers are not enthusiastic rabbiting dogs and a great many pet terriers will run to ground in pursuit of these rabbits. Ralph Hodgson of Rowlands Gill, at one time a bastion of the North East Terrier Rescue Society, related the following tale in 1980 .

> Long before the Fell and Moorland Working Terrier Club was formed I was called out to rescue trapped terriers (Hodgson was a pit official, had assisted in many pit rescues, and had a remarkable gift for predicting danger in coal faces). A woman called Mrs Finch used to keep West Highland white or Cairn terriers (I've forgotten which) that regularly ran to ground after rabbits. I dug one terrier from under fifteen feet of earth and it was almost dead when I broke through to it. Yet a week later I was called out to dig the terrier again. It was rabbit mad and I suggested that Mrs Finch or French kept the dog away from the railway lines where there were plenty of rabbits. Mrs Finch lost the terrier later that year and I'll bet it had run to ground and died in the holes.

Mrs Sheila Monkton who bred a superlative strain of Norwich/ Norfolk terrier relates she too had trouble keeping her terriers above ground where rabbits abounded. Yet despite the fact that Norwich/ Norfolk terriers are amongst the smallest of the true working terriers they are seldom small enough to crawl into a earth and seize a rabbit. Lucas (1909) tells a tale of a man who approached him with an offer to sell him tiny miniature dachshunds which he claimed were small enough to get to ground and draw a rabbit. He sent Lucas photographs of the dachshunds alongside the rabbits they were supposed to have drawn but Lucas was quick to see that the rabbits were Flemish Giants – large tame rabbits many times larger than wild conies. Yet Lucas mentions that these dachshunds were small enough to wriggle their way down a four inch wicker pipe. In passing it is worth noting that America huntress Teddy Moritz imports miniature wire-haired dachshunds from Germany and while many are small enough to work and draw woodchuck few are able to walk into earths, negotiate stops and draw rabbits.

Yet terriers do manage to go to ground and dig on to rabbits, and even bolt rabbits from some warrens. Doug Collins an Elgin based austringer and forester states that more than once he has seen rabbits run to ground ahead of his pedigree unknown Jack Russell terrier only to see the dog flash to ground, bay and bolt the rabbit. Collins, a falconry heretic, uses terriers instead of springers and pointers to work alongside the Harris hawks he flies.

In 1969 I had bred a very precocious terrier bitch called Set, a daughter of my stud dog Rupert, and at twelve weeks of age she showed an almost unhealthy interest in catching and killing rabbits. She frequently ran to ground in a grove near my cottage and bolted or drew live rabbits from burrows but as she grew older she became too large to crawl to the rabbits in the stops and needed to dig to any rabbits she intended to catch. She was certainly one of the most precocious terriers I have ever known and had she not died after a milk fever attack in 1973 my present strain of terrier would have carried many lines to her. Her puppies weaned at eight days of age as a result of the untimely death of their dam never developed as I would have liked however and I discontinued what might have been a very useful and typey sort of terrier.

Prior to 1953 few rabbits nested above ground and the majority made nests in deep established warrens. However after myxomatosis reduced the rabbit population to five per cent of its former numbers (it is estimated that Britain hosted 100,000,000 rabbits in 1951) rabbits began nesting above ground in deep gorse or bramble possibly because when myxomatosis wipes out an established warren the tunnels that constitute the said warren tend to fall in and according to Lockley discourage rabbits recolonising these warrens. Tales of a new race of rabbits nesting above ground are however ludicrous though it is a fact that many rabbits will at times build first nests in gorse and bramble and then return to some sort of warren to continue their breeding cycle.

However, breeding does should not concern the terrier man for the hunting of rabbits should be restricted to the winter months when rabbits seldom breed. However even in the depths of winter rabbits sit out in thick cover rather than run to ground and when rabbits sit out in deep cover hunting them with terriers is usually a lot more productive than the use of a lurcher would be in such a situation. If a terrier is hunted to rabbit regularly it soon develops its own special technique of dealing with a rabbit that sits tight in deep gorse or bramble. Dogs which simply charge into thick cover as soon as they scent a rabbit are seldom successful at actually catching the rabbit. A terrier that has refined the technique of catching rabbits that sit out in these conditions will often circle the rabbit several times thereby causing the rabbit to sit tightly before the terrier decides to make the thrust into the thicket to secure the rabbit. Some dogs become extraordinarily adept at nailing sitting rabbits – far more efficient than some lurchers in fact – for many supersaturated lurchers (lurchers with a high proportion of sighthound blood in their make up) never master the skill of nailing sitting rabbits.

It may annoy the purist rabbit hunter, but many terriers give tongue while hunting rabbit. It can be argued that many lurchers give tongue while hunting because they are over-matched by the quarry and the 'opening up' as the quarry escapes is simply a cry for help. Not so the terrier. The baying of a terrier hunting cover is a purposeful activity and may possibly frighten the prey into squatting or sitting tight and thereby precipitating its capture. Certainly pocket beagles, tiny hounds once used to hunt rabbits, bay frantically while drawing a thicket and are very successful at causing rabbits to squat and hence be captured.

Lucas did in fact run a couple of beagles with his rabbit hunting fox terrier pack to encourage the terriers to give tongue – though this is not a good or sound practice and will be discussed later in the book. Bill Mossman who hunts a small terrier pack in Devonshire actively encourages his terriers to give tongue (he is reluctant to keep a mute terrier) simply because not only is the technique enjoyable ('the gentle music of the pack') but the process helps to swell the bag of rabbits captured by the terriers.

However, on the subject of bags and the quality of the carcasses caught by terriers it is fair to point out that terriers are seldom soft-mouthed dogs and rarely are rabbits caught by two or more terriers worth eating. Terriers are however extremely efficient at keeping the rabbit population of a deciduous woodland (and its obligatory ground-cover of brambles and gorse) under control. A single terrier may well produce edible carcasses however and I have seen Irish terriers which would work cover well and were extremely soft-mouthed with the rabbits they caught. I hasten to add they were anything but soft-mouthed with other quarry and were quite vicious with other dogs. Some of the Irish breeds of terrier are in fact dual personalities – fierce when provoked, gentle when stroked, does in fact describe many of the breeds, created in Ireland!

Terriers can however be extremely efficient at working with ferrets particularly if the burrows to be ferreted are located in deep almost impenetrable cover. In such a situation exits and entrances to the burrow cannot be covered with nets and many rabbits which seem to have an almost instinctive gift for detecting which holes are not covered with nets, escape. I worked Set one of my own terriers to rabbit literally from the nest, and she proved a priceless ferreting companion. She would locate any hole in deep cover, whimper as if to encourage me to net the hole, and when I did not or rather could not, for at that time I worked a deep gorse patch that had resisted serious ferreting for a century or so, she simply crouched quivering next to the hole and nailed rabbit after rabbit as it bolted. She was extremely adept at the short sharp dash type catch and once took eight rabbits as they bolted from two holes deep inside a bramble patch. When she died of milk fever it left a void in my life for she was a useful and charming companion. As I write I own a young bitch called Barad – a replica of Set who even manifests the same grinning expression when she is excited but it is doubtful that she will be of the same calibre as her lookalike. When one owns a great dog it is usually great because it is an alloy of many qualities – if one of these qualities is missing the dog becomes somewhat less useful than the great dog. One tends to compare a really great dog with its lookalikes and the comparisons are always odious!

On the subject of working terriers with ferrets it is imperative that the puppy gets to know from the very outset that rabbits entangled in the nets should never be struck at or bitten. I smacked Set just once when she nailed a netted rabbit – and I seldom smack a dog hard I should add – and henceforth she never nailed netted rabbits again nor did she ever tangle in the nets which were placed over the entrances to rabbit warrens. Beltane, a sister of Vampire another excellent worker with an even better nose than Set was less stable. I start rabbiting as soon as the bramble leaves start to fall and for the first two ferreting trips of the season Beltane always nailed rabbits in the net – a sheepish look on her face admittedly – but afterwards she settled and became an excellent netting dog until the end of the season. She died at the age of fifteen but until her last season she always made the mistake of biting at netted rabbits for one or two of the season's first ferreting sessions.

For my sins I once worked Set with a lurcher belonging to a farm labourer called Arthur Doyle who claimed he was related to John L. Sullivan the boxer as well he might have been for it is a curious claim to make if it is not true, but working terriers in conjunction with lurchers is a bad mistake. Doyle owned a medium sized mongrel-bred lurcher that he insisted on calling a deerhound despite its smooth coat and greyhound-like appearance. The dog was innert and simply jogged alongside Doyle seemingly oblivious to the rest of the world. It seldom put its nose down to hunt and was not at all interested in working in the traditional manner expected of lurchers. At one time Doyle obtained employment on a very run-down farm near Market Harborough and the farm sported an enormous patch of gorse that Doyle assured me was 'teeming with rabbits'. Rabbits have a knack of making most men liars and when I arrived at the farm one Sunday I found a few scrub rabbits moving in and out of a 'seen-better-days' gorse patch, the centre of which had become a blackened tangle after someone had tried to burn out the gorse.

At that time I was decidedly short on good rabbiting country and was prepared to travel miles to secure good rabbiting – I regularly travel a hundred miles to hunt rabbit even today. However when I started to hang nets over suitable runs in the gorse – such a technique is seldom successful one should add – Doyle appeared with Bill his lurcher and suggested that he would use Bill to course any rabbit that succeeded in running the gauntlet of Set and the nets. Bill was innert and while it was not broken to ferret it showed little interest in ferrets and less still in terriers. In fact an indifference to life seemed to describe Bill's general attitude, but lurchers are often deceptively dangerous dogs where livestock are concerned.

Despite the shortage of rabbits in the gorse patch the 'whin' was undermined with rabbit burrows and Set moved from entrance to entrance as though baffled by the complexity of the subterranean labyrinth. My ferrets seemed to take an aeon of time locating a rabbit (Set followed the progress of the combat above ground) and took nearly an hour to bolt one. When a rabbit did decide to bolt it avoided Set – who continued to pursue the rabbit – and finding an un-netted run it proceeded to flee for the next patch of gorse. Bill head down, apparently dormant and always apathetic came to life, ran and caught the rabbit, and stood live rabbit in mouth tail wagging as if wondering what to do with its catch (Bill had never been taught to retrieve – or taught anything for that matter for Doyle was as innert and apathetic as his lurcher).

Set followed hot on the heels of the rabbit and seeing Bill standing rabbit in mouth, tail wagging with a puzzled look on his face promptly attacked the rabbit that she considered her property anyway for she had worked a long and tedious hour or so to ensure that the rabbit did bolt. Bills inertia was shed instantly and in the place of the limp emotionless gentle animal I knew, Bill became a fireball that took the attack to Set with a vengeance. The furious lurcher lifted Set off the ground and began shaking her. I rushed in to stop the conflict for there can only be one outcome to a battle if a terrier is lifted clear of the ground by a lurcher and with Set still screaming like a banshee Bill returned to his former state of inertia.

Terrier/lurcher combinations are seldom satisfactory and frequently result in chaos or worse still disaster. Rabbits seldom run more than twenty-five yards without seeking refuge so the lurchers catch is invariably made in full view of an angry heated terrier. Terriers are usually jealous hunters and with courage far in excess of their size or sense. Hence when they view a lurcher catching a rabbit that they consider to be rightly theirs, terriers react predictably. A lurcher faced with the prospect of an angry terrier trying to take its catch from it will seldom retrieve its catch to the owner. Most tend to run off taking their rabbits with them when faced with an angry terrier. Others will retaliate violently and no ten or twelve pound terrier endures a bad mauling from a large strong powerful lurcher. The much vaunted terrier/lurcher combination is seldom successful and often results in carnage. Yet the number of misguided hunters who purchase a rabbiting terrier to work alongside a lurcher must be legion: it is bad policy, it is an exceedingly dangerous policy. Above all the bedlam that results from using such a combination looks amateurish and is so chaotic as to give terrier-work and field sports generally an extremely bad name.

Lucas tells the tale of how he used his Sealyham terriers to work alongside both lurchers and German shepherd dogs (Lucas refers to the breed as Alsatians) but although nasty incidents must have abounded during these hunts, Lucas neglects to mention them. It is worth noting that the GSD is one of the most jealous hunters when it weds to the sport and the conflict between a terrier and a GSD will end quickly and unpleasantly.

However entering any terrier to rabbit is simplicity itself. Terriers progress easily from ragging a skin or dummy made of rabbit fur to attacking the cadaver of a rabbit to hunting live and healthy quarry particularly if they can accompany an experienced dog on a rabbit hunt. Where myxomatosis abounds the rabbits are usually incapacitated by the ravages of the disease and hence are easier for a terrier to catch. The morality of hunting diseased rabbits is questioned by many however for no more horrific sight than a myxomatosis ridden rabbit could be imagined. However whether the rabbits to be hunted are healthy or infected, catches should be despatched quickly and humanely. At the time of writing field sports are under fire from those antipathetic to hunting – to provide ammunition for such people by committing any act of cruelty intentional or not is unwise.

The Use of Terriers in Mink Hunting

It must seem strange to a reader accustomed to regarding the otter as a cossetted protected species that various agencies go to considerable trouble to protect, to find that once the otter was regarded as vermin that, in the words of the author of *Master of Game*, man brackets it along with the fox, wildcat, marten and polecat as a quarry which 'no good hunter goeth to the woods intending to hunt'.

Yet in medieval times, when perhaps freshwater fish was a more important item of food than it is today, it was the duty of some authorities to keep down the number of otters living along the banks of certain rivers. Sir Henry Savill writing in 1544 states in a letter to a cousin Plumpton that he has a servant who knows a man who will catch otters (perhaps a peripatetic otter catcher) and Savill adds 'My folks see them daily and I cannot kill them, my hounds being not used to them.' It is a curious fact that hounds not deliberately entered to otter often refuse to hunt them.

Turbeville states that bloodhounds were used to kill otter but the term bloodhound certainly referred to a pure-blooded hound rather than the bloodhounds one sees today. Rawdon Lee in his *Modern Dogs* is however of the opinion that the modern otter hound is a cross between the terrier, the Welsh terrier and the Southernhound and his theory is lent some, though not a lot, of substance by the fact that Lucas relates that when he was relatively penniless he created his own otter hounds by mating Airedale terriers with bloodhounds. Colonel David Hancock *The Heritage of the Dog* is of the opinion that the Airedale in its original form prior to its refinement by adding Irish terrier blood was indeed simply a rough-haired hound known as the Lancashire otter-hound. There is in fact considerable evidence to suggest that the Dumfriesshire otter-hounds – distinctive black-and-tan hounds were deliberately created in 1889 by mating a bloodhound male to a Griffon Vendeen bitch and produced Boatman a hound that became the cornerstone of this famous strain of otter-hound.

Otter hunting, always a poor relation of fox hunting, was practised in summertime when the water of rivers, streams, brooks etc were warm enough not to chill the terriers and hounds engaged in hunting otters, but poor relation or not the ethos of hunting otters was fascinating and inspired Henry Williamson's memorable *Tarka the Otter* though the hound Deadlock was a draughted staghound rather than a conventional otter-hound. The book describes this strange and now antiquated sport so accurately that further description is superfluous.

Alien hound blood was in fact often introduced into otter-hound packs and for good reason. Abnormalities had begun to appear in otter-hounds. Hip dysplacia, the scourge of modern breeds of large dogs, is truly rampant amongst pure bred otter-hounds and while it is customary to blame that nebulous body the Kennel Club for any peculiarities that manifest themselves in any breed of Kennel Club registered dog this is a ridiculous and unjust criticism. Working hounds were often terribly crippled by severe hip dysplacia long before the cessation of otter hunting and it was customary to introduce the odd dash of Welsh Harrier blood (a breed relatively clear of the problem of hip dysplacia) to reduce the incidence of crippled otter-hounds. In fact the highest incidence of hip dysplacia ever recorded was achieved by a working otter-hound.

When otter hunting became illegal during the 1970s there was some fear that the otter-hound may well become extinct. Interest from the Kennel Club did much to prevent the extinction of the breed, but working packs were kept alive when it was feasible to hunt mink in the place of otter.

Mink are not native to Britain though there is some scant evidence to suggest that allied species may have inhabited Britain in pre-glacial times. Mink began appearing in British rivers shortly after World War II and according to investigations carried out by the Universities of Edinburgh and Exeter the principal reason for the success of this predator was that it filled a broadly-based feeding niche that was hitherto unoccupied by any other predator.

Feral mink or usually hybrids between Alaskan mink, a large and very fertile strain, and the superior pelted Quebec strain, a smaller and less fertile type of mink, and the hybrids are cream/blue/white and beige in colour though they usually revert to the dark brown 'standard' coloured mink in the feral state. Likewise ranch mink may weigh in at six to seven pounds though feral mink are sometimes only half that weight.

Mink are voracious predators and feed on frogs, birds, fish and mammals up to the size of a brown hare. In Iceland ranch mink escapees wrought havoc on the ground nesting birds of the region which in the words of Clive Roots *Animal Invaders* 'had no knowledge of the new predator and no time to learn.' Scaup, golden eye, tufted ducks and scoter have suffered seriously from the ravages of feral mink that eat up to twenty per cent of their own weight in meat daily.

Mink nest in holes in the banks of lakes or rivers, sometimes in hollow logs and even in suitable containers found in rubbish dumps and the nests are usually lined with feathers which give a clear indication of the feeding habits of mink. Young born in May stay with the female until the following autumn and this practice may well have given rise to the tales that packs of mink hunt certain areas.

Apart from skunks and possibly polecats no wild species of animal is as aromatic as the mink. The stench of an excited mink can linger in poultry pens where the creature has entered and made a kill. Roots mentions that his earliest memory of the creature was the pungent stench left when a mink had broken into a poultry house and killed ten Khaki Campbell ducks. The scent left in a rabbitry in Oswestry where mink had tried so hard to break through the wire mesh fronts of the cages left the owner in no doubt as to the nature of the invader. Otterhounds find little difficulty in hunting this strongly scented predator which is decidedly more aromatic than the most frightened otter.

Newspaper articles that appeared shortly after World War II, alarmist as are most newspaper articles, describe the mink as being a creature capable of outfacing 'a large and fierce dog', but this description is ludicrous. Even a breed the size of a small Yorkshire terrier would have little difficulty in disposing of a three and a half pound mustelid, though the bite from a mink is out of proportion to the size of the creature and extremely painful. Few mink survive the bite of a terrier however for mustelids which are usually characterised by their slender and sinuous shapes are seldom capable of surviving an attack from any dog.

Mink climb well and when pursued will 'tree' as readily as will a stoat. In 1982 David Hancock photographed a mink hunt where a mink climbed some thirty feet up a nearly perpendicular willow and launched itself back into the river to escape both hounds and the accompanying terriers. Mink are certainly not as furious an adversary as otters (eight times the size of a wild mink) but are an agile and elusive quarry. It is also worth noting that a hole into which a small hob ferret can find refuge will also house mink and rat holes and rabbit burrows are invariably used by hunted mink.

Terriers are used to bolt mink from such holes and burrows and by dint of loud and continuous baying terriers will flush mink from galleries within a burrow so that they may be hunted and destroyed by hounds. A terrier that encounters a mink in the blind end of a warren soon despatches the mink almost as easily as it would a rat. However should a terrier encounter a mink in deep water or while a terrier is treading water the mink will inflict terrible damage on the face of a terrier that is gripping the mink. Terriers do in fact find great trouble killing a mink and treading water while they do so. Mink are hard biters by any standards and will puncture the face of a terrier many times as the dog swims to the shallows in order to shake a mink.

A terrier requires little entering to hunt mink. If the dog chances on a mink while drawing a river bank the stench of the mink coupled with the spitting fury of a mink brought to bay is usually enough to excite any terrier to wed to mink. Few dogs can resist hunting and killing mink, even dogs that have been broken to ferret which closely resemble mink in shape if not scent.

Nuttall of Holmes Chapel is considered by many, the author included, to be an authority on the pursuit of mink with terriers. He has in fact acted as terrier man to many of the mink hunting packs in Britain. Nuttall is careful to enter his young terriers to mink, and only to mink for he believes that a terrier which is not steady to rat or rabbit will give tongue on rabbit and rat as freely as it will on mink. An unsteady terrier will cause the hunter much effort with no rewards.

Fox Hunting with Terriers

At one time it was perfectly legal to hunt fox, badger and otter. Indeed Lucas' digs, recorded so vividly when the author wrote using the pseudonyum 'The Lad', attracted a host of titled guests to enjoy the activity. Geoffrey Sparrow a pillar of the community and author of the delightful *The Terrier's Vocation* likewise kept a team of badger digging terriers. Many working certificates which indicated that a terrier had proved its mettle against otter were proudly displayed by terrier owners and the masks of subterranean quarry were displayed in stately homes and museums through Britain.

These days there is considerable antipathy to the working terrier owner and the various sports associated with terrier work have fallen into disrepute. So too alas has the terrier man and every offence such a terrier man commits is blown out of proportion to the gravity of the offence by the media. Men even suspected of allowing a terrier to go to ground in or sometimes near a badger set are often prosecuted and because of the iniquitous 1985 Amendment to the 1981 Wildlife and Countryside Act which requires a person to prove he is not in pursuit of badgers rather than the prosecution proving that he is, men are often convicted on the scantiest of evidence by magistrates who fail to differentiate between badger digging and badger baiting.

There is little doubt that the terrier man has become the Ishmael of the field sports fraternity, a fellow against whom everyone's hand has been turned, but much of the antipathy the public has manifested to terrier work has certainly been invited by the terrier man.

Certain offences against badger, hideous atrocities it is best not to dignify by describing, received much and frankly just publicity by the media – but helped bridge the hiatus between digging and baiting in the minds of the public until even a field sports advocate may find it difficult to differentiate between the two activities. Furthermore badger diggers have often been foolish enough to 'video' atrocities they have committed after a badger dig and these confiscated videos have found a ready market as news items or television programmes.

Breay at Bramham Moor in 1963 stated that 'An unsavoury element is coming into the world of the working terrier' and curiously there occurred a spate of terrier thefts immediately after that date. In the same year Lucas stated that he was concerned at the number of 'obvious louts' that were keeping working terriers and recalls that prior to this time thefts of working terriers were almost unknown. By 1966 it became decidedly unwise not to install elaborate devices to keep thieves out of working terrier kennels and a number of breeders of good working dogs had their kennels literally pillaged by thieves and louts during the 1970s. John Cowen of Embleton had his premises burgled twice and it became a sensible practice not to claim to own good working terriers.

However, during the 1980s enemies appeared in the very ranks of the working terrier fraternity and these caused more harm than any body that was directly antipathetic to field sports could have contrived. During this time the dearth of books on lurchers and terriers prompted many enthusiasts to put together stapled-together booklets which were concerned with lurcher and terrier work. Many of the contributors to these publications would have been well advised not to put pen to paper. Many of the articles in these periodicals were slovenly written, of poor content and often painted a picture of the artisan hunter being a lout who was hell bent on ridding the country of all mammalian and avian life forms. Later when contributors ran out of ideas for these pathetic and badly written ego trip-type articles they began writing frenzied and personal attacks on other field sport enthusiasts and this produced 'a house divided' situation amongst lurcher and terrier owners that was seized on by bodies who wished to see an end to field sports. Some of these periodicals are so awful and badly written as to defy description, though they will certainly become collector's items by those who will endeavour to make a study of or compile a thesis on the decline and cessation of field sports at a future date. This spate of trashy magazines and booklets did more to damage field sports than can be imagined, and it is hoped that the BFSS monitored these magazines and withdrew all support for them. The damage however has been done and now the fox hunting terrier men must, in the words of Damon Runyon, 'Walk on eggs' to avoid prosecution and bring the sport of terrier work to still further disrepute.

Long before the working terrier enthusiast puts a dog to ground, indeed before he ventures out into the countryside with dogs and spade he should acquaint himself with the difference between a badger set and a fox earth and many terrier men have been prosecuted and fined because they have neglected to heed this advice. The BFSS has in fact gone to considerable trouble to provide literature and advice concerning the identification of obvious badger sets and to explain how such sets differ from fox earths. Badgers are now not only a legally protected species but a mammal which enjoys the sympathy of the general public – and whether that sympathy is a shade misdirected as some would have us believe, matters not a jot. Badgers are protected and the terrier man must go out of his way to avoid putting a dog to ground in a badger set and not to encourage the general public to think less highly of terrier sports to which the public are now more than a shade antipathetic. A tale illustrates both the ignorance and the antipathy of the public to terrier work. In 1990 Eddie Metcalf one time committee member of the Durham and Northumberland Terrier Club was asked to rid a local zoo of rats for it is not practicable to poison rats where other mammalian life abounds. Hence Metcalf took a team of ferrets and three terriers (together with some spades) to flush and dig the rats from beneath the cages in the zoo. Unwisely perhaps Metcalf agreed to work his terriers while the zoo was open to the public, and was promptly reported for badger digging by a lady who seemed upset by the sight of Eddie's spades, terriers and ferrets. Of course no prosecution resulted from the report for the owner of the zoo interceded but the tale does tend to show how ignorant the public are of terrier work and how antipathetic they are to badger diggers.

The fact that foxes often take refuge or even breed in badger sets (and they do despite the statements issued by certain badger protection groups) should not concern the terrier man for not only is it illegal to attack or kill a badger it is illegal to dig or probe into a badger set to secure a fox. The majority of convicted badger diggers once offered as defence that they were digging for foxes, but seldom is such a defence accepted by magistrates these days.

Badger sets are usually fairly extensive affairs – the badger is a habitual digger that continues to delve and excavate long after the set becomes established. Mounds of earth piled outside a hole usually indicate that a badger may be in residence. However many established rabbit warrens also manifest signs of considerable excavation yet do not house badgers. Badgers do however lie in nests of straw, hay, dried grass and more rarely bracken (few creatures seem to enjoy being bedded on bracken) and sometimes take this soiled bedding out to air. Neither rabbits nor foxes tend to build nests of grass and hence the presence of bedding on mounds of earth outside a fairly large hole is a very clear indication that the hole houses or has at some time housed a badger. Other signs such as paw impressions, latrines dug near the set and nearby trees scored by the claws of the badger are clear indications that a badger is resident in a particular set of diggings. It should also be stressed that the terrier man should avoid such places like the plague. Countless terrier men, terriers on leash, spades in hand have been apprehended by police as the diggers approached a wood that housed badgers despite the fact that these terrier men have been concerned with catching foxes and not badgers. That these terrier men have been carrying fox nets has been ignored despite the fact that badgers seldom bolt, and hence cannot be trapped with nets. It is a decidedly dangerous policy to put a terrier to ground in any district that houses a badger, particularly if the terrier man has no business being on the land! The majority of convicted badger diggers did not have permission to seek for fox or badger on the land where they were apprehended and hence have justly deserved their conviction and fine.

It is possible to contain a terrier in kennels, to never take it out until it is a year or so old and enter it to fox during its first trip off the premises. It is also fair to state that the failure rate of people who adopt this method of entering will be staggeringly high, and the number of terriers permanently ruined by this method of entering will be legion. Gradual entering adopting a process of starting a terrier at small quarry and allowing it to work small fry until it is eighteen months of age before allowing it to face a fox will reduce a handler's failure level to almost zero. Yet such is the temperament of many modern terrier enthusiasts that far too many terriers are entered prematurely, become damaged dispirited and become the stock-in-trade of unlicenced dog dealers. The majority of terriers will work well or fairly well regardless of breeding, if they are allowed time to mature and subjected to a gradual programme of entering, yet a great many terrier buffs fail with every puppy they buy and complain that no one is breeding useful terriers. The fault 'dear Brutus' is usually with yourselves not the dogs you attempt to train. Many good experienced hunt servants can produce a suitable hunt terrier simply by taking a 'free to a good home' pet terrier, subjecting it to a careful training programme and then entering the adult terrier to fox. Some excellent terriers have been produced from noisy unruly pet-bred terriers that have been properly entered and given every chance to develop their full potential.

It is not good policy to enter any terrier to quarry that can possibly hurt it before the terrier is at least a year or so old. If the terrier is left to develop until it is eighteen months of age before it is tried so much the better, but the education of a terrier should proceed from the nest onwards and it is lunacy to have a dog in kennels and then ask it to enter to fox on its first venture off the premises. A terrier that is intended for working fox should lead a full and interesting life as soon as it is innoculated and thus able to be taken hunting. Every minute of the time spent hunting a young terrier to small fry – rats, mice and even rabbits, is well spent, for it allows the young terrier to develop its full potential. Conversely a kennelised dog, even of superb breeding with an excellent working pedigree is often extremely difficult to enter. It has no experience in the field, has learned no bush craft and is often confused by its first encounter with a creature that is capable of inflicting hurt on the terrier.

A terrier that has some knowledge of the countryside, that has been encouraged to hunt small fry, will usually have acquired at least some experience of going to ground to seek out quarry and will require little encouragement to enter an earth and seek out a fox. The chances are that the terrier will have flushed a rabbit or rat and followed it into a drain or run it to ground in a large burrow. In fact most breeds of terrier still show an innate propensity to follow quarry into earths and drains and most have to be restrained, not encouraged. Terriers are certainly not the most intelligent members of the dog world but are certainly the most inquisitive. Each nook and crevice is explored by a terrier, every hole every burrow entrance and it is a strange terrier indeed that requires much encouragement to run into an earth. During the 1970s when I fielded a pack of over fifty terriers there were places where it was nearly impossible to take recently innoculated puppies for they simply vanished into a series of rabbit burrows and needed to be dug out. Any lair emits exciting scents from its depths; scents that lure a terrier into the earth to investigate the source of these scents.

I am reluctant to allow any terrier to go to ground unless it is totally obedient for I insist on dogs coming to hand even from the bowels of the earth. The logic behind 'I want a dog to stay until it wishes to come away' escapes me but the majority of working terriers are so badly trained or seldom off their couples that it is not surprising that many terrier men confuse courage with total disobedience. A disobedient dog (and these are plentiful amongst working terriers) is a terrific nuisance, and no pleasure to hunt. At some time in the 1960s I dug badger with great regularity in Leicestershire (it was perfectly legal in those days) and I stopped allowing terrier men with disobedient dogs coming along on digs. Comments such as 'Turk will stay down until he is dead' are simply poor excuses offered by people who simply cannot call a dog out of an earth. At one time when I had no car I was forced to allow an idiot with an equally idiotic dog to accompany me on a dig. His dog – a huge red fell terrier with more than a hint of Irish terrier about it – was a pest of the first order. My associate found it almost impossible to control, totally impossible to call off cats or sheep and when the dog, which he allowed to run ahead of him free of the restrictions of a leash, disappeared into every earth and stayed until dug out my friend seemed highly delighted with the animal. The fact that it is always policy to restrain a terrier with a leash when it is taken hunting subterranean quarry was explained to him, but both the handler and the dog were impossible to control and eventually I finally decided to leave him behind. It was better not to allow him to hunt with us despite the fact I had no car and I took three terriers on a bus trip to Leicestershire rather than invite such a nuisance. I have seen many dogs lie just beneath our feet, a yard or so out of reach, but in totally undiggable positions refusing to come out when called and what is worse I have waited hours for such dogs to leave their foxes or badgers while their owner boasted of the courage of his recalcitrant brute. I have owned ferrets that came out when called (I own one such ferret at the time of writing) and I certainly would not tolerate a disobedient dog that would not come out when called. Fortunately I was able to field all my terriers in my rat pack where they learned total obedience from the nest onwards.

Prior to the actual entering of the terrier to live fox a terrier should have some experience of being allowed to worry or rag a cadaver of a fox, for there is no natural antipathy between dogs and foxes. Some antipathy can be induced if the terrier is encouraged to rag a fox carcass, however. Nuttall of Holmes Chapel seldom kills a fox but utilises all the carcasses he can obtain. Nuttall encourages all his puppies to worry and shake these carcasses (Nuttall uses as many road casualty fox carcasses as he can obtain). When the puppies are well and truly ecstatic about the prospect of worrying a dead fox Nuttall hangs the cadavers just out of reach of the puppies to allow their enthusiasm for worrying foxes to continue unabated. It should be noted that Nuttall's claim to fame is that he is able to regularly produce well entered, well trained terriers. Young terriers trained in this manner, prior to entering frequently become hysterical at the sight of a dead fox and the actual process of entering them to fox is thus made easier. Terriers trained in this manner often become wild with excitement at the first scent of fox emanating from an inhabited earth.

It is extremely dangerous to allow a heated, young, inexperienced terrier to follow a grown dog to ground after a fox. The foremost terrier is soon impregnated with the musk emitted by a frightened fox and it is not uncommon for the excited youngster following behind to seize and shake the foremost terrier and inflict terrible damage to the older dog. Some years ago I observed a Border terrier terribly mangled and much of the muscle of the Border's hind legs chewed off when an excited and eager young black fell terrier was slipped behind it. The carnage to the Border's hind legs would have convinced even the most inept of terrier men the dangers of working two dogs together in a fox earth.

The initial entering of a terrier to fox is of great importance and if the terrier can be tried in a shallow earth or a place that can be easily and quickly dug to stop the combat, so much the better. A young terrier should never be over-matched during its first foray against a fox. A young terrier should in fact experience a degree of triumph after its first encounter with a fox and Shire terrier men at the turn of the century were wont to kill a terrier's first fox and allow the youngster to worry the carcass. Nuttall does not believe this process is necessary and states that if the terrier is allowed to chase or bolt the fox it experiences success enough to ensure its continued interest in fox hunting. Nuttall does in fact go to considerable trouble not to kill foxes unless the owner of the land on which the fox has gone to ground wishes to be rid of the fox.

However, should a terrier show that it is unwilling to face its first fox it should never be forced to enter the earth to tackle its quarry. If a terrier is jack-knifed into entering before it is ready the effect can be traumatic, long-lasting and sometimes permanently damaging. The act of pushing a terrier down to a fox and barring its exit with a foot or spade is particularly injurious. Yet each year dozens of terriers are forced into conflict with a fox using this method – and the number of terriers permanently mentally and physically scarred by forced entering to fox countless. When a terrier is ready to enter to fox it will usually display a great enthusiasm to do so. If terriers do not display this enthusiasm the chances are that it is not emotionally ready to enter. The terrier should be taken away and tried at another time and never forced into conflict with a fox in an effort to enter it. So many potentially useful terriers are often permanently damaged or ruined by asking too much of them too soon. It is extremely difficult to enter terriers that have been frightened by premature or ham-handed entering. At one time I specialised in re-entering terriers that had been mentally scarred by bad entering techniques, but despite the fact I subjected the terriers to a lengthy process of retraining my failure rate was unacceptably high.

When a terrier engages a fox below ground it is required to perform one of three functions. It must either kill its fox; and many fell strains or fell bred derivatives such as certain strains of Parson Jack Russell terrier are extremely adept at killing foxes below ground. The terrier may also be required to bolt the foxes and many strains of highly vocal Jack Russell terrier are wonderfully dextrous at causing even a tightly bolted up fox to leave its sanctuary to bolt. Similarly some terriers are required to find and bottle up a fox and prevent it from bolting while the handler digs to the combatants. To perform this latter feat a tenacious and if possible a vociferous terrier is required, but all types of fox hunting terriers should be tenacious and capable of staying with the foxes whether it be to kill, bolt or bottle up their foes.

A good foxing terrier should have:

a. nose to locate its quarry in any conditions and foxes may seek to go to ground in water filled drains, methanous mineworks or labyrinth-like borrans such as are found in the Lake District;
b. tenacity to stay with the fox even though thirst and bad air may cause the dog to wish it was elsewhere;
c. courage to face a foe often larger than itself and in conditions which favour the fox rather than the dog;
d. sense and aptitude to engage its foe without enduring excessive punishment from the fox;
e. voice to guide the digger to the location where the battle between dog and fox is taking place. In recent years since the introduction of terrier locators voice has become a less important consideration. At one time a terrier with a weak piping voice was considered to be of little worth.

For some reason many terrier men do not place a great importance on the nose a terrier manifests. Todd of Kendal author of *Terrier Song* usually sung to the tune 'Lal Melbrick', once told Eddie Pool that he seldom saw a dog that was a good finder and a good fox killer. This statement is often related by those who state that the nose of the typical fell terrier is inferior to that of Jack Russell terriers and other working terrier breeds yet Clapham's dictum 'no nose – no find, no catch – no kill' is singularly accurate. A dog with a poor nose will be unable to find a fox that runs to ground in a large earth full of labyrinths of side tunnels and galleries. Nose is in fact a vitally important quality in the make-up of a working terrier.

Nuttall has a heretical theory regarding the poor noses many fell terriers are said to possess. He believes that these terriers have well-developed olfactory senses, but are reluctant to engage their foxes and this cowardice or reluctance to tangle with a fox in a difficult situation is manifested by the fact that some terriers fail to find their foxes in fairly deep earths.

In point of fact when a strain or breed of terrier ceases to be worked nose is the first quality to disappear, for unless one deliberately breeds for nose, olfactory qualities tend to lessen. This can best be illustrated by reference to the unadulterated fell strains which supposedly have excellent noses and the strains of fell that have been heavily spiked with Kennel Club registered Lakeland terrier blood in which nose is often noticable by its absence.

It should also be noted that the short-lived craze for mating terriers to beagles that occurred in the 1960s was practised for purely cosmetic reasons by some – though some of the initial hybrids were anything but aesthetically appealing. However some of the best finding dogs imaginable were bred from these beagle terrier crosses and many of the very best working Jack Russell terrier lines, Mousely's Meynell strain of Jack Russell terrier trace their origins to beagle terrier hybrids though it must be said the beagle blood is now much diluted.

However, while it is generally accepted that many strains of fell terrier are low on nose few would question the tenacity and staying ability of these dogs for many fells are renowned 'stayers'. A terrier that engages its fox and stays but a little while to bay at it before coming out for air or for other less obvious reasons may find its fox has moved elsewhere in the earth or worse still has dug on to an even more inaccessible portion of the earth. Staying ability was even more prized in badger digging dogs for a badger finding itself not harrassed by a terrier made good its escape and dug on at a foot a minute in sandy soil.

There seems to be little correlation between great courage and staying ability however for many excessively courageous dogs became so injured when they confront their foxes that gaping wounds and the subsequent loss of blood often forces the terrier to the surface. Staying ability is in fact more closely related to the dogs ability to tease and annoy its fox rather than the dogs tendency to take the battle to its foe. Some of the most famous staying terriers, Cobby's Pickaxe, Capell's Pincher or

Forsyth's Pip have in fact been dogs that were seldom badly damaged by confrontations with foxes – though in his later years Forsyth's dog did absorb terrific punishment from foxes.

Courage is in fact a very important quality in the ideal working terrier, but it must be a peculiar type of courage, or rather a courage peculiar to the working terrier. The blind courage manifested by a pit dog is not desirable though many terrier men seem impressed by hideously scarred terriers. Terriers which are so courageous they will close with their foxes regardless of the damage inflicted by these foes will spend much of their time hors de combat and cost the owner the earth in vet's fees. Famous fox digging dogs such as Eddie Chapman's Sinbad and Tony Metcalf's Todd were rarely severely damaged by a hard day's work yet both were dogs of known courage and determination. A working terrier should manifest a particular type of courage, quite distinct from that of a recklessly hard dog, if the terrier is to enjoy a long and useful life.

During the late 1960s the appearance of the terrier locator made it possible for the terrier man to dig to mute terriers and as a result of this many crossed bull terriers (notoriously mute dogs) with working terriers to produce dogs with more durability. These hybrids were seldom satisfactory. Most become so terribly badly bitten that they were little use below ground and had to be retired prematurely. Many really good working terrier strains were ruined by the over-use of bull terrier blood.

Courage only when tempered by sense is a quality that should be prized in a working terrier. A sensible but brave terrier is capable of giving its owner years of service and of working each and every day. It is said that Malcolm Haddock of the Meynell Foxhounds worked the terrier Climber for ninety days without respite, earth stopping at weekends and using her as a hunt terrier on other days. The chances are she would have given him many years of service had not an unfortunate illness cut short her working life.

Voice is a debatable quality in the modern working terrier though before the invention of the terrier locator voice was an exceedingly important virtue in a working terrier. Beagle blood produced a terrier with an incredible booming baying voice that guided the digger to the place where the conflict was taking place. Prior to the days when locators were used it was not uncommon to see an otherwise good working terrier change hands at an absurdly low price simply because these terriers had a weak piping voice. Mute terriers no matter how game these terriers were or how good the dogs were at finding a fox were literally worthless prior to the invention of the terrier locator.

Terrier locators obviously caused great changes in terrier work and perhaps started a metamorphosis in the development of a working terrier. A terrier locator kit consists of a battery fitted collar and a detector unit that emits a crackling sound when it comes within range of the locator pellet. Modern locators are extremely sophisticated and indicate not only the position of the terrier but also the depth of the dig required to break through to the terrier and its locator collar. Collars that emit signals which can be detected under some fifteen feet of earth are now available to the terrier man.

Locator collars have certainly done much to reduce the death rate amongst terriers trapped below ground – and prior to the advent of the locator many terriers died through suffocation or starvation when diggers were unable to find these buried terriers. In 1948 two terriers, Badger and Butcher, became trapped in the Ullswater hunt country and a huge portion of the hillside was torn out in order to recover one of the dogs: the other was never recovered. There is a distinct possibility that aided by locator collars and receivers the diggers may have had more success in recovering the terriers, though many of the rock crevices utilised by Ullswater foxes run considerably deeper than fifteen feet. Johnny Richardson, one time huntsman for the Blencathra, told the tale of a terrier that went to ground near Glenridding to emerge from a crevice a mile distant. The Lake District is literally undermined by diggings made by copper miners and delvers who sought other minerals.

On the negative side the locator and receiver has allowed mute terriers to be used as fox hunting dogs particularly if these mute terriers display a tendency to physically attack or to close to foxes. Second-rate terriers are now able to be used by fox diggers, terriers that would not be considered to be any use before the advent of the locator. Terriers are now being bred without emphasis on the vocal qualities of a fox digging terrier and should a dog get to ground without its collar or should it shed its collar when it engages its fox (and it is not uncommon to find diggers have delved through many feet of earth fo find a collar that has been cast by a terrier) the terrier may be lost forever for it is unable to indicate its presence by baying. Many lost terriers can still be located by the sound of their baying, though admittedly it is very difficult to detect the exact position of a terrier in a tube only by the sound of its voice. It is nevertheless disturbing to realise that more and more mute terriers are being bred each year as locators reduce the value of good vocal dogs.

On the subject of fox digging it is expedient to mention some of the letters written by George Newcombe the breeder of the Rillington, Lakeland and Bedlington terriers to the sporting press. Newcombe ever the heretic but perhaps one of the most literate of working terrier men, believes that a fox earth should seldom be dug unless it is to recover a trapped terrier. Newcombe considers that the purpose of putting a terrier to ground is to test the dog not to kill the fox and for this reason he suggests that earths should be disturbed as little as possible.

Nevertheless there are times when a terrier fails to bolt a fox and it becomes necessary to dig and kill a fox that has proved a nuisance as a stock worrier. Digs should be carefully conducted forays if they are to be efficient and should not commence until the sounds of combat (or signals from the locator device) settle to one spot. A fox will often move around the earth, fighting off the attentions of the terrier pursuing it, for some time before it finds a place to settle to fight off the terrier. Hence it is pointless to begin a dig until a terrier indicates a fixed mark. Should the terrier stop engaging its fox and decide to come out for air there is a distinct possibility that a fox may move and seek another vantage point and hence excavations have to begin again in another portion of the earth.

The fact that foxes will move once a terrier ceases to engage them has made canine legends out of quite indifferent dogs. Many dogs may be bested by a fox that has found some vantage point from whence it can withstand the attacks of a terrier. Dog after dog will be tried to move this fox, but because the fox has found a suitable place to lie to fight off the terriers (a ledge or fox bench or better still a tree root) the dogs fail to bolt the fox. After a while the diggers or hunters decide to use a young green dog, inexperienced in the ways of foxes or quite an inferior animal that has proved little use at its work. The terrier is tried, a fox is bolted and the dog becomes famous for its prowess. What has happened is that during the respite given the fox while the terrier men debate as to whether to use another terrier the fox has left its vantage point and hence bolts before the fresh terrier.

When I hunted fox regularly in the Midlands it was my policy to deliberately allow a fox a respite after it had bested a terrier. After half an hour or so, with the diggers silent and the terriers taken some way from the earth another fresh terrier was tried and often bolted the fox quickly and apparently efficiently. A particular incident comes to mind. At that time Forsyth's Pip had been at stud in Lichfield and at Hancock's poultry farm in Sutton Coldfield and he had proved an incredible working dog. However on the day in question he had gone to ground in an old established earth in Dyatt Woods, taken quite a bad beating and come out for a breather. Rather than let Pip go to ground yet again, he was a ten-year-old terrier at this time, I kept the diggers silent and half an hour later I tried Pip's son Carl Pollit's Damien a ten-month-old terrier who later obtained a working certificate at the Grove and Rufford Foxhounds kennels and became an important sire of Plummer terriers. Damien entered the earth, bayed less than a dozen times and bolted his first fox. Later he was to become quite a famous terrier and the sire of Rocky Rupert and an extremely tough terrier called Lucy, but his success on the day in question was due to the fact that the fox that had bested Pip had left its vantage point and was preparing to bolt. Damien had simply precipitated the bolt.

In fact if a terrier is bested by a fox and the terrier man is determined to see the fox bolt so that it can be shot or killed with lurchers, he has but to put his terriers away and wait in silence near the earth. Foxes disturbed by a conflict with a terrier will leave an earth where they have encountered a terrier as soon as they believe that it is safe to do so. Some almost follow a terrier out so as to be clear of the earth. Dogs have little natural antipathy to foxes, but foxes are terrifed of dogs. The presence of a small vocal dog used as a guard dog around poultry houses is usually enough to deter any fox.

As to whether earths should be dug out or as Newcombe believes left unmolested is a moot point. What is absolutely certain is that earths from which a fox has been dug should be back-filled. Hunters are rarely welcome if after a visit a landowner finds huge craters on his property particularly if cattle or sheep graze on land where these craters have been dug. There is a story that in Melton Mowbray an earth was dug and not back-filled and a winning point-to-point thoroughbred horse fell into the crater and broke its hip. If an earth is back-filled the chances are that other foxes, attracted by the musk left by the previous tenant, will dig out the damaged but back-filled earth and take up residence there again.

For some reason some earths are always found to house foxes and these earths should not be disturbed for they will always provide sport for the terrier man. One such earth near Lichfield hosted an incredible number of foxes. This earth situated on a disused canal bank, could always be relied on to produce a fox on most days and seldom was the earth unoccupied for two consecutive days. Foxes bolted easily from this earth and it proved a wonderful place to start a youngster to fox. In 1980 the earth was bulldozed to produce agricultural land and never again did the place yield foxes. The spot was never used as a breeding earth however but foxes could be found at home from September to March.

On the subject as to when foxes can be found to ground, few foxes return to ground during the summer months unless a freak cold spell occurs in months when the weather is expected to be fine. Numerous terrier men have been convicted for badger digging simply because they put a dog to ground at times of the year when a fox was unlikely to be at home. Solicitors for the prosecution are now very au fait with the ways of foxes and badgers. It is in fact extremely dangerous for a terrier man to be caught digging during the warm summer months when badgers are at home and foxes are unlikely to be in residence.

Normally foxes start returning to ground in early autumn usually after the corn is cut or a chilly wind has caused the undergrowth to die back. Cubs will then often return to the breeding earths and it is not uncommon to find four or five well-grown cubs residing in a single earth at that time. As the autumn progresses litters split up again and in mid-winter it is not common to bolt a great many foxes from a single small earth.

Vixens mate at the waxing of the year and produce cubs from March onwards on the bare earth on the floor of a fox earth. Male foxes dig or find separate earths a hundred or so yards away from the breeding earth. Perhaps a close pair bonding of dog and vixen is responsible for the close proximity of these earths for there is no evidence that males deliberately seek out prey to feed the cubs (though vixens have been observed racing out of the lairs to scratch prey from males returning to adjacent earths). Fox controllers make good use of the fact that males will stay close to vixens and cubs for when a breeding earth is discovered they are fairly certain that another nearby earth will house a dog fox. Sometimes two or three males will dig or occupy earths near the breeding earth, though the practice would be counter-productive to the production of strong healthy cubs for the country around the earths would be depleted of edible game and vegetable provender by an overlarge fox population. Nevertheless certain areas always produce large populations of male foxes in the breeding season. The woods and fields around Whittington Heath invariably yielded a large male fox population from March until late June, possibly because the area was adjacent to both the Meynall and the Atherston hunt country yet the proximity of large main roads prevented either pack hunting this triangle. The woods abounded with foxes most times of the year and fox drives, the only means of controlling the fox population often yielded a high proportion of male foxes.

In recent years foxes have been observed feeding and breeding in urban areas. In fact a newspaper article published in 1981 stated that it was likely that Birmingham hosted a larger fox population than the Quorn hunt country – though how the journalist arrived at this conclusion was never explained. Ecologists tend to believe that when myxomatosis which reduced the rabbit population of Britain to a mere five per cent of its former numbers the absence of rabbits may well have prompted the movement of foxes from rural to urban districts. Indeed in 1948 the appearance of a fox in Small Heath, Birmingham merited a column in a local paper. It is also likely that the spread of the cities after World War II entrapped numerous foxes which slowly adapted to the urban conditions thrust on them. In all probability both the paucity of rabbits after the myxomatosis outbreak of 1953 and the construction of new estates in suburban districts caused the increase in the number of urban foxes.

As to the diet of the urban fox many live on large amounts of vegetable food whereas the faeces from rural foxes indicate that a mere fifth of the diet of these animals is composed of vegetable matter. Rats, mice and insects make up the majority of the animal protein eaten by urban foxes though rabbits too are now becoming quite common even in the centres of large towns. It is also worth noting that rabbits caught in these urban settings are usually slightly above average size though whether this extra size is due to better food or simply due to infusions of domesticated rabbit blood when escapee hutch rabbits have mated with wild stock has never been explored.

Urban foxes sometimes cause a nuisance and need to be removed and either killed humanely or released elsewhere. When fox trapper Barry

Jones – at one time chairman of the Parson Jack Russell Terrier Club – was interviewed by a reporter from *Country Living* he stated that he released many hundred urban foxes he had caught in rural areas, but this action certainly did not please Welsh farmers many of whom claim they are plagued by urban foxes who denied their scavenging in dustbins or the 'handouts' offered them by certain inner city householders revert to lamb worrying.

Urban foxes nest in some curious places. Rubbish piles are usually favourite spots for these foxes to breed possibly because these refuse tips are seldom disturbed by terrier men and also because rats and rabbits are sometimes plentiful in such areas. Many litters have been reared in old steel barrels or discarded household appliances such as washing machines and spin dryers. However nests beneath the floors of garden sheds and outhouses are commonly used as breeding earths by urban foxes. One litter was reared behind dustbins at the rear of a Chinese restaurant in Birmingham though it speaks volumes that the bins were left unemptied long enough for a vixen to produce and rear a litter.

However, it should be pointed out from the onset that while live trapping of foxes and releasing them in rural districts is a perfectly legal if questionable activity, hunting the same urban foxes with terriers is a decidedly illegal action. Obscure but still operative laws govern what a person can do within the confines of a town. It is perfectly legal to hunt a fox with dogs in the countryside: it is decidedly illegal to hunt foxes with dogs within a town. It can be argued that the law is an obscure one. It can also be argued that these regulations were passed at a time in our history when life was not as it is today. It must be agreed however that at the time of writing terrier men should do all they can to avoid upsetting people. To deliberately flout any regulation, however obscure and archaic that regulation may be, is to court disaster. Urban foxes are best left alone or if they become too numerous trapped by a registered pest controller. They should not concern the terrier man who should leave urban foxes strictly alone.

Once again it is time to discuss the lurcher-terrier combination as a method of securing foxes, and it must be conceded that this combination can be an extremely efficient method of securing foxes if the team is trained to work together in unison – and it is extremely easy to train a lurcher to work fox in conjunction with terrier or if the lurcher shows a strong inclination to run and tackle foxes. Basically the process consists of the terrier working below ground to bolt a fox so that the lurcher may course and catch the fox. A clever lurcher will follow the course of the battle proceeding below ground, predict the exit from which a fox may bolt and nail the fox before it has had time to run either to cover or to ground to escape capture. Some lurchers become extremely adept at 'reading' the way a subterranean battle is proceeding and snatch and kill the fox before it has run twenty yards – and it must be added that foxes like roe deer are as good as lost if they can run into woodland or put a good distance between themselves and the pursuing lurcher.

It is relatively easy to create enmity between a terrier and a fox. It is less easy to inspire that enmity in a lurcher or a longdog and many lurchers are reluctant to tackle foxes while others simply refuse to do so. A higher success rate can be obtained if the lurcher is carefully entered to fox. Once again the lurcher must be encouraged to seize and worry the cadavers of foxes and the ragging of a carcass should be treated as a game by the hunters. I never waste a road casualty fox cadaver and encourage all my dogs to rag and worry the carcass until the carcass becomes unpleasant to handle.

If the fox cadaver is attached to a length of strong twine and pulled in front of the lurcher, while the lurcher is encouraged to shake the carcass, some enthusiasm for attacking a live fox may be generated. The fact is that many lurchers do not manifest antipathy for foxes and while it is true that some lurchers, longdogs or pure bred sighthounds may well course, catch and kill the first fox they encounter, the self-same dogs would probably course and kill a smaller dog with the same zest with which they killed the fox. The majority of lurchers will pursue a fox, as indeed they will any small mammal but though they may come to terms with a fox and even shoulder the fox until it rolls clear of the jaws of the dog, few untrained lurchers (few lurchers that have not been actively encouraged to attack foxes or the cadavers of foxes) will actually attempt to kill or catch a fox. Thus the role of the handler is to generate sufficient antipathy between dog and fox for the lurcher to seize, catch and kill its fox – and some lurchers kill foxes extremely quickly – a point to remember when a lurcher engages a fox-sized terrier in a kennel fight!

If the lurcher is allowed to see another dog catch and kill a fox and encouraged to join in the battle, then it will sometimes wed to fox catching with enthusiasm. However should it be hurt through its first encounter with foxes the lurcher may decide that it is expedient not to tackle foxes. The fact is many lurchers, longdogs and sighthounds alike do not possess the disposition to run, catch and kill foxes. An early epic concerned with hunting, *The Master of the Game*, records 'A little greyhound is very hardy when (if) it takes a fox by himself for men have seen great greyhounds which might well take a hart or a wild boar and a wolf and would let a fox go.' The author was clearly aware that there was no natural antagonism between dogs and foxes.

A variety of lurchers, longdogs and sighthound types can be used to catch and/or kill foxes bolted by a terrier and straight way it is wise to remember the Irish quote 'It is not the size of the dog in the fight but the size of the fight in the dog', for quite often diminutive whippet-sized dogs will tackle a fox with gusto yet huge powerful dogs may show little enthusiasm for catching and killing foxes. Borzois are said to still show natural antipathy to wolves and foxes and a chapter in Standfast Press epic book *Coursing* mentions a borzoi which while it showed little aptitude for coursing hares or catching rabbits went wild with excitement when it saw a fox particularly when the same fox nipped the hound for its curiosity. This may well be true, for borzois have been used to course fox and wolf for many centuries and as late as 1908 the fabulous Perchino stud, advertised in *American Field*, hounds which were trained to take wild canids up to the size of a timber wolf. However the low concentration span of a borzoi and the natural recalcitrance of the mid-oriental sighthounds makes it less than suitable as a dog to work above a terrier that is trying to bolt a fox.

Track and cast coursing greyhounds, too long in the tooth to be worth keeping for competitive coursing and racing, often make excellent fox catchers particularly elderly coursing dogs which may well have encountered and killed foxes on previous forays. These hounds should always be 'suspect' in the company of terriers and other small dogs however and it is unwise to kennel a greyhound with terriers until the greyhounds temperament is established as being 'sound'. Yet excellent fox catching dogs can be obtained for a song if the hunter is prepared to take on cast and unwanted greyhounds. The best fox killing dog I have ever seen was in fact a cast greyhound bitch, a daughter of Old Kentucky Minstrel and this bitch not only ran and killed foxes, but hunted them out of woodland as freely as a foxhound might. So impressed was I with the performance of this bitch that I used her brother to mate to a lurcher bitch – with disastrous results I should add, though that is another tale.

Some lurchers are tailor-made for fox catching. David Hancock of Sutton Coldfield, the world's largest breeder of collie greyhound hybrids, breeds a particularly successful fox killing crossbred by mating a bearded/Border collie stud dog to a greyhound bitch and notes that puppies from this cross are often unusually adept at fox catching. Hancock states that one of his first bearded/Border greyhound hybrids sold to a long-netter in Kent caught sixty foxes in its first season's hunting – though it should be pointed out that most of these foxes were killed by lamping them and running the lurcher at the illuminated foxes. A fox is a fox however, in or out of the beam, and the process of catching it exactly the same.

Many mongrel pedigree unknown types of lurcher also make excellent fox killing dogs and while it is true that a careful entering programme gives the dog a better chance of becoming a successful fox catching dog, many lurchers show absolutely no propensity to run and catch foxes no matter how they are encouraged; no matter how often they are run at foxes. The early signs that the dog will never take fox are legion and these dogs will often apparently run fox with great enthusiasm but fail to tackle or come to terms with them.

Once it is known that the longdog, lurcher or sighthound will tackle fox with gusto it should be subjected to an intensive training programme to allow it to give of its best when working it with a terrier. When a terrier is to ground the hound should be kept close in to prevent it wandering away from the earth and when the fox does bolt being in the wrong place at the wrong time. Many fox hunters insist that their hounds sit and remain sitting while the conflict proceeds below ground. This is a counter-productive method of training however as it does not allow a dog to use its natural ability to predict where the fox may bolt. A better technique is to restrain the young dog in a standing position, with a hand beneath its loin for instance, until the dog comes to understand that it is required to stay near the earth during the duration of the time a terrier stays beneath the earth. In a very short time indeed a lurcher learns that it is better employed staying near the earth than wandering abroad to seek other game. I teach the 'freeze technique' but allow a lurcher to tread gingerly around the top of the earth to ascertain the course of the battle beneath its feet. A lurcher's sense of hearing is so superior to that of a human beings that it can detect sounds that are inaudible to the terrier man. This superior hearing should be made use of, not curtailed, by insisting that the dog sits near the earth in a spot dictated by the terrier man.

To watch a lurcher work with a terrier, one harrassing the fox below ground while the other covers the exits through which a fox is likely to bolt, is an exciting sight, particularly if the team has been trained to a degree of efficiency. Some greyhound blooded dogs become so efficient at freezing to total immobility without moving a muscle or blinking an eye that a fox will endeavour to creep past them as if unaware of the presence of the dog guarding the exit. It is my belief that the incredible concentration span required of a dog that performs in this manner is not related to intelligence and pure bred sighthounds often learn to perform this spectacular caper as readily as a well bred lurcher will. I should add that my own lurchers mark the progress of a subterranean battle superbly but show little inclination to pursue and capture foxes.

As soon as the lurcher, longdog or sighthound chases and catches the fox the terrier man or an assistant must rush to the scene of the battle to forestall further cruelty to the fox or the dog. Battles between the antagonists should not be allowed to continue a second longer than they need to. The foxes should be despatched quickly and painlessly or bagged so that they may be released elsewhere, but no element of cruelty, intentional or unintentional cruelty, should bring disrepute to any facet of field sports.

Shortly after World War II it became popular to net foxes that bolted before a ferret. Foxes bolt quite readily before a ferret, particularly a persistent hob and some fox hunts used ferrets instead of terriers to bolt fresh foxes. Lucas mentions that Mr McNeill master of the Grafton for seven seasons used a 'buck' (hob) ferret to flush foxes. Many foxes bolted before ferrets entangle in the purse net set to catch rabbits. Hence it was not unreasonable that fox hunters began to make larger stronger nets to entrap bolting foxes, though unless the fox hits the nets quite vigorously nets often fail to entrap foxes. Foxes that become au fait with nets and the way nets work often become singularly adept at lifting nets with their muzzles and slipping under the nets to safety.

A lurcher that attacks a fox that is entrapped in the nets is a great nuisance but easily restrained from the practice. On hitting a net foxes struggle but briefly before falling into a type of catatonic trance, a possum-like gesture that often saves the lives of medium-sized predators under attack from larger more aggressive foes. Few lurchers, longdogs or sighthounds are enthusiastic about attacking a prostrate non-moving prey and hence as soon as the fox ceases to struggle in the meshes of the net many lurchers will automatically cease to attack the fox. A slap or word of reproach is usually enough to deter a lurcher from attacking a struggling fox and lurchers and longdogs alike are extremely sensitive to reproach of any kind.

Terrier work produces a type of elation few other field sports manage to produce and within five years of owning terriers a great many tyro terrier men consider it may well be worth while them becoming professional terrier men. It is quite unrealistic for a person in a world where poisons, fumigants and toxic substances exist to imagine that he can make a living as a pest controller using only his terriers and spade to remove vermin. Those would-be pest controllers who insist on using only natural methods of controlling pests are deluding themselves for no landowner will pay a man to ferret a field for four days when gassing the rabbits can be done far more quickly and far more efficiently. In fact the majority of 'pest controllers' use their titles to obtain some hunting permission and cannot make a living from their interests in terrier and lurcher work.

A terrier enthusiast may however find full time employment and a chance to indulge in his passion for terrier work at a hunt kennels, but the job of a terrier man is both hard and mentally taxing. Furthermore the pay such a hunt servant might expect is little short of pitiful. Eddie Chapman, one time terrier man for the Cattistock, records that in 1986 his net wage was £48 a week though he lived rent free and had the use of a vehicle, but only during his working hours.

It is also noteworthy that the hours a hunt servant is required to work are out of proportion to the salary paid them. Chapman recalls that during cub hunting he began work at 3.30 am and finished work at 9.00 pm – a terribly long day though from May until September a terrier man might expect to work from 7.00 am until 5.00 pm. Days off were rare for stock needs to be fed and cared for seven days a week and should a fellow hunt servant be ill, Chapman was required to double up to help fill the void left by the absence of his colleague.

Basically a terrier man must know the country, the pack to which he is attached, is required to hunt and the night before a meet seek and block the numerous earths, sets and burrows into which a hard-pressed fox is likely to run. Tom Easy, a horseman and fox hunter of some note, is reputed to have said that an efficient terrier man seldom needs to dig on a hunt day for by good earth stopping he will have prevented any fox getting to ground. Cecil Alden, one time master of the Old Berkshire, is said to have devised a novel method to ensure that few foxes ran to ground. He paid his terrier man 2/6d (12½p) for every fox taken by hounds and deducted 1/-d (5p) for every fox that went to ground. Alden himself bred some excellent terriers and realised that a terrier man might welcome a dig at a fox while the field waited impatiently nearby!

Earth stopping, or rather efficient earth stopping, is far from easy. It is policy to approach every earth to be stopped silently and allow the terrier to work the earth so that foxes are walled out rather than walled in. The earth should then be carefully stopped with stones, stakes or earth clods and a fox should be unable to find its way back into the earth. On the eve following the 'hunt' passing through the hunt country the earths must be unblocked to allow foxes to return to ground again. Badger sets must be subject to meticulous stopping and unstopping so that the badgers suffer as little inconvenience as possible. Badgers are terrific burrowers and if the earths/sets are not properly blocked, badgers will remove the stakes and stones thereby allowing foxes to run to ground. I earth stopped for our local hunt for some five years and while the task gave scant use for my terriers, the process of earth stopping can be extremely tedious and tiring.

Hunt service may be considered one of the last bastions of feudalism. The hunt servants year begins on 1 May and continues until the following 30 April though notice to quit must be given by 1 February. Hunt servants who leave half way through the season find it extremely hard to find work in hunt service elsewhere. The hunt offers an almost obligatory social life and many newcomers find it hard to adjust to the world of hunt service.

At one time a terrier man was required to bring half a dozen terriers to hunt service, for the terrier man was required to remove badgers from sets as well as bolt foxes. These days a terrier man must not allow his terriers to go to ground in badger sets and must on no account dig badgers, so perhaps he may be able to get by with fewer terriers. Hunt terriers are required to go to ground and bay at foxes to bolt them or 'fix' them so that the terrier man can dig to them. Hunt terriers in the South and Midlands at least are not required to kill foxes or damage them so badly that they cannot afford the hounds a run.

A terrier man's work does not however solely consist of working terriers to fox or for that matter earth stopping. Terrier men are usually required to help out in kennels, to collect the cadavers of fallen animals (and incidentally only hound kennels or licenced greyhound kennels are allowed to feed fallen stock to dogs of any kind) and to perform the somewhat odious task of skinning out and preparing the meat of the fallen stock as feed for hounds. Kennel work is tiring and the would-be terrier man must consider this before he applies for a post in hunt service. Sales of hides and grease (the waste bones, skins and fat from the cadavers of fallen beasts do provide some perks for the hunt staff, but quite often terrier men receive no money from these sales). In fact in recent years, since the restrictions on the use of animal waste products, it is now quite a problem to get rid of the offal from fallen stock and hunt servant's perks from offal processors may well be a thing of the past.

On the credit side the full time terrier man has a house provided free of charge and may have the use of the hunt vehicles: sometimes outside working hours. He has the opportunity to use his terriers regularly and to a certain extent to enjoy a lifestyle of his choice. His lifestyle involves him being out of doors quite a lot – a dubious distinction when he finds himself hauling a dead steer out of a bog in mid-winter – and he usually maintains his terriers free of charge.

On the debit side the terrier man occupies the lowest echelon of hunt service, well below that of huntsman or kennelman. He is poorly paid receiving often half the wages of an agricultural worker, and even when his name is well-known through the pages of the Hunt Service Registry he has little chance to negotiate his salary or to improve his terms of contract. A terrier man may find himself 'on call' twenty-four hours a day and the work he is required to perform is exhausting.

The lot of the part-time terrier man is a shade better in some respects. Part-time terrier men are paid pocket money to cover expenses, but are free of the commitments that be-set full-time hunt servants. Seldom is accommodation provided and a part-time terrier man usually has to use his own vehicle even on hunt days. Some, such as Wally Wyld of the Grove and Rufford Foxhounds, are held in high regard by the staff and hunt followers alike. Others, who sometimes serve a mere season, enjoy a dubious reputation for illicit fox digging and allowing hordes of undesirables to gain access to properties hunted by the local pack. Questionable characters seldom last out a season in hunt service where a good name is of paramount importance to the reputation of 'the hunt'.

The lot of the hunt servant with a fell pack is less desirable still. Fell packs, the traditional poor relations of the world of hunting, are hunted on foot and a huntsman usually provides his own terriers or uses hunt supporters terriers – and these are fairly numerous amongst the followers of most foot packs. Fell pack hunt servants are paid only during the time when the pack is hunted. In Summer they are literally cast adrift to fend for themselves and are usually engaged by nearby farms to help at hay making etc. and return to hunt service only as the hunting season approaches. Fell pack hounds are usually 'put out' to local farmers in much the same way as hunt servants are one should add! Hunt service from the fells to the shires is a tough life that is not to everyone's liking. Each year a spate of terrier men leave their well-paid jobs in industry to seek employment in hunt service. Few renew their contracts on 1 February and most return to heavy industry with a glad heart after 30 April.

From time to time terrier men endeavour to obtain working certificates for their terriers. A working certificate may be an ornate card of the sort furnished by the Atherstone Foxhounds two decades ago or a scrap of paper of the sort issued by Dermot Kelly when he was MFH for the Meynell Foxhounds. The merits of obtaining working certificates are several. Firstly it acts as a sort of proof that the terrier one keeps can perform the tasks for which it was intended. Secondly it can enter working certificate classes at hunt and working terrier shows. Lastly it is a means of checking records of the merits of certain dogs that may be used in future breeding projects. At one time one of the Border terrier clubs did much to encourage members to obtain working certificates for their dogs, but now this working certificate scheme seems to have fallen into disuse.

A working certificate is usually signed by the master or huntsman of a particular pack and certifies that the dog has either:

a. worked for a season or so with the pack and acquitted itself well during that season or
b. has been seen to be a good worker by either the master or the huntsman who has observed the dog work either in conjunction with the hunt pack or privately.

Personally I place quite a high value on working certificates and at one time I owned seventy such certificates some of which were admittedly for dogs long dead. My best stud Rupert bred forty-two working certificated offspring and I encouraged people who bred from him to obtain certificates for his progeny.

Conversely there are those who decry such paper qualifications, though I have never understood why. The working terrier world bristles with machismoism although many of those who display this characteristic are fearful inadequates who have neither working certificated terriers nor personal dignity. Hunt and working terrier shows rarely stage classes for working certificated stock these days simply because, despite the boasts of certain terrier men as to the merits of their stock, these working certificate classes are badly attended.

Working Terrier Packs

Whether or not terriers were bred to be run in packs can of course be debated for the terrier is by definition a dog that is capable of going to ground to destroy or oust subterranean vermin, and the damage caused to the foremost dog pushed into a fox by the dogs behind it has been described in an earlier chapter. Nevertheless in the last few years the hunting of small packs of terriers to rabbit, rat and mink has become a fairly popular and highly entertaining sport.

However, hunting terrier packs are by no means a recent phenomenen. Alys Serrell, *With Hound and Terrier in the Field* (1904), (edited by equestrian and hunting authority Francis Slaughter), recalls how she hunted her pack of fox terriers on the River Lyd in Dorset in 1888. Miss Serrell hunts all quarry from rat, the waterhen (waterhens run a considerable distance before considering taking to the wing) and to otter. The book, written in a rather stilted style, does however give a picture of terrier work during the golden age of hunting, though it gives little indication of how a terrier pack should be controlled or trained.

In the 1920s Sir Jocelyn Lucas, prompted like as not by Miss Serrell's book (he makes frequent reference to the work), hunted first a pack of fox terriers and later a pack of pure bred Sealyham terriers to rat, rabbit, stoat and otter. Unlike Miss Serrell, Lucas had excellent control over his terrier pack though Cartwright once stated that all this control vanished once a cat sprang up in front of the pack. For some reason Lucas never managed to make his pack steady with cats – and the subject of cats will be dealt with at a later stage – and all hell broke loose when a cat was sighted by Lucas' terriers. In his book, *The Sealyham Terrier*, he gives some small indication of the trouble he had with his terriers attacking cats but passes over the subject fairly quickly.

During the 1960s Ruth Haw – a great terrier enthusiast from Market Deeping, and an expert on terrier conformation – remarked that she had witnessed a pack of small terriers some of which were less than ten inches at the shoulder hunted by a lady mounted on an Exmoor pony drawing some woods near Worth Maltravers, Wiltshire. The lady was in fact Joan Begbie whose Seale Cottage strain Jack Russell terriers were descended from dogs she was given by Annie Rawle who kept house for Arthur Heinemann. Miss Begbie's dogs were carefully inbred to a particularly tough and hardy bitch, Seale Cottage Welcome, said by John

Cobby to be one of the hardist bitches alive at the time. Later, when the Seale Cottage strain were becoming less typey, Miss Begbie did in fact use a son of Cobby's famous Pickaxe to tidy up her strain. By the time I encountered Miss Begbie she was quite an old lady and simply used her pony to exercise her terrier pack as much as hunt it, but as a mounted hunter she experienced terrific difficulties when her pack regularly ran to ground on badger in the huge sets surrounding her house. She apparently lost her stud dog Seale Cottage Wizard for four days when he disappeared into a set during an exercise period – and hunting a terrier pack in an area that boasts a great many earths, large warrens or sets can often be a nightmarish experience.

In America where large, fierce predators are still found, at one time small packs of Airedales were used to bring bear, wolf, pig, cougar and jaguar to bay. Plott hounds, Birdson, Bluetick and Walker hounds were found to be more effective however, probably because the wild and sometimes insane courage of the Airedale often proved its downfall when it rounded on fierce quarry such as Prussian boar and razor-back pigs. Ben Lilly one of the huntsmen on Rooseveldt's Teddy Bear Hunt once remarked that he would not use Airedales because their courage often brought them to grief though the Oorang strain bred down from a rather untypey male, King Oorang, enjoyed some twenty years of successful predator hunting before Plott hounds ousted the Airedale from its popularity.

Airedales, of course, pack well possibly because of their otter hound ancestry or if Hancock, *Heritage of the Dog*, is correct because they were a relatively pure form of the Old Lancashire Otter-hound. If Hancock is correct then the addition of Irish terrier blood to an already potent mixture of bull terrier and hound would have had a devastating effect on the Airedale's ability to hunt large dangerous predators for not only would the Irish terrier blood have produced excessively and dangerously game Airedales but would have had a ruinous effect on the packing instincts of these 'refined' Airedales (and packing instinct with all its subtle ramifications is vitally important if dogs or hounds are used to bring bears, boars and large species of cat to bay). It is thus understandable that Plott hounds were preferred to pure bred Airedale terriers by the varmint hunters of the mid and far-west of America.

However, even pure bred terriers have been used to good effect at the sport of hunting medium and large predators. Lucas records that Major Doig who obtained his initial terrier breeding stock from John Russell and Arthur Heinemann, and hunted small fry, antelope, gazelle, species of wild pig and even leopard with his pack of leggy Parson Jack Russell-type terriers.

It should, however, be pointed out that many breeds of terrier will not only hunt well but pack and work together as a unit rather than as a group of individuals all intent on performing separately without concern for the other terriers in the pack. Scottish breeds of terrier: Cairns, Scotties, West Highland white terriers, are notoriously bad at packing and it can be a nightmare experience hunting a team of these terriers particularly in country that hosts a large number of rabbits, badgers or foxes and a correspondingly large number of burrows, sets and earths.

I hunted my own pack of terriers to rat and rabbit, but rarely mink, from 1965 until 1985 when a coronary incapacitated me for six months and my pack was disbanded. My own pack ranged from thirty to fifteen couple and were hunted four nights a week and at weekends. In 1980 we hunted seven nights a week during a bumper rat breeding year and succeeded in taking a huge haul of rats, though only five rabbits as weekend hunting was curtailed. Terrier packs can be extremely effective at mink hunting, far more effective than huge and often cumbersome otter-hounds one should add, but for some reason it is very difficult to secure rights for a terrier pack to draw a river bank. It is also worth noting that when my pack drew a bank for mink we also took a large haul of rats and water voles.

My terrier pack held together remarkably well, possibly because these terriers had a strong trace of beagle blood in their ancestry – between one-sixteenth to one-eighth part hound – and from 1968 onwards I took a great deal of pleasure hunting a level typey sort of animal. Hunt meets were strictly invitation-only and the process of selecting the field was intricate and complex. In twenty years of hunting not one unsavoury character turned up to spoil the evenings hunting and the field was composed of writers, actors and actresses, film stars, ballet dancers, opera singers and professional boxers. We fielded not only a team of first rate typey terriers but as good a band of hunt staff as one could imagine or wish to meet. The social life associated with the meets was excellent and the selection process used to thin out the field was a guarantee no one disreputable ever appeared at meets. Over fifty newspaper men recorded the meets: journalists from as far afield as Tokyo to San Francisco and while the write-ups we obtained were often bordering on the bizarre, not one reporter stated that he did not enjoy the hunt or find the field and hunt staff any less than totally delightful. This period was certainly the happiest time of my life and I have no regrets about spending my nights following my terrier pack. If I regain health, vitality and hunting country I shall certainly field another pack of identical terriers.

My pack were kennelled at Huddlesford and, because of the high standard of obedience the pack displayed, I am deeply suspicious of trencher-fed packs of terriers and would not countenance hunting such a pack. A trencher-fed pack is composed of animals housed and fed off the premises and brought together only to hunt. This type of pack, be it composed of hounds, terriers or bobbery, is seldom efficient or a pleasure to hunt. Some terriers will be well trained and others less so. Worse still, some may not be steady to stock – and if just one terrier is not stock steady in no time the whole pack will be rioting on sheep, cats, poultry or other farm livestock. Worse still some trencher-fed terriers may not be steady with ferrets and no vice is more infectious than ferret worrying. Even terriers that have been reared alongside ferrets and worked regularly with them react with hostility to ferrets when they see a ferret killed by other dogs. I am always suspicious about hunting a terrier with ferrets after it has witnessed the worrying of a ferret by other terriers. In 1966 I ran my terriers with a man who owned two Border terriers which were the wildest Border terriers I have ever encountered; for Border terriers are usually easily controlled and hence well mannered. I tolerated the idiosyncracies of the Border terriers simply because I did not own a car and felt marooned in Huddlesford. My tolerance became stretched to breaking point when one of the Borders killed a ferret and I found my own team staring hard into my ferret cage for a week or so after the chaos. I demand a high standard of obedience from my terriers, – but I find most people are less demanding. The majority of working terriers are far from well trained and the caper with the Border terriers left me decidedly against including other people's terriers in my pack. It became even more imperative not to allow other people to bring their terriers when I ceased hunting maggot factories and began running my terrier pack through live poultry as the prospect of a dog that is not stock broken running riot in a poultry pen is too hideous to contemplate. The reputation of a trencher-fed pack of terriers rests on the least trained of its dogs.

What is even more of a problem with trencher-fed packs owned by two or more terrier men is that the majority of owners insist on either hunting their own dogs within the pack or giving advice to the person nominated to hunt the team. The result is usually total bedlam and not only does the scene of several enthusiasts hunting their own terriers within a pack look bad, but the efficiency of the trencher pack is usually decidedly below par. In theory a trencher-fed terrier pack trained by several competent terrier men should be more efficient than a similar sized pack trained by one person, but in practice utter chaos results when such a pack is fielded. A single terrier not working in accord with its owner looks bad. A team working erratically goaded on by a band of equally erratic owners looks terrible. I have hunted with five trencher-fed packs or teams of terriers and each time I have returned to my kennels and rejoiced at the uniformity and obedience of my own pack.

'Building' or assembling a private terrier pack is both interesting and complicated. The nucleus of the pack – for choice a mature and sane bitch rather than a male – should be superbly trained and must come to call instantly and without question. My mature bitch, Beltane, was well enough trained to compete in obedience tests and because she was so obedient and her hunting ability never questioned by the others in the pack, when I shouted and she came to hand instantly, the rest of the pack drifting with her, never questioning that what she was doing was the right thing to do. The entire pack, thirty or more terriers, would come clear of any poultry house at a single command or return to the dog carrying trailer whenever they were required to do so. It is important to train these 'magna mater' bitches totally and thoroughly so that the pack, even if it questions the wisdom of the owner, never questions the common sense of the senior bitch. If she is trained thoroughly, there will be little problem in controlling a terrier pack.

It is policy to add to a terrier pack slowly, increasing the number of terriers hunted by one, or at the most two terriers. My own terriers (I added two terriers to the team at a time when the whelps were twelve weeks old and innoculated) were taken on leads to watch the hunting to soak up the ethos of ratting and rabbiting and kept on leashes until I considered they were ready to enter to rat. I trained puppies separately every afternoon when I returned from school, though never to the standard that I trained the pack leader Beltane. They were only allowed to hunt, free of the leashes, when they came instantly to hand during the afternoon training sessions. Only once did I attempt to introduce three terriers at the same time and the result was so disastrous that I was forced to give one terrier to friends. As it happened the bitch I gave away bred Omega my best rat catching terrier.

As to the calling in of the pack or rather the method of calling in a pack I have never favoured the use of whistles or horns to control or call in a terrier team. It is bad policy to allow a terrier pack to hunt at a great distance anyway, for nothing finds trouble as easily and readily as two or more terriers, besides which the sound of the human voice is less impersonal than the call of the horn or whistle. I find a repetitive short sharp staccato yell is best to call in wayward terriers and this cry is best taught the pack by uttering it when the pack is being fed in kennels ('I find a good YUT to be the best', Jack Ivester Lloyd).

A peculiarity of a terrier pack is that within days of hunting two or more dogs in unison the pack stratifies or rather polarises into hunters and catch dogs. Some terriers are natural hunters who seek to make use of their natural olfactory gifts. Others polarise to become catch dogs which are more keen to take the fight to their prey rather than simply seek out the quarry by scent. This is not to say that in a typical rat pack some terriers will deliberately fight shy of killing rats, but once a pack settles – and it does so in days after a pack comes together – it is to the benefit of the pack that its members should specialise using the skills each member possesses. Old magna mater bitches tend to gravitate to become hunters rather than simply catch dogs. A similar process of polarising occurs in packs of wild dogs and wolves, and it is worth noting that when the hunters are withdrawn from the pack situation confusion occurs but lasts only a short while after which the catch dogs stratify to secondary hunters and catch dogs. When the hunters return to the pack the secondary hunters return to the role of catch dogs. If one might appear anthropomorphic it is possible that 'hunters' occupy a higher status in the pack than do 'catch dogs' and a whole pack may be swayed by a decision of an elderly esteemed hunter. Beltane had terrific 'pack respect'. Her decision was never questioned by the rest of the pack which trusted implicitly in her nose and her wisdom. When she was removed from the pack by way of an experiment Pagan took over her role: when Beltane returned to the pack Pagan reverted to secondary Beta position. If both Pagan and Beltane were withdrawn from the pack Vampire adopted the role of the Alpha hunter. Henceforth each and every terrier would be withdrawn from the pack until only Omega and another terrier would be hunting/catching but it was only when Omega was fielded singly did she consider 'hunting' as well as 'catching'.

Although at one time I hunted thirty couple of terriers this is far in excess of the ideal number of terriers to hunt. The number in a terrier pack should be able to be assessed at a glance and a missing dog identified instantly. If the pack has to be counted every few minutes it is too numerous for the hunter or handler, or that particular hunter. I was instantly able to assess that I was fielding fifteen terriers – if I fielded more I needed to count them every time we drew a field or poultry house. If the number fell below fifteen, I felt 'edgy' as if I sensed the pack was falling short of the right number. Clearly seven and a half couple of terriers was the correct number for me to hunt. Others might be able to assess a greater number of terriers at a glance easily; others far fewer than seven and a half couple.

It is, however, very important to be able to assess instantly if the pack is intact or if the pack has split when hunting a country that has a great number of earths, sets or warrens. Terriers, as their very name implies, are likely to run to ground after any creature that tends to inhabit a subterranean lair and it becomes extremely dangerous when two or more terriers run to ground in a set, earth or warren. If the lair is inhabited by a fox or badger the damage done to the foremost terrier when other terriers push a dog into the very jaws of a fox or badger can be terrible, particularly as the foremost terrier cannot retreat and must suffer the terrible bites from its foe. My pack experienced such an accident in 1968 when Penny, a none too brave bitch, ran to ground in a deep set and was followed to ground by Spidey and Colt. Penny was dreadfully bitten and a huge goitre-like abcess appeared below her jaws, a goitre that burst and exuded a large amount of pus and blood and left a five inch scar that never completely healed.

What is even more dangerous is the possibility of a terrier team following a rabbit to ground in a mature warren; the ramifications of which often resemble the structure of the Metro. A rabbit will not of course retaliate against a terrier, but it will lead a terrier deep into the warren and encourage the terrier to dig its way into a blind tunnel or 'stop' to extract the rabbit. If several terriers go to ground behind the lead terrier the foremost dog becomes well and truly jammed into the tunnel, particularly as the terrier will dig itself in deeper to attempt to get to the rabbit. A 'stop' is a blind-ended tunnel and because of this contains only a limited amount of air. The frenzied digging of the terrier not only walls off the terrier from an outside supply of air, but the exertions of digging to the rabbit rapidly uses up the air within the stop. More terriers die of suffocation than from the bites of foxes or badgers.

While discussing the terrier pack and its problems it is perhaps expedient to touch on the subject of bobbery packs, packs composed of various breeds of dogs and hunted to all manner of quarry. Basically a successful bobbery pack – and I confess I hate bobbery packs – should be composed of three main elements:

a. dogs small enough to get to ground or to work beneath bramble cover to flush game;
b. dogs with accutely developed noses to locate game;
c. dogs which have speed enough to pursue and catch game bolted by the other two types of dog.

I must admit the very sight of a bobbery pack sets my teeth on edge and while I have hunted with a good many bobbery packs I have yet to return from a hunt not in a state of tension because of the bedlam that results when such a pack attempts to work together. A bobbery pack always looks bad, always looks ragged, and rarely do the three separate elements within the pack fulfil the roles expected of them. Lurchers within such a pack will often push headlong into cover, irritated by the reluctance of the terriers to face the cover perhaps, while scent hunters furiously and fruitlessly chase after game pushed out of cover by lurchers.

During the late 1970s and early 1980s Jack Ivester Lloyd wrote cleverly constructed pieces concerning the Bagley Rat Hounds, a curious band of dogs comprised of a black fell terrier a Jack Russell terrier and a collie and the exploits of the Bagley Rat Hounds caused such interest that *Shooting Times* lost a great deal when Ivester Lloyd ceased writing of the adventures of 'the hounds'. However Ivester Lloyd's writing was meant to be purely entertaining for there was no way he would consider his pack as efficient or the performance the pack gave as being anything akin to a pageant. Yet Ivester Lloyd wrote so well and convincingly of the exploits of his rat hounds that people wrote to him to apply for membership of the Bagley Rat Hounds!

Allowing the general public to attend a meet of any pack is thwart with danger and once (and only once) did I 'go public' so to speak. My pack of terriers had begun to breed true to type a few years previous and by 1970 they had begun to level out at twelve inches at the shoulder and a fiery red and white colour that I found incredibly attractive. During the early years of the pack I was flamboyant enough to run a cat, a pig and a fox amongst the terriers I hunted but as my type of terrier began to breed true to type and my pride in the creature I had created increased, my desire to be ostentatious diminished and cat, fox and pig together with uneven members of the pack were draughted until my kennel consisted of some sixty even and very typey terriers.

I took great pleasure in merely looking at the team: the same pleasure Mary Shelley's Frankenstein must have felt regarding his creation I thought at the time, and the fact that the pack also worked splendidly became an added bonus. When they fanned out to draw a thicket they looked spectacular and as the beagle influence was strong at this time the terriers held together well. I was justly proud of my team and perhaps my pride invited the troubles that were to follow.

At that time we acquired the rights to hunt Green Rock Farm a few hundred acres of run-down pasture, gorse and duck flight pools that were riddled with rabbits and the banks of the pool hosted a healthy population of rats. It was a delightful place to hunt, particularly as our hostess was a charming lady who expressed great surprise at the level nature of our terrier pack. As a result of a monumental error in judgement however I heeded the hostess' suggestion and 'went public' or to be more explicit I allowed a field (not personally invited by me) to watch my pack at work.

I owned some really lovely, evenly marked, terriers at the time and hence when I appeared with my hostess for a press interview she had arranged I took eight terriers which milled around our feet as we chatted to the press. The upshot of the interview was an article which spelt my name PLUMBER and credited my hostess with the ownership of the pack – but the euphoria of appearing in public with my beautiful pack of terriers made me overlook inaccuracies in the article.

Thus it was I arrived home from work on the Friday night and set to cleaning my dog trailer until it glistened while my terriers danced around the vehicle as if they were aware that an extra special hunt was to take place on the Saturday. Had any of us the gift of foresight we would have been a shade less happy about the prospects of the Saturday's hunting.

We arrived at Green Rock Farm at exactly 10.00 am driving to the meeting point where a field of over a hundred had gathered to watch us hunt. The group composed of friends of the hostess, and perhaps friends of friends, and were a delightful crowd who peered into the trailer congratulating me on the quality of my terriers. However, just as it takes only a handful of rowdy children to create chaos in a school, a similar number of trouble makers can ruin a day's hunting and we had five spectators ready and waiting to cause as much trouble as they could.

I glanced around the crowd and saw five lads, tattooed arms akimbo, and crossbred pit bull/fell terriers straining at the leash. My terriers, hot fiery and excited by the prospects of a day's hunting would have milled around these dogs and triggered off a furious fight – a fight that could only have one outcome for some of these dogs were thirty-five pounds in weight and more than a match for twelve pound terriers.

I eyed the band of youths, sensed their hostility and gently approached them requesting that they crated their terriers to prevent trouble. With a sneer the leading lout uttered 'Are you afraid of the competition from' – he stepped aside to reveal an ugly black brute, most of the face of which had recently parted company with the skull 'Turk'! I explained that 'Turk' would not be allowed to run with the pack anyway but the sneers of the quintet convinced me that they had every intention of allowing these monsters to run with my terriers. Politely I returned to the trailer, uncoupled it to turn it (I believe that trailers take on a life of their own when hitched behind my car) to take my pack home, when I noticed my hostess had approached the thugs and was administering a verbal whipping to the band of louts, who sheepishly took the vile looking crossbred back to their vans. I thanked my hostess, turned loose my terriers, and basked in the admiration of the field as a flood of identical red and white terriers poured out of the trailer.

We set off towards one of the flight pools, my terriers running head down on the scent of rabbits and moorhens but glancing back I observed the leading lout with a greyhound on a slip – a greyhound that lunged at every terrier that approached it. To complain, to ask the lunatic to put the greyhound back in the car, or to crate my terriers to go home would have caused bedlam, so I shrugged my shoulders and hoped the louts wold keep the damned greyhound under control.

To cut a very long unpleasant tale short, one of my terriers marked a rat near the pool and I put in a very good jill ferret. Two rats bolted and were snaffled up by the terriers. Curiously the greyhound showed not the slightest interest in the rats but broke clear of the slip and slew my ferret before it ploughed into my terriers, lacerating two before I could prevent it doing more damage. I crated my dogs, headed for our local vet and vowed never to 'go public' again. Henceforth I vetted each and every visitor and never allowed anyone I did not know to attend a meet. Other dogs were expressly forbidden and I turned away anyone who brought an uninvited pet terrier to a meet. Henceforth we experienced no further trouble, though once my pack had witnessed a dog killing a ferret I never really trusted any of the team for months after the incident.

Thus the terrier pack, its pleasures, its problems, and the curious band of people such a pack will attract. A mistake made when a pack is hunting is magnified thirty-fold as the other terriers join in the game, so a terrier pack needs to be totally under control when hunting or at rest – and if fights are to occur it will be when the pack is at rest! If a pack is hunted hard and regularly then it will seldom be cursed with fights and it is only during inactivity that bad battles between terriers occur. Lucas once said that he once hunted so often he seldom needed to clean out his kennel runs. A well disciplined pack is always a pack that is hunted regularly and kept always under control.

The Law and the Terrier Man

Ignorance of the law has never been regarded as a form of defence in any part of the world and in no country are the laws more complicated than in Britain. In a country with a very congested population where many people are required to live in close contact with each other, many laws and regulations are required to protect the rights of the individual, and few countries are as thickly populated as Britain.

Every square inch of the islands of Great Britain belongs to someone and there is literally no such thing as truly common land, land on which a person can do exactly as he pleases, regardless of how he might upset or annoy others. Thus before a terrier man seeks out land on which huntable quarry lives he must first seek out the owner of this land and obtain permission to hunt the property.

Actually the act of simply trespassing on someone's land is usually regarded as a civil tort (or wrong) and will not be prosecuted in the criminal courts, but this should not encourage the terrier man to wander abroad as he will. In fact certain statutory bodies such as the British Railway Board are entitled to prosecute trespassers on their land – for fairly obvious reasons one should add – and it is extremely difficult for anyone other than those who work for the British Railway Board to obtain permission to hunt on railway property. I have yet to hear of any British Railways employee who has been given permission to dig or disturb the soil on such property I should add. Yet many youths and tyro men deliberately seek out railway embankments which often act as sanctuary for foxes and rabbits in the mistaken belief that they have every right to hunt such property. Such was the incidence of trespass by children on railway property in the Midlands that many schools brought in police officers to give lectures on the dangers of hunting on railway embankments and property.

Likewise the Forestry Commission. In many areas of the British countryside every square foot of wasteland is bought up by the Forestry Commission and planted with trees. Immediately such places are purchased they become subject to Forestry Commission Byelaws of 1982 under which it becomes an offence to:

Dig up or remove any soil.

Allow a dog to disturb, chase any bird or animal.

Net, destroy or take any bird, fish or animal.

Disturb, damage or destroy the burrow, den, set or lair of any wild animal.

Thus to all intents and purposes Forestry Commission land is *verboten* to any terrier man and must not be hunted. Yet each year several terrier and lurcher enthusiasts are apprehended for hunting on forested land on which they have absolutely no right to be.

Furthermore because the density of the population of a town or city is greater than that of a county district certain laws apply to hunting quarry of any sort within the boundaries of a town. It is against the law (1847 Town Police Clauses) to allow any animal to attack or worry another animal such as a fox, rat or rabbit in a town, though it is perfectly legal to hunt such animals in the countryside, providing the owner of the land on which these wild animals normally reside has given the hunter permission to pursue such quarry. Thus it is not legal for a terrier man to allow his dogs and ferrets to kill rats residing under a neighbours shed or poultry house, should the said neighbour reside in a built-up area that might be considered to be a part of a town. Likewise, the ludicrous caper of a fox hunt in the series *Coronation Street*, (January 1991), where a mongrel dog was encouraged to seek out a pigeon killing fox which constituted an offence under this 1847 Act. Yet numerous terrier men hunt foxes in the middle of Birmingham without knowing that by doing so they are committing offences – and ignorance of the law can not be offered as a defence in a criminal court. Acts of Parliament, obscure and antiquated as such Acts may be, will eventually be used by those antipathetic to field sports to bring terrier work into further disrepute.

On the subject of bringing field sports (or rather quasi-field sports) into disrepute the 1911 Protection of Animals Act did much to prevent some of the barbaric cruelty that masqueraded as hunting. The act of tipping a quantity of rats into an enclosure from which the rats had no chance of escaping, and setting a dog to attack and kill the rats in the enclosure, became illegal – it was argued for the defence for the first rat pit prosecution in 1912 that the pit was used as a training aid for the dogs performing in the pit. However as the pit allowed no opportunity for the pitiful, hapless rats to escape this defence was not accepted.

In the same year the curious Waters v. Meakin case which caused considerable interest at the time cast an extremely grey light on the activity erroneously known as 'rabbit coursing', that in no way should be associated with true field sports, despite the decision of the court. It appears that rabbits were released in a three acre field that was netted to prevent the escape of the rabbits but the fence was punctuated by small escape holes. Crated rabbits were released and two dogs (whippets and cross-bred terriers) were allowed to chase and capture the rabbits. Of the fifty-five rabbits 'coursed' (an inaccurate expression) not one escaped capture even though some endeavoured to run up the netting in order to escape. The fact that rabbits run well-known routes in order to escape capture and the rabbits did not know the field on which they were released and hence had no possible chance of escaping was overlooked by the court, who decided that while there had been unnecessary suffering and cruelty perpetrated on the rabbits, there was no offence as the action formed part of coursing.

Fortunately in 1921 an amendment to the Act made the coursing of animals in a confined space strictly illegal.

It is however not illegal to release a captive wild animal in front of dogs which are encouraged to pursue or kill the animal providing that the animal is not subjected to terror, is not released in an exhausted state, or mutilated or incapacitated in any way. The animal must also be allowed some chance of making good its escape. Yet despite the fact it is not strictly illegal to course captive animals (rats, rabbits, hares etc.) it is inadvisable to do so. The pursuit of captive game is a pointless rather inane activity and should not be associated with true field sports.

The act of putting a terrier to ground to bolt, bottle up or kill a fox is, however, perfectly legal but nevertheless it does leave the terrier man in a legal limbo if the dog is badly injured by its encounter with a fox. It can be argued that the unnecessary and unreasonable abuse of any animal may amount to an act of cruelty. The cup for the Best Battle Scarred Veteran offered in 1984, once and fortunately only once, did in fact give tremendous ammunition for those who would like to see field sports brought to an end. Some hideously disfigured terriers, the faces of which had almost parted company with the boney skull tissue, were paraded around the ring by proud but exceedingly brainless owners and the maimed and badly disfigured animals were carefully photographed by many people who wished to see field sports made illegal! I feel very strongly about this cup for I was asked to judge the class of scarred veterans. I declined, and it would have been better for field sports if the exhibitors had decided not to bring their terriers to the show to compete in this class. Any activity that brings field sports into disrepute should be avoided by all terrier men.

An interesting case involving the prosecution (under the 1911 Protection of Animals Act) of a young terrier man from Doncaster occurred in the autumn of 1985. The terrier man had found a fox to ground in a rocky hillside near Doncaster and had blocked the exits of the earth prior to putting two terriers (Border-X-Lakeland hybrids) to ground. The terrier was scarred by the encounter and the youth was charged under one of the complex ramifications of the 1911 Act. It was an historical case for, had the prosecution proved successful, the case would have effectively outlawed field sports. The defence stated that the youth was endeavouring to rid the land of the foxes (the youth had no permission to hunt the land one should add), but this was overlooked by the prosecution, and required his terrier to kill the foxes. It was also pointed out that the Lakeland or Lakeland-type terrier was bred to kill, rather than bolt, foxes so it was practice to prevent the escape of the fox by blocking the exits to the earth. The court decided that the youth had no case to answer, but had the Director of Public Prosecutions decided to explore the subtle ramifications of the Rowley v. Murphy case of 1963 (certain acts of dominion constitute captivity) the youth might have fared less well. Parkes and Thornley's *Fair Game* quotes an interesting interpretation of a similar case where a fox engaged in a conflict with two terriers for an hour may well be considered to be in a state of captivity if all the entrances to the earth were blocked. 'If, however, the entrances are netted to catch a bolting fox to be taken or killed humanely, there is probably no offence'. Each year courts seem more and more willing to broaden the concept of 'captivity'.

Terriers often run to ground in deep or almost undiggable earths and refuse to come out or, more often than not, are unable to come out. To deliberately leave such dogs to ground not only constitutes an offence but it is barbarically cruel to allow a dog to suffer a lingering death from hunger and asphixiation in the eternal darkness of the bowels of the earth.

Thus every terrier keeper, be the dog kept as a pet or a working dog, should join a terrier rescue society, and at the time of writing there are many such terrier rescue societies or working terrier clubs that lend both muscle and machinery to dig out trapped terriers. The first terrier rescue society, The Fell and Moorland Working Terrier Group, was formed to rescue terriers trapped in the deep borrans or tin and copper mines of the Lake District, but since then most districts in Britain boast terrier rescue clubs and societies that will assist in the rescue of trapped terriers. Ralph Hodgson was regularly called out to rescue two trapped West Highland white terriers that ran to ground in any earth or burrow in Durham.

Some clubs have gone to incredible measures in order to extract trapped terriers and have employed earth moving equipment and dynamite to delve to dogs, and while it must be added that many trapped terriers would not be trapped if their owners had been careful where they allowed their terriers to run to ground, it is essential that a working terrier owner – or indeed owner of any terrier for most breeds of terrier will run to ground if they are afforded any chance to do so – joins a terrier rescue group. The membership fees for such clubs are very reasonable and totally out of proportion to the incredible services such clubs can furnish to rescue trapped terriers.

It would be literally impossible to discuss the legal implications of terrier work without mentioning the badger and the hunting of this the largest British stoat. Prior to 1973 it was perfectly legal to hunt, dig and kill badgers. Indeed badger digging clubs were not only accepted by society, but often held in high esteem. Sir Jocelyn Lucas organised badger digs as social events and these digs were attended by titled ladies and socialites, but in the late 1960s it was suggested that the otter was in danger of becoming extinct and thus needed protection if it was to survive in Britain. Otter hunting ceased in the years following the public interest in the welfare of otters and packs of otter hounds were either disbanded or were hunted to mink.

Why the badger received the protection it now enjoys is still a mystery. The general public would certainly not have been aware how, since earliest times, this creature has suffered the torment of the damned at the hands of hunters and baiters alike. The creature seemed tailor-made for those interested in baiting. As a mustelid the badger inherited the furious courage from the common stock that had spawned stoats, weasels, otters and polecats, but unlike other mustelids it acquired a shape that was more ursine than musteline, a form that was capable of surviving savage maulings from dogs and man alike, and because of this endurance, because of this fiery disposition, it became the ideal animal to bait. Stoats, weasels, otters and even polecats seldom survive the terrors that accompany capture and expire if subjected to human curiosity let alone cruelty.

Badgers alas are made of sterner stuff, and the horrors perpetrated on the beast were legion. The pluck of bull terriers was tested to the full when these dogs were matched against badgers and flesh, bone and fur was ripped asunder by the badgers awesome bite. The jaw of the badger, the mandible of which was hinged into a cavity of the skull, was seldom dislocated by conflict (skulls of badgers are usually found with the lower jaw still attached to the cranium) and hence the beast could be subjected to a great deal of ill treatment before death afforded the captive badger a merciful release from its tormentor. Curiously the physique and disposition that enabled the badger to survive attacks from larger predators almost brought about its extinction at the hands of man.

Or did it? Prior to 1973 the badger had become far more numerous than the public had realised. In 1941 the first badger was dug near Ullswater. It is likely that it had been brought in from Lancashire by Lakelanders who wished to introduce the species as a sporting quarry. Yet despite the enthusiasm of Cumbrians for the chase and terrier work, the badger not only survived in the Lake District but became numerous. Troutbeck became undermined by the delvings of badgers, and foxes ran miles to reach the sanctuary afforded by the deep badger sets in this district.

Derbyshire boasted a huge population of badgers. In Etwall, Bill Brockley purchased land that held two artificial earths constructed by the nearby Meynell hunt to harbour foxes. In one year (1967) I removed some sixteen badgers from one of these 'earths' yet badgers continued to invade the woods surrounding these 'drain and kennel' constructions – though foxes rarely ventured up the pipes of these earths.

Roads around Lichfield frequently sported road casualty badgers, but the deep sets around Whittington were always inhabited. Some disease, possibly a Laidlaw and Dunkin Virus A distemper killed many badgers in 1966 but while the decayed cadavers of badgers were found around many sets badgers continued to be numerous in Staffordshire even after the epidemic.

Thus the badger was far from being an endangered species as 1973 dawned, but it was to receive a form of protection seldom enjoyed by any species before that date. The 1973 Badger Act makes it an offence to wilfully kill, injure or take any badger or attempt to do so (Section 1/1) but the terrier man will not be guilty of an offence if he can show to the court that his action in digging the badger was necessary to prevent serious damage to the land. Serious damage might be construed as meaning damage to corn (badgers play by rolling in ripening corn) poultry, lambs (there is little factual evidence to support the notion that badgers seek out and kill lambs, though there is ample proof that they will eat the carcasses of dead lambs or even exhume buried cadavers of lambs) or undermine the land so that livestock may fall into the burrows and damage itself. If this can be proven, and it is exceedingly difficult to prove that the damage done by badgers can be considered as 'serious', the landowner may apply to

a. the Nature Conservancy Council or
b. the Ministry of Agriculture Fisheries and Food

for a licence to remove and relocate the offending badgers though the likelihood of such a licence being granted is small and these bodies usually advise preventative measures rather than grant a licence to remove the badger.

It is an offence under Section 1(2) of the Badgers Act 1973 to possess a dead badger, skin, skull or part of a badger, unless it can be shown that such trophies were obtained under circumstances that do not contravene the Act. If a badger is killed as a result of a road accident it is wise for the terrier man to drive on by leaving the roadside cadaver for another for it is exceedingly difficult to provide proof that the badger was killed as a result of a road accident – particularly if the owner of the trophy has terriers of any sort.

However it is a far more serious offence to be found in possession of a live badger (Section 3, 1973 Badgers Act). Parkes and Thornley, *Fair Game*, state that there is a considerable market for live badgers to bait with dogs of all breeds and to a certain extent this is obviously true. However it is ludicrous to imagine that the £1000 a badger suggested by the tabloid press has ever been obtained by diggers – if such a price was obtainable the badger would certainly become an endangered species!

If a terrier man is found in possession of a live badger most courts impose huge fines to deter the act of baiting these badgers, though a licenced contractor mmay transport badgers to and from certain sites or take a badger to be treated by a veterinary surgeon.

Under Section 2 of the 1973 Badger Act it is an offence to cruelly ill-treat a badger and this can mean setting dogs to ground in a badger set or taking a badger alive, bagging or boxing it, or containing a badger in a car boot or cage. It is also an offence to seize a badger with tongs – a curious piece of equipment resembling sugar tongs used to seize a badger by its neck or fore-paws.

It is also illegal to shoot a badger with a shotgun of less than twenty bore or a rifle using ammunition having a muzzle energy of less than 160 ft/lb and a bullet of less than 38 grains – though a special dispensation must be granted in order that badgers might be killed.

The usual defence of those found digging for badger is that they were seeking foxes in the earth or set they were attempting to excavate, but the Wildlife and Countryside (Amendment) Act 1985 strengthened the Act of four years previous by insisting that the accused must prove he was not digging for badgers. It is an instance of where the accused is literally deemed guilty until proven innocent and this Act has been the cause of much concern to both law makers and terrier men alike.

The attitude of magistrates towards badger diggers is interesting and the fines imposed by those magistrates an indication of the attitude of the public towards badger diggers and possibly field sports generally. In 1981 the now famous Appleby incident resulted in three youths being tried for digging a badger in the Lunesdale Hunt country. The youths claimed that, despite the fact they had no permission to be on the land, they were digging for foxes. They were fined £85 apiece. In 1984 another group of men were apprehended under identical circumstances at Shining Cliff Woods, Belper – they received fines of £2500. This should alert terrier men of the danger of hunting near a badger set even if they are in pursuit of foxes or rabbits.

The spate of convictions of men supposedly digging for badgers has terrified the various terrier clubs and the BFSS, and to discourage badger digging or to deter terrier men from seeking foxes in places which may house a badger the BFSS, in conjunction with the National Working Terrier Federation, have published five rules for the terrier man.

1. Learn all signs of badger and avoid them.
2. Obtain permission of farmers, landowners or occupiers of land.
3. Do not run away if challenged.
4. Join a recognised terrier club.
5. Observe club codes of conduct.

The BFSS and the National Working Terrier Federation are to be commended concerning their efforts to prevent further prosecutions for badger digging, yet each and every week badger digging offences are prosecuted and staggering fines meted out by magistrates. Badger diggers are hastening the cessation of terrier work and field sports generally. When laws exist those laws must be obeyed.

Terriers are small dogs and hence are frequently transported in the boots of cars. As to whether transporting animals in this way is illegal is one of the grey areas of the law. If transporting animals in this way causes distress (and personally I do not believe it does if the boot is well ventilated, and the animal is not subjected to exhaust fumes) and it can be proven that the animal is distressed then a prosecution may result from carrying dogs in this manner. It should be pointed out that magistrates often have a rather strange notion of what actually constitutes cruelty. So antipathetic to terrier work are many magistrates, that these days it is unwise to carry dogs in the boot of a car while out hunting. If a terrier man is charged with badger digging – and many are accused of the offence even though it is patently obvious that they are well clear of badger sets, the fact that the terriers were carried in the boot of the car is certain to be mentioned by the police, and equally certainly the bench may well be swayed in their judgement by the possible cruelty involved transporting dogs in this manner. It is wise to tread carefully in a world which is becoming increasingly hostile to the ethos of working terriers.

Thus the sporting terrier, the breeds the art of working these dogs and the present laws which dictate the way such terriers can be worked and kept. Each year it becomes more difficult to find legitimate work for these dogs and each year the terrier man must strive to work his dogs yet not offend or break the law. It is indeed a difficult gauntlet to run.